THE KROBO PEOPLE OF GHANA TO 1892

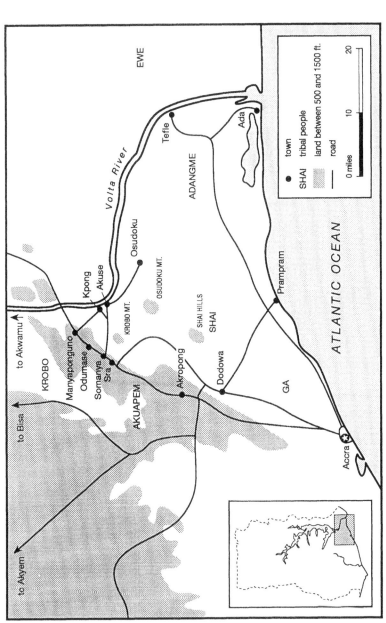

Sketch map of Southeastern Ghana

THE KROBO PEOPLE OF GHANA TO 1892

A Political and Social History

by

Louis E. Wilson

Ohio University Center for International Studies
Monographs in International Studies

Africa Series Number 58
Athens, Ohio 1991

Library of Congress Cataloging-in-Publication Data

Wilson, Louis Edward.
    The Krobo people of Ghana to 1892 : a political and
social history / by louis E. Wilson
        p.   cm. − (Monographs in international studies.
Africa series; no. 58.)
    Includes bibliographical references (p.   )
    ISBN 0-89680-164-0
    1. Krobo (African people)–History.
        I. Title. II. Series.
DT510.43.K76W55   1991
966.7'0049633–dc20   91 - 13764
                                                CIP

This volume is dedicated to

Nene Azzu Mate Kole
Konor of the Manya Krobo
from 1939 to 1990

to
Judy, Bennett, Mark

and to
Rebecca McKenzie Wilson

CONTENTS

TABLES

CHARTS

xi

PREFACE

The author carried out field work for the present study in two stages during the years 1973-1974 and 1983-1984. During these years he conducted extensive interviews with a number of people: the late Nene Assu Mate Kole (1939-1990), konor of the Manya Krobo during his lifetime; the Padi Oketeku Akrobetto II, konor of the Yilo Krobo between 1955 and 1977; the Okumo; and the Very Reverend E.L.M. Okjidja (Rtd), former Moderator of the Ghana Presbyterian Church. The author consulted archival material in the Balme Library of the University of Ghana, Legon, including the Furley and Africana Collections; at the Institute of African Studies Library in Legon; and at the Accra, Kofordua, and Cape Coast branches of the Ghana National Archives (GNA). Konor Azzu Mate Kole made available to the author the family papers at his residence and at the Accra branch of the GNA. He also made available the private collection of Konor Emmanuel Mate Kole (1892-1939) in Odumase-Krobo.

I wish to express my deep thanks to the Ford Foundation which assisted me with my dissertation work in 1973-1974. Thereafter I received support from the University of Colorado at Boulder and in 1983-1984 from the Fulbright Fellowship Program.

In addition, I also wish to state my deepest appreciation for the support given me by the Krobo themselves as well as by numerous people at the University of Ghana, Legon, and by the people of Ghana. Furthermore, I would like to acknowledge the critical nature of the information gained from numerous interviews with Konor Oketeku Akrobetto III and with the late Nene Azzu Mate Kole. More important than the interviews with him was the personal and moral support which Konor Mate Kole accorded me.

Finally a word to the scholars who assisted me during the years this work was in preparation, to Earl Phillips, Boniface T.O. Ranger, Hugo Huber, David Northrup, and A. Adu Boahen as well as to James L. Cobban, editor of the Monographs in International

Studies, Hope Hendricks, and Nancy Basmajian for their painstaking work in preparing the manuscript for publication.

1

INTRODUCTION

During the twentieth century, though numerically small compared to the rest of the population of Ghana, the Krobo people have determined events in southeastern Ghana more than any other ethnic group. The century began under the leadership of Konor Emmanuel Mate Kole, OBE, who reigned from 1892 until 1939. He was succeeded by his son, the late Konor Azzu Mate Kole, who reigned until his death in 1990. These two konors were the paramount chiefs of the Manya Krobo. During the colonial era of the twentieth century, they were the rulers of a people who were the preeminent producers of palm oil in Ghana. Earlier, during the late 1880s, eager to continue their economic advantages, aggressive and shrewd Krobo farmers had adopted cocoa as an additional crop for export. In Kroboland, however, cocoa failed to replace palm oil as Ghana's main export crop, partly because cocoa thrives best in forested regions and such regions were unavailable to the Krobo. Besides their dominance in palm oil, the Krobo thrived because of their influence over educational institutions which were established first by the Basel missionaries during the 1880s and because of their control of the valuable trade along the Volta River.

Critical to the expansion and prosperity of the Krobo during the twentieth century was the quality of their leadership. Konor Emmanuel Mate Kole was educated at one of the Basel Mission stations. He ruled vigorously for forty-seven years and in 1934 became the second African in Ghana, the former Gold Coast, to receive the Order of the British Empire from the British monarch. Azzu Mate Kole succeeded his father in 1939 on the eve of World War II and reigned for fifty-one years. He prompted the continued growth of the Krobo which had begun with the palm oil trade of the nineteenth century. Many changes occurred in Ghana during his reign: the end of colonial rule, the flourishing of nationalism, the rise and fall of President Kwame Nhrumah, and the decline of the Ghanian economy and political institutions. Throughout this time, Azzu Mate Kole became a symbol of traditional authority not only for the Krobo but for all Ghanians. At his Golden Jubilee on the stool the whole of Ghana celebrated the history of the Krobo. In his speech, recorded in the newspaper *West Africa*, he stated: "We are young eagles. Look up at the rising sun of the twenty-first century civilization and flap, again flap your wings and soar high beyond the dark clouds of suspicion, mistrust and envy, and emerge at the grand dawn where a haven awaits you" (May 21-27, p. 835).

A comprehensive history of Ghana (formerly the Gold Coast) has yet to be written. To date, we have only a series of case histories, primarily of Akan states. But Ghana's history is more than a collection of stories of Akan chiefdoms or of separate states. These states, both large and small, engaged in dynamic interaction: their institutions were constantly changing, their people moving about, the people's ideas developing and evolving. This book attempts to present a broad analytical framework for the history of southeastern Ghana through a representative study of the Krobo, still one of the region's most important political and economic forces.

The modern state of Ghana comprises several language groups, including Akan, Ga, Adangme (Adangbe), Dagomba, Gonja, Mamprusi, and Ewe. The slightly more than 150,000 Krobo are the most numerous of the Adangme-speaking peoples and form the fourth largest ethnic group in Ghana.[1] Since the middle of the nineteenth century they have been also economically and politically the most important group, because of their dominant role in commercial crop production for export. How their rise to prominence came about and how it illustrates local responses to wider forces for change in West Africa form the focus of this study.

Methodology

Traditionally, historians of West Africa have concentrated on the study of large political entities. The power and far-ranging influence of such states in part account for the attention they attract. So does the availability of considerable written documentation, especially for those states with access to the coast, which in turn provided direct contact with European traders after about 1650. By comparison, the smaller stateless societies and those like the Krobo in the process of developing toward statehood—of which there were hundreds in West Africa—have received little attention, particularly for the period before the nineteenth century when many were still in the formative stages of their political and cultural development.[2] Partly because of the nature of the historical evidence and partly because of the presumed unimportance of these societies, historians and other scholars have avoided them.

Recently, however, historians of Africa have expanded their interests beyond the mere reconstruction of political histories and have devoted more attention to economic and social change. Methodological advances in the use of nondocumentary sources such as oral tradition, linguistics, and archaeology have opened the way to more effective handling of these essential areas of the historian's concern. Small-scale societies deserve study not only because they figure so prominently in the total number of societies in West Africa but because of their crucial role in the social and economic history of the larger region. To understand the political environment of a state such as the Akan kingdom of Asante or the Yoruba kingdom of Benin, one must consider the interrelations between these larger states and their smaller tribute-paying chiefdoms and independent neighbors. No state existed in a vacuum; each was part of a complex system that involved many other societies. In this respect, a close analysis of the formation of a society such as the Krobo in Ghana can provide a microcosmic model of West African history.

Until recently, histories of the region focused on the centralized, matrilineal Akan states that occupied the forest regions of Ghana, or on their interaction with surrounding neighbors.[3] The importance of the Akan, especially the Asante, the Fante, the Akwamu, and the Akyem, in the reconstruction of Ghana's history cannot be disputed.[4] Moreover, a general abundance of material exists on the various Akan states, and the fact that these were centralized societies clearly added to the availability of information on them. If, however, historians ever are to construct a complete history of Ghana, they must give more emphasis to the study of all Ghanaians.[5] This study thus is also a plea for additional intensive work on small-scale societies in Ghana and throughout West Africa.

3

The Ethnography of the Region

The Krobo are surrounded by the Akuapem to the west and northwest, the Akyem Abuakwa to the north, the Ewe to the southeast, and other Adangme, the Shai and the Osu, to the southwest and the southeast.[6] The Akan peoples—the Akuapem and the Akyem Abuakwa—outnumber the Krobo and other Adangme and arrived earlier in the region west of the Volta. Highly centralized chiefdoms with a strong political structure, the Akan have been traditionally the politically dominant group in the area, followed by the Ewe. While Akan often fought Adangme groups, relationships between the Adangme and the Ewe historically have been cordial. Indeed, Adangme traditions speak favorably about the migration through Ewe chiefdoms in present day Togo; moreover, the patrilineal Ewe contributed much to the religious structure of the Adangme. However, because the Ewe concentrated their political activity on the lower Volta, some Adangme, namely the Krobo and the Shai, had little direct contact with the Ewe after settling their respective ancestral homes on the Krobo Mountain and the Shai Hills.[7]

The Physical Setting

The Accra plains, the Volta River, and *Klo-yo* (the Krobo Mountain) were the important geographical factors that shaped the earliest Krobo history and set the Krobo apart from other Adangme.[8] Rainfall in the northeastern portion of the Accra plains, part of the coastal savannah, averages forty inches per year. The heaviest precipitation occurs between March and June. A second rainy season, *Gie*, begins in August and lasts until early November. The heavy rains turn the red laterite soil on the flat plains into a swamp, a condition frequently aggravated by flooding of the Volta River from Ajena to Amedica. *Hlabata*, the dry season, begins in mid-November and ends in late February, with temperatures averaging in the high ninety-degree range. The intense heat turns the soggy swamplands into parched ground. The climate of Kroboland tended to separate the Krobo economically from their fellow Adangme, forcing the former to rely more on trading with Akan peoples, on hunting in the forested Akuapem Mountains, and on symbiotic economic relations with Ewe fishing villages along the

4

Volta.[9] Of all the Adangme-speaking people, then, the Krobo had the greatest contact with Akan groups.

The most important geographical element in the entire Eastern Region is the Volta River. "The river Volta winds through the plains," observed nineteenth-century missionary Jakob Heck, "in a broad silver band bordering the east of Krobo until it disappears behind the Noja [Yogaga mountain]."[10] During peaceful times the villages along both sides of the Volta provided a natural environment for trade among the Akan, Adangme, and Ewe peoples. However, strong currents, shifting sand bars, and crocodiles made navigation of the Volta difficult at times. Fish from the Volta, obtained either directly or through trade, formed an important part of the Krobo diet, but water was secured from the nearby Okwei Stream, not from the Volta. Krobo farmers made little direct use of the Volta's gifts until the nineteenth century, during the declining years of the Atlantic slave trade and the rise of agricultural production for export, when the Volta became a major year-round transportation route.

The Krobo Mountain is the ancestral home of the Krobo. Reaching 1,108 feet, the mountain is an impressive granite inselberg in the southeasternmost portion of the Accra plains. Klo-yo was one of three such outcroppings on the plains described by Basel missionary Johannes K. Auer in 1855:

> Little Krobo land has several peaks. They are overhangs of the Akuapem mountains like the huge Yogaga or 'high peak' looking like a huge guard at the northern gate of Krobo land . . . . It rises 1430 feet [sic] above sea level. In the jungles behind the Yogaga a few elephants are said to live according to the Krobo—other mountains rise as colossal rocks directly above the plains without connection to the main mountains, thus standing like lonely outguards. . . . They are the Noja at the Volta, the Osudoku, and the Shai, both 1,400 feet high. The Krobo [mountain] . . . according to English measurement, [is] 950 feet [sic] high.[11]

In the valley of the inselbergs two Adangme groups, the Krobo and the Osudoku, evolved from what can be termed their proto-Adangme origins.[12] The Krobo Mountain, although not the

5

highest of the inselbergs, was better suited for habitation than the others and more accessible. All provided defensive fortresses. Ascent of the granite and gneiss Krobo Mountain was extremely difficult, except along two narrow paths, which today are hidden by heavy overgrowth. The more accessible and older path is located on the northeastern side of the mountain; the other path is on the southwestern side.[13] The locations of these steep, narrow paths were closely guarded secrets. Sharp rock formations, often covered with thick vines, leaves, and heavy brush, interlaced the pathways, impeding visibility. During the rainy seasons, slippery footing made access even more difficult. Under ideal conditions, ascent along the northeastern path took about one-half hour, whereas ascent up the steeper, higher southern path took about three-quarters of an hour. "We climb from rock to rock," recorded the missionary Auer in 1855. "I wonder how the women can carry up water."[14] Herein lies one of the major weaknesses of the fortress: all water and most food, found or acquired on the plains, had to be carried up the mountain.

Massive rocks and rock formations cover the acropolis-like mountain, especially on its northern and southern sides. Some of these rocks acquired religious importance for the Krobo. For instance, the all-important *Dipo* ceremony, or initiation of young girls into womanhood, is still performed at formations on the eastern side known as *Anikaka* and *Tegbete*.[15] A deep gorge divides the plateau portion of the mountain into two distinct and unequal sections. The larger, northeastern portion was the site of the earlier settlement of Dose, from which the present-day Manya Krobo developed. The southwestern section, smaller and more rugged, was the site of the later Bose settlement, whose present-day descendants are known as the Yilo Krobo.[16] Each settlement eventually divided into six subtribes.[17]

Auer provides us with a description of Manya habitation on the mountain:

> Mount Krobo and the village here are very interesting. The little houses are situated in groups between huge rocks, each house again between rocks, so the roads themselves are rocks, [and] you have to climb on all fours.[18]

Johannes Zimmermann described Krobo houses as being "like eagles' nests," with one room, and constructed of swish (a composition of clay and grass).[19] The doors, mats, and windows were constructed of palm branches tied together; the roof, held up by poles, was made from interwoven palm branches.[20]

The Krobo's mountain residence afforded an almost impregnable haven in the midst of the flat Accra Plains. From the seventeenth century to the first quarter of the nineteenth century, repeated warfare, triggered by political expansion and slave raiding, shook the region. Political disputes arose primarily among the various Akan states—the Akyem Abuakwa, the Akwamu, the Akuapem, and the Asante.[21] In this era of the Atlantic slave trade and the Asante wars of expansion, the Krobo developed their own system of defense. Sentinels watching from all the vantage points sounded an alarm at the threat of enemy attack.[22] All the Krobo then rushed back from fishing, hunting, or tending their small family farms adjacent to Klo-yo. Once on the mountain, "they [would] await the attack of the enemy." If the enemy did attack, "a small group of armed men could impede any African army from penetrating the mountain."[23] The technique of siege apparently was not used as a military strategy, at least not successfully.

The success of the Krobo's defensive strategy is impressive. They withstood attacks from the Akuapem in 1755 and 1758 and from the Asante in 1771-1772, 1811, and 1816, and held out against the combined forces of the Danes and the Akuapem in 1835-1836.[24] Only the introduction of rockets and accurate rifle fire by the British in 1858 resulted in a military defeat of the Krobo. Not until 1892 was the mountain occupied permanently by hostile forces. As a result of more than a century of military successes, the Krobo, not without reason, considered themselves warriors par excellence.

This prolonged series of wars of expansion and/or independence produced significant cultural adjustments. As the immigrant Krobo on Klo-yo absorbed Akan refugees, the Krobo came to include more peoples of ethnically and linguistically Akan heritage than did other Adangme groups. In time, the need for constant military preparedness gradually strengthened the role of the supreme war chief (*konor*) and of other secular leaders such as the chiefs of subtribes (*matse*) in a polity where the supreme authority had been that of a priest (the *okumo*). Two additional

7

factors further expanded and solidified the konor's authority: a new system of land tenure (the *huza*) and colonial rule.[25]

The evolution of a unique system of land tenure, the huza, by the end of the eighteenth century, followed by the Krobo's involvement in the international trade in palm oil by the second decade of the nineteenth century, marked a definite break with its past. In the eighteenth century and before, agriculture had been mostly subsistence production on small family farms adjacent to the mountain.[26] By the 1830s the Krobo, led by the Manya, acquired land progressively farther from the Krobo Mountain. The population was divided between the Krobo's old residence, Klo-yo, and new farms along the Akuapem foothills. During the same period the Krobo began to engage in the commercialization of palm oil products for export.

During the second half of the nineteenth century Krobo institutions changed radically, partly because of the increased presence of Europeans—traders, colonial officials, and members of the Basel Missionary Society—and partly because the Krobo had become the major cultivators and producers of palm oil for the whole of the Gold Coast. The basis for all these radical changes was the huza, which had become the center of all life, in part because it offered a way of participating in the new distribution of wealth, which in turn became the new basis of political power.

Sources

A wide range of sources documents this history—oral traditions, linguistics, archaeology, mission records, colonial records, and the observations of traders and travelers. Noa Akonor Agai Azu (c. 1835-1917) wrote the earliest and most comprehensive work based on traditions.[27] A similar study was written in the Ga language by another Basel-educated Manya Krobo, Thomas Harrison Odonkor (1865-1918).[28] Both are in fact reconstructions from oral sources of specific political and cultural developments, with an obvious bias toward the present royal clan of the Manya Krobo. Odonkor Azu (c. 1835-1867), the first paramount chief recognized by the Manya Krobo, was the father of Noa Azu and the grandfather of Thomas Odonkor; Odonkor Azu's successor, Konor Sakite (1867-1892), appointed Thomas Odonkor chief of Kpong (1885-1915), a major trading village along the Volta River. Enoch

8

Azu's *Adangbe Historical and Proverbial Songs* provides important primary materials from Krobo traditions.[29] These *Klama* songs are remembrances of the earliest period of Adangme and Krobo history as told through proverbs. They contain few references to the Yilo (Bose) Krobo, primarily because four of the six Yilo subtribes did not arrive on the Krobo Mountain until the early eighteenth century.

Subsequent studies of Krobo society have relied heavily on the works of Noa Azu and Thomas Odonkor. Margaret J. Field, who traveled widely in the 1930s and the mid-1950s among the Ga, the Krobo, and the Akyem-Kotoku, wrote a number of important works.[30] Leading the list is her unpublished study "The Krobo Constitution in Relation to the Nyewe-Ogome Dispute and the Significance of Priestly Stools" (1942), which drew on additional primary testimony as well.[31] She also wrote less detailed but important studies on the Osudoku, the Shai, and the Nungwa. Several colonial officials also contributed to early ethnographic knowledge of the Adangme: D. A. Sutherland and F. G. Crowther, both district commissioners, and S. W. Saxton and Roger E. Page of the Gold Coast Political Service.[32] In a separate class is the extensive study of Gold Coast land tenure by R. J. H. Pogucki, important for its analytical use of oral traditions and written documents.[33]

The well-known work of Carl Christian Reindorf, *History of the Gold Coast and Asante* (1886), provides limited but valuable discussions of the political events of the eighteenth and nineteenth centuries and of related Adangme peoples.[34] Reindorf is occasionally a useful check on other nineteenth-century studies. Before the work of Hugo Huber, no definitive study had been conducted on any aspect of Krobo society. His *The Krobo: Traditional Social and Religious Life of a West African People* (1963) is the major ethnographic study of the entire Krobo society. In the post-independence era, Ghana set out to reconstruct its history. The Dangbe Research Project (1964), a product of this effort, also proved useful to this study. The published works from this project include T. N. N. Accam, *Klama Songs and Chants, and Dangbe and Klama Proverbs Part I*, and M. E. Kropp, *Comparative African Wordlist: Ga, Adangbe, and Ewe (Lome)*.[35]

Linguistic and archaeological work is as yet spotty. A limited use of lexicostatistics suggests that the Krobo dialect began to

9

diverge from other Adangme dialects by perhaps the middle centuries of the first half of the present millennium (i.e., about the fourteenth century), and so gives some indication of how far back particular Krobo oral traditions may reach.[36] In southeastern Ghana, archaeological sites are few; hence we are limited to the work of Paul Ozanne.[37] James Anquandah has been conducting work on the Shai Hills settlements of Ladoku, Ayaso, Dawhenya, and Prampram.

Archival Documents

The Danes provided the first, albeit brief, written view of the "Crobo" in 1733, in the annual report by Governor Andreas Waero.[38] Danish sources are useful in providing an overall view of "Danish Guinea," but their references to the "Crobo" or the "mountain negroes" are limited.[39]

European presence among the Krobo increased significantly after 1835, when the Basel Missionary Society established its main interior station at Akropong; both Ga and English were used as languages of instruction. As a result there is voluminous material collected by missionaries to be found in *Der Evangelisches Heidenboten der Basler Mission, Der Evangelisches Missions-Magazin*, and *Jahresbericht der Evangelischen Missionsgesellschaft an Basel*. A number of other mission works touch on the Krobo: Paul Steiner, *Saat und Ernte der Basler Mission auf der Goldküste* (1896), and *Kulturarbeit der Basler Mission in Westafrika* (1904); G. A. Wanner, *Basler Handelsgesellschaft, 1615-1899* (1959); I. Bellon, *Die Gewaltsame Vertreibung der Basler Missionäre von der Goldküste* (1918); W. Schlatter, *Geschichte der Basler Mission 1815-1915*, (1916); and Paul Eppler, *Geschichte der Basler Mission, 1815-1899* (1900). References to the Krobo are infrequent but provide important insight into the culture and internal dynamics of the society during the latter half of the nineteenth century. Krobo history before the missionaries' arrival is not discussed, and the early reports tend to be pro-Manya Krobo and anti-Yilo Krobo.

The Basel Missionary Society and European colonial officials (first Danish and then British) became interested in Krobo society at about the same time, but for different reasons. By the 1850s the region and most especially the Krobo were associated with palm oil

10

production. British sources concentrate overwhelmingly on the political and economic aspects of Krobo society and the Krobo's relationships with surrounding peoples. Traders left few records, as the United Africa Company archives indicate.[40]

2

The Formative Era of Krobo Society: From the Earliest Times to the Early Eighteenth Century

Considerable debate surrounds the fundamental question of the origin of Ghana's inhabitants. Two schools of thought predominate: the "migrationists" and the "antimigrationists."[1] The migrationists, including J. B. Danquah, Eva Meyerowitz, and W. Balmer, contend that Ghana's present population migrated to the region from as far away as the Tigris and Euphrates in Mesopotamia. The antimigrationists, W. Ward, F. M. Bourret, and R. Mauny, suggest that peoples such as the Akan and the Ga-Adangme migrated to Ghana not from outside the African continent, but from within, namely from the Chad-Benue region. The two schools thus agree essentially that Ghana's inhabitants are immigrants, but disagree fundamentally over whether they migrated to Ghana from inside or outside Africa.

Linguistic and archaeological evidence, however, does not support either school. Recently Professor Adu Boahen, of the History Department of the University of Ghana, has postulated another theory. Citing linguistic data, he concluded that all of Ghana's various ethnic groups evolved from "cradles" within Ghana.[2] The history of the Adangme's migration to their present location seems to suggest that both the cradle theory and a variation of the antimigrationist theory have some validity.

The Adangme Migration

The Krobo trace their origins to a migration of the patrilineal, numerically small, Adangme-speaking people from the "east," perhaps from present-day Togo or the Republic of Benin.[3] The

Adangme, or correctly the proto-Adangme, probably reached the area remembered as Lolovor (Tagologo) in the Accra plains well before the fourteenth century. The Lolovor Hills (*Merna* and *Papla-yo*) were located about twenty miles southeast of the Akuapem foothills. The group of villages known as Lolovor became the cradle of Adangme culture. The Adangme prospered there, living in small patrilineal family groups ruled by patriarchal religious leaders. From this settlement sprang all the Adangme-speaking peoples—the Shai, the Ada, the Prampram, the Ningo, the Osudoku, and the Krobo.

Adangme oral traditions record little about the Lolovor period. Among the Krobo, Madza is the first high priest remembered from the Lolovor period.[4] Two of his descendants, Lanimo and Chayi (Shayi), became the priestly rulers (*wono*) of the Krobo and the Shai respectively.[5] After the Lolovor period, many Adangme families resettled in the nearby Shai Hills, on the Osudoku Mountain and the Krobo Mountain (Klo-yo), and along the coast at Ningo, Prampram, and Ada. According to Odonkor,

> Adangbe consisted of several small kingdoms or priestdoms. . . . the Krobo, the Shai, the Osudoku, the Ada, Prampram, Ningo, Poni. They found land on all sides, land into which they could continue to expand.[6]

In the absence of archaeological data from the Lolovor area itself, excavations at the contemporaneous or, more likely, later Shai Hills settlements of Ladoku and Adwuku provide some understanding of the Lolovor settlement and period. The coastal settlement of Ladoku was the older, as one would expect from its location nearest the original migration routes. According to archaeologist Paul Ozanne, Ladoku, now Prampram, was established during a period that he called "Phase M1," ca. 1200-1400 A.D.[7] James Anquandah, however, has carbon dates of local artifacts from a few centuries earlier. Adwuku, a fortified village on a small hill about four miles northeast of Ladoku and less than ten miles southwest of Lolovor, was also settled during the latter part of "Phase M1 . . . dating possibly from the fourteenth century or earlier."[8]

By the fifteenth century, and through the seventeenth century, the Shai Hills villages of Adwuku and Ladoku enjoyed prosperity. Farming and an extensive pottery industry, involving trading with neighboring Adangme and Akan communities, formed the foundation of their economy. Ozanne's excavations also uncovered a collection of beads, gin-bottles, gunflints, lead-shot, and tobacco pipes, including some made by Gauntlett of Amesbury, England (c. 1680-1700).[9] Despite relatively secure positions, neither Shai village could resist the powerful Akan kingdom of Akwamu, located in the nearby Akuapem Mountains. The Akwamu exacted tribute in commodities and slaves from the Adangme until the former were driven from the region in the late 1730s by the Akyem.[10] Unlike the Akwamu, the Akyem had little or no interest in the Shai, or for that matter in any other Adangme. The Akyem's political attention was directed north and west against a rising new power, the Asante.

Lolovor itself was peaceful and prosperous, but endemic warfare plagued the region around it. Anticipating eventual involvement in these neighboring wars, the Adangme left Lolovor and established settlements in easily defensible or remote locations. Their choice of sites was limited to the three inselbergs amid the Accra plains, the highland regions around what are now known as the Shai Hills, and the coastal area farther away from the Akan. All three mountain fortresses afforded the Adangme some protection from Akan warfare, which was centered in the hinterland. As groups of Adangme left Lolovor, they established their own geographically and, later, linguistically distinct societies. Traditions recall this as a period of expansion and opportunity. On linguistic grounds, the breakup of the early Adangme society and the beginning of the Krobo settlement on the mountain seem to date from around the fourteenth century (Chart 2.1).[11]

The Krobo Settlement

After leaving Lolovor, the Krobo, who call themselves "Kloli" or "Klonc," established their own settlement on a nearby tortoise-shaped mountain, which they named Klo-yo or Klo-wem.[12] Taken together, Krobo traditions of origin indicate that the mountain was from the beginning a heterogeneous settlement. One tradition states that Muase, while hunting on the Krobo Mountain, discovered that this uninhabited inselberg would be suitable for settlement by his family and friends.[13] Another tradition has it that

14

Lolovor's priestly rulers sent two hunters, Muase and Madza, to explore the mountain and ascertain its suitability for settlement. The rival Muase and Madza traditions may represent the arrival on Klo-yo of two Adangme groups at about the same time. A Klama song says something still slightly different:

> Muase lighted the fire for Madza
> so that he saw the mountain
> Madza claimed that the mountain is his
> But Muase is the owner of the mountain.[14]

Chart 2.1

ADANGME LANGUAGE TREE

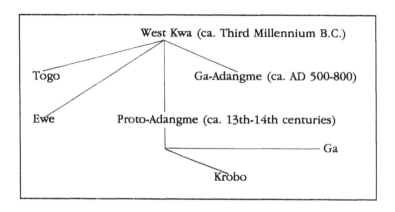

Muase's prominence in these legends is due to the latter-day political prominence of his descendants as the first group of priestly rulers, and he must be counted as representative of a slightly later era of settlement than that of Madza. Madza's name is associated with the original possession of the mountain, as the song in its veiled manner also conveys. Madza and his people were apparently only the first immigrants to seek refuge around the mountain in the succeeding centuries.

The first series of settlements, established between roughly the fourteenth and late seventeenth centuries, consisted of small groups of Adangme and later of Ewe who ritually and culturally became Adangme. In addition, some evidence suggests that the

Krobo ritually admitted a small number of Akan—possibly Akyem, Kamana, Apirede, or Kotrope—into their society. According to Field and to oral tradition, these disparate groups of settlements became known collectively as Dose. Whereas their original residences were located along the eastern side of the mountain, many of their shrines were established on the western, less inhabitable side.

The second settlement stage probably occurred between 1700 and the 1740s, when large numbers of people of Akan ancestry were admitted to the mountain as refugees from the Akan wars.[15] They settled on the smaller, rockier, western side of the mountain, called Bose (beyond the thicket). After this second wave of settlement, Krobo society no longer was composed primarily of people of Adangme origin. Dose remained predominantly Adangme, but Bose became overwhelmingly Akan. Because of basic ethnic and cultural differences between the two settlements (which will be discussed in the next chapter), around the mid-eighteenth century the Krobo split into two politically independent chiefdoms—Manya and Yilo.

To determine the history of the Krobo settlements requires an understanding of the Krobo pattern of social groupings and of authority (Tables 2.1 and 2.2). The Krobo's record of their past is a composite of all family and clan traditions. Furthermore, because the Dose Krobo were ruled by a theocratic oligarchy until the 1840s, it is also essential to understand the interconnection between the various clans and the appointment of an elite group of priests—the *djemeli*.[16] Adangme traditions unanimously agree that the earliest rulers were priests (wono). The simplicity of this statement, however, is misleading. Throughout the early history of the Adangme, and specifically of the Krobo, these priests also exercised or delegated to others limited secular authority.

Every Krobo belongs to three social units—the *wetcho*, the *kasi*, and the *we*.[17] The largest, the wetcho (family tree), unites a number of patrilineal kingroups, not all usually claiming descent from the same ancestor, under one name. For this reason the wetcho may be classified as a subtribe rather than a clan, according to Hugo Huber and Konor Azzu Mate Kole.[18] In the nineteenth century twelve wetchos existed, with no overt gradings among them.[19] Originally, a wono, a religious patriarch, led each wetcho (chapter 3).[20]

Table 2.1

MANYA KROBO SUBTRIBES, CLANS,
LOCALITIES, AND DEITIES

Subtribe (wetcho)	Clan (kasi)	Locality* (ma)	Deity (Djemawo)
Djebiam	Nam	Odumase	Kole
		Adome	
		Abude	
		Abodonya	Leete-Na
		Saisi	
		Blonuanya	
	Agbom	Agbom	Likpotsu
		Asite-Kpose	Kpenitse
	Ogome	Salosi	Nadu
		Atua	Totroku
			Medoku-Aye
			Lalo-Bake
		Agomanya	Nadu/Meet
	Yokwenya	Asite	
		Adzikpo-Yokunya	
Manya	Lomodze	Agomanya	Nause/Otu
			Manya-Tete
	Dodze	Agomanya	Medoku-Aye
		Manya-Kponuno	Lalo/Bake
	Petsi	Manya-Kponuno	
	Setsunya	Manya-Kponuno	Se (Stool)
	Agbasi	Manya-Kponuno	Totroku
		Atua	
	Nanmla	Manya-Kponuno	
		Atua	
	Tesano	Agomanya	
Akweno	Konya	Akweno-Mampon	Se (Stool)
		Atotsonya	
	Asemdua	Akweno-Mampon	Okumo
	Masi	Manya-Kponuno	
	Sainya	Manya-Kponuno	Lanma
	Wekpeti	Koletsom'	Kole

17

Susui	Alabonya	Kodzonya	Nana Kloweki
(Suisi)		Manya-Kponuno	Atsuwayo
		Nuaso	
	Yono	Manya-Kponuno	Hiono
		Kodzonya	
		Atotsonya	
	Wekpeti	Kwekpe	Ayawa-Dade
		Meneko	
		Koletsom	Kole
		Nuaso	Adumuli
		Kodzonya	Me/Lalo-Bake
		Otalenya	
	Kukunya	Menekpo	
Piengua	Yokweno	Yohe	
	Wekpeti	Sokwenya	Omessu
	(Mitsom')	Lom	Odente
		Madam	
		Takpe	Osieku/Onyoku
		Anyinma	
		Fodzoku	
		Mampon	
Dom	Memlessi	Salem	Se (Stool)
		Nauso	Nako
		Asite	Nadu
			Medoku-Aye
	Kolenya	Salem	Kole
		Nuaso	
		Asite	
	Konopiem'	Manya-Kponuno	Katapani
	Tesanya	Nuaso	Mani
		Asite-Kpose	

*Village location along the Akuapem foothills.

18

Table 2.2
YILO (BOSE) KROBO SUBTRIBES, CLANS, LOCALITIES, AND DEITIES

Subtribe (*wetcho*)	Clan (*kasi*)	Locality (*ma*)	Deity (*Djemawo*)
Bonya	Nakodzeli	Sawe Sum Sra Adzikpo-Basayono	Nako/Kleme Bleku
	Badzebii	Sawe	Ayebida Lalo-Bake
Ogome	Matebii Neubii Nanebii Odeyoku	Ogome Ogome Ogome Nuaso	Se (Stool) Dika

Okpe	Wekpeti
	(Ago)
	Okpe-Piem'
	Okpe-Lowe
	Gbekomanya
	Adzikpo-
	  Aduman
	Nakuyo-
	  Ledze
	Betesi
		Okpe
		
		Somanya
		Okpe
		Gbekomanya
		Adzikpo-Aduman
		
		Nakuyo-Ledze
		
		Betesi
			
			Anate/Agla
			Kole
			Atsekeni
			
			Aku
			Kofi-Dade

Bunase	Dono
	Hulakonya
	
	Sekwenya
	
	Alamsakwonya
	Agvenya
	Odave
	Amlakpo
		Adzikpop-Dono
		Adzikpo-
		  Hulakonya
		Somanya-Salosi
		Kpom-Kpoo
		Adzikpo
		Somanya-
		  Agavenya
		Adzikpo-Odave
		Adzikpo-Amlakpo
			Dika
			(at Ogome)
			
			Dzaobo

Plau	Lamsanya Tsatsuk-plenya Nakpe/Plau-Kpom'	Somanya Somanya	Kofi-Obonuma Kaklago
Nyewe	Kplade Abokobi Trom Sra Yokono	Kplade Abokobi Trom Sra Yokono	Kotoklo Otroku Medoku-Aye Lanma Dasuma

The next smaller social unit is the kasi (clan), whose members reputedly descend from a common ancestor or from an immigrant kinship group.[21] There are primary and secondary kasi. The Djebiam subtribe, for example, has four primary kasi: Nam, Agbom, Ogome, and Yokwenya. Each of these is further divided into secondary kasi or subclans; Yokwenya's subclans are Agomanya, Asite, and Adzikpo-Yokunya. Like the wetcho, the kasi are neither exogamous units nor exclusive cult groups. The names of kasi were frequently derived from the location of either their settlement on the Krobo Mountain or their ancestral farm, but usually not from the ancestral founder. Collectively, the family heads, elders, and priests govern the kasi. Of these ruling elements the priests exercise the greatest authority.

Each kasi is composed of a number of we (houses), the we being the minimal lineage or maximal family group whose members all descend from a particular male. Namlii (children of Nam's house), for instance, are all descendants of Nam through the male line. There was probably little clear distinction between we and kasi until the late eighteenth century, when the population had increased significantly and become more stratified. The subtribe (wetcho), the clan (kasi), and the family (we) each had its own leader (Table 2.3).[22]

Assisted by the elders and the heads of the smaller units—the asafo-tse (subchief) and the we-nokotoma (house elder)—each matse (chief) controlled the judicial functions of his respective subtribe. The asafo-tse whose authority paralleled that of the matse, headed the next social unit, the clan (kasi). With the assistance of the elders and heads of his clan, and of the heads of the respective families, the asafo-tse maintained order in secular

Table 2.3
PRINCIPAL SOCIAL GROUPINGS

Unit	Ruler/Authority
Subtribe (*wetcho*)	*Matse*/secular
Clan (*kasi*)	*Asafo-tse*/secular
Family (*we*)	*we-nokotoma*/secular/religious

matters affecting the clan (lineage/house). The asafo-tse was also the clan's military leader.

The family or house (we), ruled by its most senior male member, the we-nokotoma, formed the smallest social unit. Unlike the matse and the asafo-tse, the we-nokotoma was not elected. Moreover, the house elder's domain included both secular and religious issues. Thus, when a particular family's deity achieved importance on the clan or tribal level, the corresponding house elder (we-nokotoma), as well as the deity's priest (wono) or priestess (*woyo*), became especially important to its worshippers.[23] For instance, Nana Kloweki was first introduced into Krobo society by a member of the Alabonya clan of the Susui subtribe, and authority over Nana Kloweki is therefore under the house elder of Kodzonya, the locality associated with the Alabonya clan.

Chronology of Migrations

By the eighteenth century the Dose Krobo were governed by a theocratic oligarchy composed of the djemeli and the okumo, who was primus inter pares among the djemeli.[24] Not all Krobo priests were djemeli; the djemeli were selected from some of the earliest Dose (Manya) Krobo clans. Oral traditions provide little evidence to explain the evolution of the priestly oligarchy or the historical seniority of various subtribes, clans, and families (chapter 3). Cultural analysis, however, may be used to suggest a relative chronology of their emergence.

All Krobo deities were introduced into Dose Krobo society by a particular family. Certain deities are considered older than others; the oldest deities are associated with the oldest clans, which brought them to Klo-yo (Table 2.4). This kind of evidence makes it possible to suggest broad periods during which these deities and ceremonies "arrived" on the mountain, and thus to estimate roughly when specific clans or families associated with these deities and ceremonies became part of Dose society.

Table 2.4

MAJOR KROBO DEITIES

Deity	Subtribe or Clan Affiliation
Major Deities:	
Nana Kloweki	Susui, Akweno, Dom,
	Djebiam-Yokwenya
Nause	Manya-Lomodze
Nadu	Djebiam-Yokwenya, Dom
Oldest Deities:	
Nause	Manya
Nako	Bonya
Nana Kloweki	Susui
Hiono	Susui

In other words, the elaboration of the djemeli may be interpreted as a response to a succession of new immigrants to the mountain, with the more senior djemeli commanding the more important religio-political positions in Dose society because religious institutions were focal to the successful social integration of the immigrants. At some point the body of djemeli ceased to expand, and later immigrants failed to produce djemeli of their own. Similarly, the physical disposition of participants in the society-wide Anikaka Council (chapter 3) early became formalized, and this positioning too provides a relative dating for groups within Krobo society.[25]

The First Settlements

The oldest Krobo families and clans can be found in the Manya, Bonya, Susui, and Akweno subtribes. This conclusion is implied by the seating positions for representatives of the different subtribes during general councils of the whole society. The priests

22

from each family grouping convened around a large square-shaped rock on the mountain called Anikaka, sitting in the pattern indicated in Chart 2.2.[26] The Anikaka Council apparently took shape at a time when just four subtribes composed Dose society: the Akweno, Manya, Susui/Dom, and Bonya all had their own positions on the Anikaka Rock, while the other subtribes sat behind or were attached to one of the original four.[27]

Until the creation of paramount chiefs in the middle of the eighteenth century, authority remained in the hands of this council. All important Krobo matters were discussed and resolved at the "Anikaka high-court" and council. If the court deadlocked or an individual wished to contest the court or council's decision, the matter was appealed to "the Old Lady," the priestess of Nana Kloweki. Her decisions were uncontestable.[28]

Chart 2.2

SEATING ON THE ANIKAKA ROCK
(KLAMA TE EWIE)

Okumo	
Dome Tsatsu Te (Domeli/Susui)	Manya Te (Akromause Stool) (Manya)
Ogome Te (Bonya and later Bose/Yilo)	Akweno (Piengua, Djebiam)

Of the four clans represented in the council, tradition explicitly indicates Manya as the first. The legendary founding father of the Krobo, Madza, is also the patriarch of the Manya subtribe; and Nause of the Manya-Lomodze clan is universally recognized as the oldest Krobo deity. The same reasoning suggests that Bonya developed as the subtribe of the second significant group of immigrants to the mountain, since Nako, the deity of the Nakodzeli kasi of Bonya, is considered the second oldest god of all Kroboland.[29] The Yono clan of the Susui subtribe, whose deity Kiono is considered by many to be the third oldest, may thus originally have been composed of the third set of arrivals there.

23

The Cultural Revolution

The arrival of the founders of the Alabonya clan of the Susui subtribe appears to have marked the beginning of a period of major changes in the still forming society. These immigrants introduced Nana Kloweki and its accompanying Dipo ceremony.[30] Nana Kloweki was not just another deity.

> It is said that the repertoire of Krobo rituals was greatly enriched by the addition of the cult of *Nana Kloweki*; not only were the millet-'eating' ceremonies introduced, but the *Dipo* initiation was also organized as a more magnificent performance. Many other deities have, through their priests, adopted the ritual practices of *Nana Kloweki*.[31]

The rise of Nana Kloweki illustrates how immigrant groups added to the existing pantheon, and how such an "immigrant deity" expanded its influence beyond the boundaries of a particular family. While the potential for such a phenomenon always existed, no other deity affected the politico-religious authority of the priesthood as did Nana Kloweki.

Among the early Krobo there was probably little distinction between the sacred and the secular. As A. K. Quacoo has noted concerning another Adangme group, the Shai, "religion permeated all life, all exigencies and all conditions."[32] In the words of the venerable Konor Nene Azzu Mate Kole of Manya Krobo, (1939-1990): "Originally the administration of the Krobo tribe was in the hands of the priests and carried out by heads of clans [and] heads of families."[33] Before the introduction of Nana Kloweki, authority over the Dose resided in the hands of shadowy figures remembered as priestly kings (*madja*). Little is known about these rulers, although the title has remained. *Okumo Majano Atreku* (ruler of the town) is remembered as a descendant of one of the legendary founders of the Krobo Mountain.[34] The madja probably presided over the Anikaka Council at its inception.

The rise in power of the priestess of Nana Kloweki and the accompanying djemeli challenged the Majano's secular authority. The priestess of Nana Kloweki could not herself rule, because she was prohibited from interacting personally with strangers and was confined to the shrines associated with Nana Kloweki. Such restrictions, however, did not prohibit the djemeli from emerging both as the representatives of the religious community in the broadest sense and as spokesmen for the secular community. Before the establishment of paramount chiefs in the mid-eighteenth century, the djemeli were the most important group of priests. According to anthropologist Hugo Huber, the djemeli stand out among priets as "one chosen group whose members, more than any other priests, influence public worship and the religious life of the people particularly in the past." Not wishing to remain confined to ritual matters alone, the djemeli expanded their secular authority. As their agent they selected a member of their own ranks from Akweno or Susui families. This official was known as the okumo. "Among the *djemeli*," Huber noted, the "*Okumo* ranks first." The okumo perceived his rule as continuing the line of previous rulers linked to madja and, equally importantly, himself as "*Kloweki otsiame ke labia nua*" (spokesman and head-assistant of Kloweki).[35] This relationship has been preserved in one of the Krobo's many proverbs (Klama):

> *Okumo* priest,
> father of the *dipo*-girls
> guard us!
> *Kloweki* priest,
> husband of the *dipo*-girls![36]

Like the madja, the okumo presided over the Anikaka council and court, and also served as executioner.[37] But the okumo's secular and religious authority was greater than that of his predecessor. The increased importance of his secular authority marked a break with the original group of priestly leaders, who had been selected from Manya families and had no association with Nana Kloweki; the okumo was the spokesman for Nana Kloweki and the djemeli.

The okumo functioned as both the secular head of the Anikaka Council and as a priest. In each capacity he had limited access to the general Krobo population. He was restricted to the mountain and the farmlands adjacent to it; and, like the priests, he was forbidden to interact personally with strangers, especially the Akan, who were "unclean"[38] (uncircumcised). The okumo was also forbidden to participate in warfare. However, before the expansion of the Krobo population in the eighteenth and nineteenth centuries, these prohibitions did not inhibit the successful function of either the okumo or the priesthood. Indeed, as long as the Krobo lived on the mountain and on small family farms at its base, the isolation of priests tended to reaffirm their unique social importance. Not until the Krobo began to move well beyond the mountain in the late eighteenth century did they take another major step toward the secularization of their system of government.

Table 2.5

KROBO SUBTRIBES c. 1700

1. Manya
2. Susui
3. Akweno
4. Dom
5. Bonya
6. Piengua
7. Djebiam

Many of the Akweno ancestors must have arrived in the same general wave of migration as the Susui, since their descendants shared in the control over Nana Kloweki and the Dipo ceremony, which together lay at the core of the theocratic oligarchy. Not only did the Akweno provide the major djemeli for Nana Kloweki and the Dipo ceremony, but the okumo was selected from the Akweno. Just when this "revolution" took place cannot be precisely determined, but the social and religious structures created by the Susui and Akweno migrations were in place before the sixteenth- and seventeeth-century settlements of later Djebiam and Piengua clans. Since the original Manya settlement may date back to the fourteenth century, the Susui-Akweno "revolution" might best be placed in the fifteenth or perhaps the early sixteenth century; but that can be only a most tentative suggestion. By the year 1700 the Krobo were made up of seven subtribes (Table 2.5).

The Later Dose Settlements

The Dom and Piengua wetcho appear to descend from a relatively early settlement era, but from non-Adangme forebears. The Dom or Ohwe (valley dwellers) were primarily *Aniboi* (people from the east, that is, Adangme) immigrants from Awuna,[39] who were led to the mountain by the patriarch Akada Kwadzo. Field claims that three of the four Dom clans—Kolenya, Konopiem, and Tesanya—came from Togo. The Dom-Memlese clan, however, point to Akropong in Akyem as their place of origin.[40]

Initially, according to some traditions, the Dom attached themselves to the Akweno subtribe. Along with the Akweno and Djebiam-Yokwenya, the Dom provide djemeli for Nana Kloweki. The Dom-Memlese supplied the djemeli who was responsible for "bringing millet-beer to priests of *Nana Kloweki* during the millet festival, and also [for providing] new grasses for covering the hut of *Likpotfu* during the annual yam and town blessing ceremonies."[41] The priest of Nadu is selected alternately from the Dom-Kolenya, Djebiam-Ogome segments and Djebiam-Yokwenya. The Dom's role is the more important; they also provide the "playground" (*Dom Mano*) for the celebration of this national deity. The Dom's religious and military importance in the society strongly suggests that their integration into Dose society may well predate that of any Djebiam clan except possibly Yokwenya. That is, Dom probably emerged as a Dose wetcho before the sixteenth century.

The presence of deities of Akan origin in all three Piengua clans supports Field's inference from oral testimony that the Piengua and the Dom-Momlese were part of the same Akyem group.[42] The development of the Piengua and the incorporation of the Momlese kasi into Dom may therefore reflect a seventeenth-century movement of people, perhaps refugees from the Akyem's wars with the Akwamu.

Of the Dose Krobo subtribes, Djebiam is the largest and shows most clearly the composite origins of the early Krobo subtribes. Djebiam consists of four very distinct clans: Yokwenya, Ogome, Nam, and Agbom. The Djebiam-Yokwenya, who trace their origins to Biam, along the coast, appear to have been the first of the four clans to settle on the mountain. Their deity, Meete, is associated with Nako, the Krobos' national symbol; djemeli from

27

the Djebiam-Yokwenya, along with those from the Akweno and Dom subtribes, alternately serve as the djemeli for Nana Kloweki, the single most important deity. Moreover, the Yokwenya, Akweno, and Dom provide the sanctuaries and shrines for Nadu, the Dose Krobo's war god.[43]

The Yokwenya may have been incorporated into Dose society in the fifteenth or sixteenth century. Tradition associates Yokwenya clan migration with a peaceful period. Sometime before the mid-sixteenth century is therefore probable, because after the 1640s recurrent Akwamu raids in the region should have generated traditions of forced migration.

Like the Yokwenya, the Djebiam-Ogome were immigrants from the "east," more specifically from Lekpono at Ada, and were also of Adangme ancestry. According to their traditions, Nadu, the Dose Krobo's god of war, was brought to Klo-yo by an Ogome woman. In more recent times, the priests of Nadu have been selected alternately from the Djebiam-Ogome, Djebiam-Yokwenya, and Dom-Asite. The association of the Djebiam-Ogome with a war god conceivably may indicate that they joined the Dose settlements after the Yokwenya, during the widespread political instability of the seventeenth century, or it may reflect earlier events of which we have no record. Djebiam-Ogome is also associated with the Dipo ceremony, part of which is performed on the Tegbete (*Totroku*) Rock, which is under the protection of Djebiam-Ogome.

The Nam clan of Djebiam is a special case. First, since the middle 1850s it has been the royal clan of the Manya (formerly Dose) Krobo. Moreover, many of the recorded oral traditions come from two members of this clan, Noa Akonor Agai Azu and Thomas Harrison Odonkor. The Nam (Namlii—people of Nam) claim descent from Muase, contemporary of the founding father, Madza, but other evidence suggests that the ancestors of Djebiam-Nam were from the north or west and were probably Akan. Thomas Odonkor favored "Dodi in the Asabi Kingdom,"[44] whereas Manya Krobo Konors Emmanuel Mate Kole (1892-1939), Azzu Mate Kole (1939-1990), and Margaret Field support the assertion that Kamanda was the source of the original Nam immigrants.[45] Neither area is or apparently ever was Adangme-speaking country.

Leete-Na, the clan deity of Djebiam-Nam, is generally considered one of the oldest deities of the Dose, but this belief probably reflects recent Nam preeminence rather than actual chronology. Leete-Na is worshipped on Friday, whereas Adangme deities are normally worshipped on Thursday or Sunday. Furthermore, priests of Leete-Na are not members of the djemeli. Kole, the particular deity of the Nam-Odumase family, the royal family of the Manya Krobo, does appear to have originated in Ada, an Adangme area, but is probably a later adoption by them from other Krobo groups, for the deity also belongs to the Dom-Kolenya, Susui-Wekpeti, and Akweno-Wekpeti clans. The connection with the Wekpeti kasi, now found in two subtribes, suggests that they may have been the original bearers of the deity.

Djebiam-Agbom's heritage is similar to Djebiam-Nam's. The Agbom claim origins in the area around Fante in the central region. There are also significant Ewe elements in the Agbom tradition, for Likotfu, the clan's deity, is of Ewe origin. The Djebiam-Agbom thus give the appearance of having arisen from an amalgamation of Ewe immigrants from the east and Akan from the west and north. The relative age accorded their deity suggests a fairly early arrival, perhaps during the era of early Ewe expansion, in about the sixteenth century. If so, the composition of the djemeli may already have become established as early as the sixteenth century, since no djemeli is selected from either of the two Agbom we.

The backgrounds of the four Djebiam clans thus reflect the incorporation of groups of Adangme, Ewe, and Akan origin who settled on the mountain before the end of the seventeenth century. The varied origins suggest the existence of some sort of policy in early Dose society of overcoming the disruptive potential of immigrants by attaching them as corporate groups to already established clans. The established group in this case would seem to have been the Yokwenya, who not only appear to have been the earliest of the four, but also came, as the attribution of Biam origins must mean, out of an ethnically akin Adangme-speaking background.

The Eighteenth-Century Migrations

The second major wave of immigrants, arriving in the first decades of the eighteenth century, were Akan refugees remembered as "Denkyira Krobo."[46] (Although they were in fact mostly Akyem, Krobo tradition insists that some were indeed

29

Denkyira, whose kingdom was located in the central region.)[47] These late immigrants formed clans that came to be grouped into four subtribes: Nyewe, Plau, Okpe, and Bunase (Table 2.6).

Table 2.6
KROBO SUBTRIBES BY THE 1740s

Dose Krobo	"Denkyira" Krobo

Akweno
Susui
Dom (Ohwe)
Piengua
Bonya
Djebiam-Nam (Nambii)
    Ogome
    Yokwenya
    Agbom
	Nyewe (Langmasi)
	Plau
	Okpe
	Bunase

Table 2.7
KROBO SUBTRIBES FROM c. 1750
TO THE PRESENT

Manya (Dose)	Yilo (Bose)

1. Djebiam-Nam
        -Agbom
        -Ogome
        -Yokwenya
2. Susui
3. Akweno
4. Piengua
5. Dom
6. Manya
	1. Nyewe
	2. Okpe
	3. Plau
	4. Bunase
	5. Bonya
	6. Ogome

30

The incorporation of the four Denkyira Krobo subtribes in the early 1700s raised the number of subtribes to twelve and permanently altered the ethnic composition of Krobo society. The djemeli became in effect even more exclusive, systematically denying admission to members of these four subtribes. The deities of the Denkyira Krobo played and have continued to play only a minor role in Krobo religious ceremonies. Since the middle of the eighteenth century the Krobo have developed two still larger groupings: the Manya and the Yilo (chapter 4). Each of these has six subtribes and a number of families (Table 2.7).[48] Furthermore, all important sacred meeting places, objects, and shrines belonged to or were under the protection of various Dose clans and were part of the Dose settlement on the mountain's eastern side or under its authority (Table 2.8).[49]

Table 2.8

MAJOR SACRED OBJECTS, ROCKS, AND SYMBOLS

Sacred Object	Purpose	Location
Anikaka Rock	Council meeting	Manya Krobo
Tegbete/Totrotu	Dipo ceremony	Manya Krobo
Lomodze-Te	Sacred rock in sacred grove of Nause	Manya Krobo
Ball-Python	Sacred animal of Bonya and Susui	

The conditions for admission to the mountain, listed below, clearly functioned to speed the acculturation of immigrants into the Adangme tradition (Table 2.9).[50] Their intent was at least threefold. First, as far as was possible all Krobo should undergo the initiation ceremonies for men (circumcision) and women (the Dipo ceremony). Second, core Adangme traditions, such as language and personal names, took precedence even though non-Adangme were permitted entry into Krobo society. Finally, the security of the mountain and the secrecy of its access paths should be protected from potential spies.

Table 2.9
CONDITIONS FOR ADMISSION TO MOUNTAIN

1. Male circumcision
2. Speak only Adangme on the Mountain
3. Girls must undergo the *Dipo* ceremony
4. Must take Adangme names, especially children
5. Non-Adangme immigrants could not leave or send messages from the mountain without permission

The Krobo migration to the mountain represents but a small part of an Adangme tradition of group migration and amalgamation. Because all Adangme shared a willingness to accept newcomers, each group came to reflect the geography and ethnicity of its own locale, incorporating varying proportions of Ewe and Akan elements while maintaining a general sense of cultural Adangmeness. Even Noa Azu, with his strong pro-Djebiam biases, recognized the varied origins of the Krobo. In a tone that reflected his Basel mission education, he called on all Krobo to "rejoice in the coming of these *Aniboi* and *Moboi* [Eastern and Western] refugees, for without them the Krobo would have not been able to defend itself [*sic*]. . . . All these tribes formed together as one, is what we now call Krobo."[51]

3

THE KROBO AND THEIR NEIGHBORS
FROM THE SEVENTEENTH CENTURY TO 1835

The Krobo were part of a larger political and cultural landscape during the eighteenth century. In 1701 the name "Crobbo" made its first cartographical appearance on a rough map of the region.[1] Otherwise, the first specific reference to the Krobo in a written source dates from 1733, when Governor Andreas Waero noted in his annual report on trading conditions in the Eastern Region of Danish Guinea that

> it is certain that all of Fante, Accra, Adampe [Adangme], and Pramprams get their trade from Crobbo and Crepe which border the [Volta] River. . . . Above Crobbo the River divides into three parts.[2]

Given the comparatively small "Crobbo" population of that era, it is surprising that they were noticed at all by the coastal Europeans. Among peoples of the Eastern Region they were more prominent, as will be demonstrated below and in the following chapter.

When a serious disruption of trading occurred in 1748, the Danish governor blamed Krobo "bandits."[3] Krobo banditry continued well into the mid-1760s. Lacking gold, slaves, or other valuable trade commodities, the Krobo apparently stole what they needed or desired from unsuspecting itinerant African traders traveling to or from the coast. By 1750 the Krobo made their appearance on other European maps. M. D. Anville's 1760 map of the Gold Coast identified the "Crobbo" northeast of the "Landingcour" kingdom.[4] L. F. Rømer also identified "the mountain negroes [Krobo] who border on the river Volta, and who trade with Keta."[5] Despite continued trade-related references to the Krobo, the Ladoku (Le), Ningo, Ada, and Keta along the coast

33

coast received the greatest recognition from Africans and Europeans, because these Adangme villages were centers of the European trade connections.[6]

Since at least the seventeenth century, various Akan states have dominated southern and central Ghana. During the seventeenth century, the Denkyira, the most powerful kingdom, had tributary control over the entire central and southern region. In a series of wars beginning in the late 1690s, the Asante defeated the Denkyira. By 1701, the Asante began to consolidate and expand their influence throughout Ghana, surpassing the former kingdom of the Denkyira. With the rise of the Asante and the fall of the Denkyira, several states, Akan and non-Akan, scrambled to fill power vacuums or challenge the authority of states formerly under the Denkyira. The Akwamu, the major political force under the Denkyira in the southeastern region, managed to hold on to their power until the mid-1730s, while the Asante were extending their authority throughout central, western, and southern Ghana.

Before the coming of the Akwamu, the La kingdom of Ladoku, of which little is known, was the most important center of commercial activity on the coast between Accra and Ada.[7] Archaeological data indicate that Ladoku, which dated from the eleventh century, was the largest and most important of the Adangme villages. Portuguese trading accounted for the expansion of Ladoku, which by 1500 measured over a mile long and more than half a mile wide. Trade in ivory, gold, and a variety of European goods peaked around 1680. By this date, the region had come under the suzerainty of the Akwamu, with an economy based on the exportation of slaves and gold, both collected from the Akyem forest region. According to Ivor Wilks, the Akwamuhene Ansa Sasraku "effected the conquest of the kingdom of Ladoku in 1679."[8]

Thereafter, Akwamu expansion continued under Akwamuhenes Ansa Sasraku (c. 1660-1689) and Basua Ado. By 1693 the Akwamu kingdom included a number of other Akan states (Akyem Kotoklo, Akyem Abuakwa, Akuapem, Jakiti, Apirede, and Kotrope), most of the small Guan chiefdoms of the southeastern region (Kamana, Bunu, Equea, Aburi, and Latebi), the Ga, and all the Adangme-speaking peoples. Nor did the Ewe escape the aggressive, expansionist policies of the Akwamu. By 1710 many of the trans-Volta chiefdoms, including Peki, Krepi, Ho, Kpandu, and Kwahu, were part of the Akwamu empire.

Unlike their successor, the Asante, the Akwamu did not establish a strong administration. Nor were they efficient traders. Their rule was harsh: "Everywhere power was abused."[9] Led by the Akyem and the Ga, a combined force of Akan, Ga, and Ewe warriors resoundingly defeated the Akwamu in a series of battles in the Akuapem Mountains in 1730. Fearful of the wrath of their revengeful former subjects, the Akwamu fled the region, crossing the Volta and establishing their present settlement. Peace did not follow the Akwamu, however; in the course of the next century or so a series of wars involving the Akyem and the Anlo Ewe, among other peoples, further eroded the Akwamu's political force in the southeastern region.

Throughout the period of Akwamu rule the Krobo were merely one Adangme group of no particular geopolitical significance. Although they shared the general hostility to Akwamu rule, the Krobo did not participate in their defeat, but more important benefitted politically and materially from their exodus. In the aftermath of the Akwamu's defeat, the Krobo began to feel secure enough to expand gradually into lands between their ancestral home, Klo-yo, and the Akuapem foothills. This expansion in turn permitted the Krobo to cultivate more foods for domestic use and for sale.

Many of the chiefdoms of the Eastern Region made political and economic advances, thus filling the vacuum left by the Akwamu. In the region south of the Akyem, between the Akuapem escarpment and the plains, the Akuapem assumed political leadership. In Accra and the immediate area, the Ga predominated. The Adangme communities, too, were again freer to pursue their political and economic programs.

Krobo Political Expansion in the Eighteenth Century

For the Adangme peoples the eighteenth century was a time of territorial expansion, rapid population growth, and new economic opportunities. The Adangme were not, in general, major participants in the Atlantic slave trade, because they were militarily weaker than their neighbors who engaged in slave raiding and because they had no commodities to trade for slaves for export.

Slavery, however, certainly existed within Adangme societies. The Adangme along the coast—the Ningo, the Ada, and the Prampram—did engage in the Atlantic slave trade, probably as middlemen, as well as in trading generally. The interior Adangme—the Osudoku, the Shai, and the Krobo—were not involved in the trade in slaves, relying more on subsistence farming. The defeat of the Akwamu diminished the threat of large slave raiding parties and encouraged the movement of these groups away from the protective shadow of their mountain homes. The Shai gradually descended from their fortified hill residences, as did the Osudoku and the La. The Krobo began moving into areas vacated by the Akwamu and their allies, the Jakiti, Kotrope, Kamana, Apirede, and Begoro, many of whom fled the Akuapem Mountains together with the Akwamu, leaving unoccupied large parcels of land—land subsequently purchased by the Krobo or occupied outright by them (chapter 5). Between the 1750s and the 1850s the Krobo farmers expanded from the base of the Krobo Mountain north and west into the Akuapem foothills and valleys and south along the Volta. It is estimated that the area they appropriated during this hundred-year period covered about 200 square miles.

Cheap cultivable land, the absence of oppressive political authority from chiefdoms such as the Akwamu, and the introduction of new food crops from the Americas—maize, lima bean, cassava, peanut, sweet potato, pumpkin, squash, red pepper—led to a natural increase in the Adangme population. The eighteenth-century Akan wars produced refugees. For example, Rømer observed that about one hundred Akwamu families settled along the gorge of the Volta after their defeat in 1730.[10] All the Adangme settlements, especially those in direct contact with the Akan, such as the Krobo, the Osudoku, and the Shai, admitted refugees into their societies. These various Akan immigrants are remembered collectively as Denkyira. Among the Ada these Denkyira constituted the Kabiaweyumu clan, whereas another group of refugees from Kamana constituted the Kabiawer clan.[11] The largest number of Denkyira refugees settled among the Krobo, because of the Krobo's geographical proximity to the Akan. In all Adangme societies, these immigrants formed their own familial units rather than becoming integrated into the existing Adangme clans (chapter 2). The Akan wars, therefore, led directly to an unexpected increase in the total

Adangme population, especially among the Krobo. Of course, not all refugees were Akan; some were Ewe.

The forced exodus of the Akwamu and the Akan wars generally led directly to a rapid Krobo population increase and territorial expansion. Both developments prepared the ground for economic stability among the Krobo. First, the accumulation of land outside the protective shadow of the fortress-like Krobo Mountain afforded an increasing number of Krobo farmers an opportunity to cultivate crops—which now included maize, millet, yams, and cassava—above subsistence level. Also, fishing increased when the west bank of the Volta came under the suzerainty of the Krobo.

Obstacles to Krobo Expansion:
The Geopolitical Background

Territorial and economic expansion did not proceed without occasional political challenges from neighboring peoples. Although removed from the western side of the Volta and reduced in numbers and strength the Akwamu remained a major force in the region. Moreover, they hoped to regain economic control over the lucrative trade along the Volta in foodstuffs, firearms, ironwork, and spirits—a trade that was now in the hands of various other groups, including the Osudoku, the Anlo Ewe, the Krobo, and the Ada. To protect their economic interests, the Adangme, including the Krobo, formed a military alliance with the Ga against the Akwamu/Anlo.[12] Intense economic competition and chronic warfare between these forces during the 1750s and 1760s intensified after 1775.

The Krobo and similar small chiefdoms of the region feared incorporation by the larger Akan chiefdoms such as the Asante, Akyem, and Akwamu. Although there is no record of a tributary arrangement between the Krobo and the Akwamu or their successors, the Akyem Abuakwa and the Asante, it seems likely, given the political realities of the day, that the Krobo probably did pay homage or in some way acknowledge the power of the Akwamu and the Akyem. But the Krobo, although numerically small, were making their own political and economic bid for part of the region. They began to form politico-military alliances that increasingly involved them in conflicts among the Akwamu, the Akyem, and the region's greatest power, the Asante.

The Krobo were the beneficiaries of the Akwamu's vacated land along the Akuapem foothills, but the Akyem filled the power vacuum created by the Akwamu's defeat and exodus. Fortunately for the Krobo, the Akyem did not regard political or economic control of the Krobo or other Adangme as a high priority. Economically, the Krobo were of little or no importance, since they had neither gold nor slaves. Moreover, the Akyem were land rich, so when small groups of Krobo farmers occupied or purchased vacant lands on the southern fringes of their newly established chiefdom along the Akuapem foothills, the Akyem Abuakwa were not alarmed.[13] Instead, the Akyem Abuakwa attempted to consolidate their holdings throughout the forested areas and prepared to do battle with the expanding Asante from the Central Region.

Throughout the eighteenth and into the early nineteenth century, the Asante challenged the Akyem's expansion schemes and even their independence. Robert Addo-Fenning's recent analysis of eighteenth- and nineteenth-century Akyem Abuakwa relations with their neighbors shows that the Asante were the Akyem's superiors during the nine eighteenth-century wars.[14] The conflicts that preoccupied the Akyem also produced Akyem refugees who were ritually admitted into Krobo, Shai, and Osudoku societies.

Krobo accumulation of land along the Akuapem foothills did not result in military conflict with the Akyem Abuakwa or their clients the Jakiti, the Apirede, and the Kotrope. The Akuapem, however, did offer resistance to wholesale Krobo expansion. This smaller Akan neighbor to the northwest viewed itself as the dominant political force in the region (a view unsubstantiated by historical evidence) and demanded tribute from the Shai and the Krobo. For a time the Krobo avoided any direct conflict with the militarily more sophisticated and numerically superior Akuapem by ignoring the latter's claim of overrule. This was easier for the more eastern Manya Krobo than for the Yilo, located on the border between the two chiefdoms. More important, without gold or abundant land the Akuapem were the Krobo's logical competitors for the vacant lands of the Akuapem foothills. The Akuapem presence posed less of a hindrance to the expansion of the Manya Krobo, who purchased lands from the Kotrepe, Jakiti, and other nearby neighbors, than to that of the Yilo, who were trying to purchase from the same chiefdoms more easterly lands that the Akuapem claimed for their own. By the late 1820s, the adoption of palm oil as a cash crop in the region and the declining importance of slave export had made land more valuable and ended any possibility of peaceful economic coexistence between the two groups. Also, in 1826, the Asante had been driven from the southeastern region after their military defeat near Dodowa, and the Akuapem were thus freed from fear of attacks from the northwest. The Dum War of 1835-36, named after the Danish governor, provided a military resolution to the dispute over political dominance between the Akuapem and the Krobo.[15]

In 1742 the Asante defeated both the Akyem Abuakwa and the Akuapem, thus becoming part of what Kwame Arhin has called Greater Asante.[16] By the 1750s the Asante were the undisputed dominant power throughout the Gold Coast.[17] Their empire encompassed an area from the Atlantic in the south, to the trans-Volta in the east, to Baule country in the west (present-day Ivory Coast), and to Gonja and Dagomba country in the north (present-day Burkina Faso). Administratively, Greater Asante consisted of provinces, protectorates, and tributaries. Provinces included Accra, Ada, Aowin, El Mina, Nzima, and Bana. Tributaries were states "who were expected to make annual contributions to the Ashanti economy and manpower."[18] Asante control and interest diminished successively from the level of provinces and protectorates to tributaries. For example, the Dagomba had only a resident tribute-collecting agent who had no other role in Dagomba society.[19] There were no Asante officials among the Krobo, who at the time were of such minor geographical and political importance as to be outside the Greater Asante administrative structure. Even at the zenith of their power, the Asante had only indirect economic interest in the Krobo. Two Krobo villages, however, Akuse and Kpong, were part of Asante's elaborate trading network.[20]

Akuse and Kpong not withstanding, the Krobo posed no political or economic threat to the Asante; they were however, an annoyance. The Asante's major concern in the eastern region was the Akyem Abuakwa, who not only refused to accept the Asante's suzerainty but vied with them for regional dominance in the wake of the Akwamu. In some of the inevitable Asante-Akyem Abuakwa conflicts, the Krobo sided with the Akyem Abuakwa, with whom they needed to maintain cordial relations in order to continue purchasing land.[21] In 1749 the Krobo joined forces with the Akyem Abuakwa in an attempt to drive out Asante, Akwamu, and Anlo (Awuna) traders from the region along their paths and along the Volta. The allies' plan was to restrict the flow upriver to the Asante of valuable European goods, especially guns and ammunition, and to keep for themselves the profits from the sales of fish, salt, ivory, and slaves. Akyem Abuakwa and Krobo commercial cooperation reached its climax between 1760 and 1770, during which time the allies actually captured Asante traders, many of whom were sold into slavery. For most of 1772, for example, virtually all Asante trade through the region had ceased. Such cooperation suggests that the Krobo had learned to form strategic alliances with competing and often hostile neighbors. The Krobo's general support of the Akyem Abuakwa against the Asante, and their alliances in the region, may also help to explain why the Krobo were able to acquire hundreds of acres of land from the Akyem Abuakwa in the late eighteenth and nineteenth centuries.

The Asante Wars

Most of the Asante wars of expansion or consolidation affected the Krobo and other Adangme only indirectly. As the Asante attempted to fill the political and economic vacuum left by the exodus of the Akwamu in 1730, the Asante increased their influence over all the peoples in southeastern Ghana, including the Krobo and Adangme. The Krobo, the Osudoku, and the Ada resisted as best they could the Asante's attempt to monopolize trade in the lower Volta. In one such conflict, the Ada-Anlo War of 1769-1770, the Krobo joined the Ada forces against the Ewe chiefdom of Anlo and its allies the Akwamu and the Krepi. Later the Akyem Abuakwa and the Ga joined the Ada, and the Asante supported the Anlo-Akwamu alliance. Asantehene Osei Kwadwo, the famous administrative reformer who claimed suzerainty over all the antagonists except the Anlo, summoned Akyemhene Obre Coran, Akuapemhene Obuobi Atiemo, and Akwamuhene Daako to Kumase. Fearing the wrath of the Asantehene for fighting among themselves, none of the feuding leaders except Akwamuhene Daako obeyed the summons. In retaliation for their disobedience, the Asantehene committed approximately 20,000 warriors to the field on the side of the Anlo-Akwamu forces.[22] The fearful Akyemhene Obre Coran fled south to Christiansborg, and then to the Fante, forfeiting several hundred prisoners.[23]

Some of the people of the lower Volta sought accommodation with the Asante, others resisted. Of the latter group, the Akyem Abuakwa, Akuapem, Krobo, Ada, and Ga more than held their own against the larger and militarily more sophisticated Asante-Anlo-Akwamu forces. However, after the desertion of Akyemhene Obre Coran, the remaining forces also retreated. Obre Coran had left many of his wives and children under the protection of the Krobo on Klo-yo.[24] The Asante pursued their military advantage and attacked the mountain—an event considered worthy of note by Britain's Cape Coast governor David Mill. Writing in 1780, Mill described the Krobo as "inhabiting a hill of great natural strength" and reported that the Asante's attack proved to be a mistake.[25] Other European accounts simply recorded the Asante defeat.[26] Merely to have been the direct object of attack by the Asante meant that the Krobo had achieved some status among the many chiefdoms in the region.

Although Asante tradition does not confirm this war, the Krobo recorded it in their Klama (proverbial) songs as their first Asante war. Bana, the leader of the Asante force, first attempted to negotiate with the "king" of the Manya Krobo by making a "visit" to the mountain. The Manya Krobo "King" Osom Boafo reputedly led a combined force of Manya and Yilo warriors against an Asante host ten times greater in number than the Krobo.[27] In a surprise attack, the Asante were routed, and Bana killed. A Klama joyously recorded: "The Asante have killed Bana; Never can they kill Krobo!"[28]

Two years later, in mid-December 1772 the Asante accused the Krobo of supporting the Akyem Abuakwa in interdicting Asante traders. Gyassewahene Adusei Tsatsa, mindful of Bana's mistakes, laid siege to the Krobo Mountain rather than attacking it.[29] Although the siege lasted three lunar months, it ended in failure; the Krobo apparently anticipating the siege tactic, had stockpiled water and provisions. Indeed, if Krobo tradition can be believed, the Asante forces suffered more from the prolonged siege, which caused some desertion. Gyassewahene Adusei Tsatsa is reported to have said: "Let the Krobo take my men to the mountain and feed

41

them freely, for I shall one day claim all of them back after I have invested those cages [sic] on the mountain."[30]

When the siege failed to bring the Krobo to terms, the Asante forces, composed of peoples of the eastern region including the Akwamu and the Juaben, attacked. As small groups of Asante attempted to ascend the mountain along the southeastern footpaths, the Krobo poured palm oil on the rocks and then attacked from well-concealed positions with spears and bows and arrows. Many Asante perished in the assault, and the remaining forces fled in disarray, abandoning their camp, their dead, and their many weapons. Krobo traditions have a further disappointed Asantehene Osei Kwadwo commenting: "It has been bad with us! We tried all in our power, yet the mountain is still standing. We went in groups and returned in scattered order."[31] This second victory over the seemingly invincible Asante boosted the Krobo's self-esteem. On the other hand, it underlined the continual need to strengthen their military forces. During the eighteenth century, intensified military conflict, combined with a growing population, much of which was of Akan ancestry, contributed to the Krobo's greater reliance on their war chiefs (chapter 4).

Throughout the late eighteenth century and into the first two decades of the nineteenth century, the Asante continued to have difficulty in containing rebellions in the southeastern provinces, Akyem Abuakwa and Akuapem. A major revolt began in 1810, and by February 1811 the Asante provincial administration for the region had collapsed. Kwame Adua of Asu, the Asante revenue agents, and an Asante group of 90 peaceful traders were killed.[32] An infuriated Asantehene Osei Bonsu recalled Boakye Yam and Odenkyem, commissioners to the southeast stationed at Accra. Immediately thereafter, in late February 1811, Adusei Kra, the Atene Akotehene of Kumase, led an estimated 20,000 troops against the rebellion at Amani and Saman. Akyem Kotoko and Ga forces were then joined by a second Asante army of about 15,000 under Gyassewahene Opoku Frefre, son of former Asantehene Opoku Ware. With the arrival of the Asante reinforcements under Opoku Frefre, Akuapemhene Kwao Safora Twe escaped by traveling along "small and unfrequented paths"[33] via Shai to Ada, where he eluded the Asante, and then back to Akuapem, where he took refuge at Abonse.

Unable to locate the Akuapemhene, the Gyassewahene thought the Krobo had again offered refuge to one of his enemies. The Asante may also have considered this an opportunity to defeat the Krobo at last. But the small band of Krobo warriors on Klo-yo held their own against the determined Asante. After two unsuccessful assaults, Opoku Frefre altered his tactics and sought negotiations.[34] Not trusting the Asante, the Krobo permitted several Ga,[35] then allies of the Asante, to search the mountain for the Akuapemhene, who they determined was not there.[36] Once again the Krobo had become embroiled in the political affairs of the powerful Akan chiefdoms. The Krobo were now the major factor in the political events of the region, and their military confidence grew with each failed attempt by the Asante to take the Krobo Mountain.

Even as the Krobo were gaining respect as formidable soldiers in the eyes of the Asante and others, the political authority of the Akyem Abuakwa declined. The century of war with the Asante was beginning to take its toll. The Asante had defeated the Akyem Abuakwa in 1744, 1770, 1774, and 1811. A few years later, in 1816, the Ga joined the Asante in a major defeat of the Akyem Abuakwa in the brief Thursday War.[37] This war ended the Akyem Abuakwa's claim of suzerainty over the Ga; but although Akan dominance over the southeast, which had begun with the Akwamu in the early seventeenth century, was now on the decline, it was still preeminent in the forest region.

The Asante's threat to the Krobo ended in 1826, when the Asante were defeated by an alliance of forces united by their fear of expanded Asante control over southern Ghana. At Akantamansu, just southwest of Dodowa, a combined force of Akyem, Akuapem, Ga, Adangme, British, and Danes defeated the Asante and their allies.[38] While the Europeans and the Africans were not in total agreement on the reasons why the Asante had to be driven from the south, all agreed that the defeat of the Asante was essential for the continuation of their respective interests in the region. The British and the Danes considered the Asante an impediment to trade in goods other than slaves—what the Europeans termed legitimate commerce. The Asante were the major slave sellers in Ghana at this time. Of course, all major powers, especially the Akan, including the Akyem, the Akuapem, and the Akwamu, all allies of the Europeans against the Asante, were also major slaving states. For the British, the primary issue was to prevent Asante control the economy in the south, with a secondary motive of avenging the death of Governor MacCarthy, killed by the Asante in 1824. For their part, the Africans who fought against the Asante in 1826 were primarily concerned with breaking free from the Asante empire; and indeed, after the war, "Greater Asante" rarely formally extended beyond the Pra River, at least in the southeast. The victory at Akantamansu ended a major chapter in the political history of the region: Asante expansion had been checked.

The British divided their force into three units. Captain Purdon commanded the center (main) force; the left wing was commanded by Fantehene Kwado Tibo, and consisted of Fante, Denkyira, Asin, and Agona. Akwamuhene Akoto commanded the right flank, composed of Krobo and other Danish allies, including the Ada, Osudoku, Shai, Akyem, Prampram, and unidentified "river-side people."[39] Though the Krobo achieved no great military fame, their involvement was noteworthy: "Each Krobo chief contributed a number of fighting-men to the Ga army to help in clearing away the Ashanti nuisance."[40] Some remembered as fighting in this war were Osom Boafo of Manya Krobo and Kole Brepong of Bonya among the Yilo Krobo; others included Akapo Azu of Okpe, Padi Konor Oketeku of Nyewe, and Ogom and Huadzi of Susui.[41] Captain L. G. Poulsen, the Danish commander, reported to Purdon that it was the bravery of the "natives from the eastern region that carried the day."[42] An estimated 12,000 Africans fought in the war. The Krobo were only one of many small-scale polities who sent warriors. Because they seized the opportunity, however, the Krobo were the greatest beneficiaries of the economic changes that emerged in the post-1826 era, while other larger competing chiefdoms, including the Akyem Abuakwa and the Akuapem, sought to fill the political vacuum left by the Asante.

The Dum War

Despite the leading role of the British in the 1826 war, the eastern region remained under Danish influence until 1850. The Danes attempted to capitalize on their role in the defeat of the Asante by increasing their trade in gold, in palm oil, the new cash crop, and in Danish manufactured goods. While the Danes aggressively encouraged the Africans to engage in legitimate commerce, the Akuapem tried to increase their share of this trade and to replace the Asante and the Akyem Abuakwa as the dominant political force in the region around the foothills. These were lands occupied by the Shai, the Krobo, and the Osudoku. The Akuapemhene Ado Dankwa deemed it a propitious time to establish or reestablish (depending on which tradition is to be believed) Akuapem authority over the Krobo and the Shai. The Akuapem claimed that the Krobo and the Shai had been clients of the Akuapem since the sixteenth century.[43] It should be recalled that in 1788, under Akuapemhene Obuobi Atieno (c. 1765-1792), Paul E. Isert acting for the Danish government had signed a treaty with the Akuapem for the creation of a commercial plantation in the region called the Krobo Colony.[44] Clearly, therefore, even before the Dum War of 1835, the Akuapem had considered the Krobo to be under their authority. There is no evidence, however, to suggest that the Krobo accepted their tributary status.

By the late 1820s, Akuapemhene Ado Dankwa began to collect tolls from traders travelling through his chiefdom, a right exercised by most chiefdoms. Furthermore, he demanded from the Krobo a tribute, payable in local commodities such as palm oil and other foodstuffs and in imported textiles and spirits. The Krobo refused to recognize the Akuapem's overlordship, and the Akuapemhene established a precedent by seeking mediation of the matter by the Danes. In 1835, Ado Dankwa took his claim to Christiansborg, an indication of the rising importance of Europeans in the political affairs of the day. Basel missionary Andreas Riis, who had recently been stationed at Akropong, was already in Christiansborg at the request of acting governor Frederik Siegfried Mørch.[45] Riis undoubtedly informed the Danish authorities that the Akuapem was a "progressive" chiefdom and had been supportive of the "civilizing mission" of the Basel Mission Society. He also supported the Akuapem's allegations and their claims of hegemony over the Krobo.

For different reasons both the Akuapem and the Danes were interested in extending their authority over the Krobo. The Akuapemhene accused the Krobo and the Shai of repeatedly refusing to recognize his overlordship and of interrupting trade. The Danes were particularly interested in stopping such alleged disruptions in trade, especially in palm oil, which had only recently become an important export item because of its new-found uses in

Europe as a lubricant and in soap making. The Akuapem were less interested in the palm oil export trade than in political domination over the Krobo. For his part, Governor Mørch was concerned about the encroachment of the British stationed at Cape Coast. In their respective ways, the Akuapem, the Danes, and the Krobo were all attempting to take advantage of the politico-economic vacuum left by the Asante.

In late November 1835 Mørch summoned the Shai and Krobo chiefs to Christiansborg to answer to the charges made by the Akuapemhene. The Shai travelled the long journey to Accra, but the Krobo chiefs did not. Apparently realizing that it would not be judicious to ignore completely a summons from the Danes, they indicated a willingness to discuss the issues at hand, but invited the governor to do so in Kroboland.[46] Mørch rightly considered this reply a complete rejection of the Danes' authority over the region. He prepared for a military confrontation with the Krobo "to put a stop to the bloody deeds poisoning the relations of the two tribes [Krobo and Akuapem]."[47] Once again the Krobo prepared for an attack against the mountain. This time, however, for the first time, European forces were involved. The Krobo had now gained a measure of recognition outside the African community—a mixed blessing.

Publicly Mørch stated that he was coming to the famous Krobo Mountain for civil purposes, not military ones. His preparations, however, suggest that Mørch expected to use force against the Krobo. In early January, Mørch set out on the fifty-mile trek to the Krobo Mountain. His African auxiliaries included Osu, La, and Ga; the Akuapem joined the force just east of Dodowa. Mørch's European forces consisted of two sergeants, the Reverend Riis, and Danish merchants John Richter, George Lutterodt, Christian Svankiaer, and Holm. Military hardware included muskets and a few pieces of artillery.[48] Such preparations were hardly necessary for what Riis described as a purely civil expedition, given the fact that the Krobo were not a major military force, nor were they well armed.[49] By 12 January 1836, the Krobo on their traditional Krobo Mountain fortress, found themselves confronted by between 600 and 800 Danish-led Africans.[50] However, the Krobo had two advantages; as in the past, the Krobo warriors were defending their home; and except for the few European merchants and two sergeants, their African adversaries were undisciplined and poorly coordinated.

Information on the subsequent Krobo-Danish (Dum) War is far from complete.[51] (A discussion of the effects of this war on the production of palm oil, and on Danish-British relations, may be found in chapters 5 and 6.) Sources agree on one fact: although the Krobo lost the war, they won impressive battles against the Akuapem until the latter were rescued by the Danes. By one account, about fifty Krobo fighters were killed and an equal number wounded. Traditional Krobo military tactics proved less than successful against European military equipment, which finally penetrated their previously impenetrable mountain fortress, although the mountain escaped occupation.

Lack of preparation impeded Krobo resistance. The Yilo Krobo were in the process of selecting their fifth konor, Ologo Patu, when the war erupted, and the Manya Krobo were completely without a supreme military leader, the office of konor of Manya Krobo having not yet been established.[52] The aging Muala Okumsra, the apparent head of the clan chiefs, was not a military leader. According to Noa Azu, admittedly a questionable source, Muala Okumsra deferred to a younger, more energetic man, Odonkor Azu, his chief linguist and matse (clan chief) of the Djebiam-Nam clan.

In the wake of the war, the Danes fined the Krobo thirty-two rixdollars (15,000 cowries), payable in palm oil.[53] The British, on behalf of their own economic interest and the well-being of British merchants in the eastern region, now entered the scene. The British governor, George MacLean, vehemently but diplomatically protested the sanctions imposed against the Krobo. Specifically, the governor objected to the method of payment of the fine, which he considered to be tantamount to ensuring a Danish monopoly of the now valuable palm oil from Kroboland.[54]

The war gave impetus to the rise of a new political figure among the Manya Krobo, the tall and ruddy complexioned Odonkor Azu.[55] "After this Odonkor Azu was hailed by the whole Krobo tribe and proclaimed King over all the 12 tribes as Nimuo or Emperor in the same year, 1832 [sic]."[56]

Krobo as a whole emerged slightly stronger in the aftermath of the Dum War. Once more, as they had done since earliest times, the Krobo had withstood the attack of a larger, better equipped army. The Krobo Mountain, their ancient, sacred home, remained in their possession, and security returned to their farms and villages along the Akuapem foothills and valleys. They continued to be independent from domination by any of their neighbors, notably the Akuapem or the Dancs. Finally, both the Danes and the British recognized the central position the Krobo occupied in the commercialization of palm oil for export for the eastern region.

By the late 1830s, the Krobo had developed from merely one of the Adangme-speaking peoples into the most important political and economic factor in the development of the eastern region. This process had begun at least by the early 1700s, when the Krobo had established themselves as effective allies of many of the region's major Akan chiefdoms and as formidable foes to their enemies. Moreover, the decline of other Adangme states, especially of Ladoku and the Shai, as well as the decline of the Akwamu, the Akyem Abuakwa, and the Akuapem in the region, provided politico-economic opportunities that the Krobo seized. The chronic wars between these and other Akan states diverted attention from the Krobo. Taking advantage of this neglect, the Krobo expanded territorially and increased their trade with their neighbors, especially those in the southeast. Furthermore, the Akan wars provided the Krobo and other Adangme with immigrants, such as the famed Denkyira Krobo, who augmented the Krobo population and brought additional military skills. Despite the endemic wars of the eighteenth century, the Krobo managed to establish farms and later villages to the west and northwest of the mountain along the foothills and valleys of the Akuapem hills, an expansion that accelerated in the nineteenth century.

The Krobo cannot be considered to have become a major political or military power by the end of the eighteenth century, or even by the 1830s. Later in the nineteenth century, however, they emerged as the dominant economic power of the region because of an advantageous geographic position, their accumulation of farms (huzas), and the increased economic importance of palm oil, indigenous to Kroboland, as an overseas export commodity.

4

FROM A THEOCRATIC OLIGARCHY TO SECULAR RULE: THE KONOR'S TRIUMPH OVER THE OKUMO AND DJEMELI

Nowhere in West Africa is the institution of paramount chiefs or kings more firmly established than in Ghana.[1] The literature gives considerable attention to the Asantehene, king of the Asante Kingdom; to other Akan rulers such as the Fantehene, the paramount chief of the Fante; and, to a lesser extent, to paramount chiefs of other peoples, including the *manche* of the Ga and the konor of the Krobo. But despite the pervasive presence of secular rulers in many modern West African societies, some of the earliest rulers were priestly in origin, while other secular rulers ruled jointly with priests. We know, for example, that the Asante kingdom was founded by the cooperative efforts of a warrior, Osei Tutu, and the "far-famed fetish priest, Okomfo Anokye [Komfuo Anotchi]," who gave the Asante the Golden Stool (*Sika Dwa*), the symbol of a new united state—Asante.[2]

While the Asante had no equal in the sophistication and complexity of their state organization, almost all of Ghana's chiefdoms have developed paramount chiefs. The Krobo and other Adangme, who presently have paramount chiefs (konors), borrowed heavily from their Akan neighors.[3] However, the evolution of paramount chiefs among the Adangme, including the Krobo, was not merely an attempt to copy the Akan. The creation— or, more correctly, the evolution—of the Krobo paramount chief was a gradual process, growing from the need for change within the Krobo community.

The first major modification in the governing structure of the Krobo after the introduction of the okumo (traditional ruler of Klo-yo) came as the result of increased warfare in the region during the eighteenth century (chapter 3). The threat posed by their powerful neighbors, the Akwamu, prompted many Adangme-speaking people, including the Krobo, to delegate more authority to their war chiefs—the asafo-tse.[4] However, individual asafo-tse were empowered only to defend their own settlements. The entire group needed a supreme military leader. Accordingly, the Krobo established a paramount military officer called the *konor* (one who is carried into war on the people's shoulders).[5] The konor had no religious authority, and most sources suggest that the original konors were selected by the Okumo from minor families and clans. Here the Krobo followed the general pattern among other Adangme of selecting military leaders from families with Akan ancestry because of the greater sophistication attributed to the Akan chiefdoms in military matters.

The creation of the konor by the okumo and the Anikaka Council did not signal a decline of the theocratic oligarchy. On the contrary, it suggests that the okumo felt secure enough to delegate significant secular authority to another officer. By appointing the konor, the okumo demonstrated that although a priest, he could still ensure the physical protection of the people.

Traditions do not suggest that the advent of the konor occurred amid internal chaos. In fact the opposite is implied: that is, Krobo society continued to expand in the sixteenth and seventeenth centuries, despite wars between the Adangme and the Akwamu during this era of slave trading. The defensive mountain and hill sites of the Adangme settlements—Shai, Ningo, Osudoku, and Klo-yo—reflect the insecurity of the time. Richard J. H. Pogucki referred to this phase of the Adangme's political history as a period when "kinship groups recognized the need of stronger cohesion" and therefore created a more formal political organization.[6]

The First Konor

Over centuries of change, most societies modify their original system of government in response to internal and/or external pressures. The Krobo were no different. During the first four centuries or so on the mountain, rulership shifted from the original kin groups to later arrivals, who elaborated and modified the system of government, albeit within the priestly structure (chapter 2). The first major departure from priestly rule came in response to a seemingly unrelated event: the Akan and Asante wars of the eighteenth century.[7] These wars increased insecurity among the Adangme, especially the Krobo, who bordered Akyem Abuakwa territory.[8]

The warfare also produced a number of refugees, mostly Akan. Because of their proximity to the many Akan chiefdoms, and because of the protection offered by the fortress-like mountain, the Krobo received more refugees than other Adangme—a mixed blessing for the anti-Akan Krobo.[9] Breaking with tradition, the Krobo conditionally[10] admitted to the mountain a large number of Akan immigrants, who became collectively known as Denkyira Krobo, although they were in fact a composite of Denkyira and other Akan groups, especially Akyem (chapter 2).[11]

Given the history of hostilities between the Krobo and other Adangme and the fact that the patrilineal, farming Adangme are very different culturally from the matrilineal, trading and farming Akan, it is not surprising that the Krobo admitted Denkyira Krobo only conditionally; it is surprising that the various Akan refugees were admitted at all. But the Krobo leaders apparently believed that the militarily more sophisticated Akan immigrants would help build a stronger and more secure Krobo. Additionally the inclusion of people of Akan ancestry among the Adangme would possibly lead to greater economic cooperation between the two groups.

The depth of the Krobo's concern for security after the admission of a relatively large number of Akan refugees (enough to have created four additional clans) is made evident by the allocation of land for these Denkyira Krobo and by the method by which they were governed. As to settlement, the Denkyira Krobo were methodically physically separated from the existing population. They were permitted to settle only the western side of the mountain, which was separated by a deep ravine, an area larger but less suited for habitation. The area was called Bose (beyond the thicket), a reference to the brush which acted as a kind of curtain.[12] The Denkyira Krobo were not pleased with their unequal treatment, and there were said to have been riots.[13] There is no evidence of any bloody conflict such as a civil war. Thus during the 1740s and early 1750s, the Bose Krobo and the Dose Krobo shared an uneasy peace.

By roughly the 1740s four of Bose's six subtribes—Nyewe, Bunase, Okpe, and Plau—were composed essentially of people of

Akan origin. The remaining two—Ogome and Bonya—were of Adangme origin, and held, by virtue of their origins and delegation of authority from the okumo, an elite position in Bose.[14]

In an apparent effort to insure control over the Bose refugees, the okumo appointed Matse (chief) Saki of the Djebiam-Ogome clan to be the supreme secular authority over Bose (Appendix A). He had no ritual or religious authority; the Ogome claim that he was the first konor of the Bose people, but the okumo and the Bose people insist that he was merely a kind of regent. As Chapter 2 explains, the four Denkyira Krobo subtribes had no priests among the djemeli, no representation on the Anikaka Council, no voice in choosing the okumo, and no share in the control over sacred meeting places, objects, and shrines. They had, in other words, no effective role in the theocratic oligarchy; unlike their predecessors, the eighteenth-century oligarchs did not expand their numbers to accommodate new immigrants. And, although the Denkyira Krobo accepted the pantheon of existing Krobo deities, they also retained their own. Their deities were of Akan origin, especially Kotoklo, their war god. To some extent Kotoklo became the focus of their religious and cultural difference with the Dose. The Denkyira Krobo created their own culturally separate community; in no meaningful way were they made to feel politically part of the old Dose Krobo community. In this respect, the Dose Krobo's policy toward the Denkyira Krobo differed radically from any previous Krobo policy toward immigrants.

The Denkyira Krobo apparently objected strongly to continued exclusion from positions of secular and religious power.[15] This is evident from the fact that by the early 1750s, the okumo's monopoly of authority over the Bose had declined. The first serious challenge to the okumo's secular authority came from an unexpected source. Shortly after assuming direct administrative control over Bose, according to traditions, Matse Saki attempted to steal the okumo's stool, break with the okumo and establish himself as paramount chief of Bose.[16] Although the story remains unproved, the contemporary Ogome of Bose (Yilo) have an okumo's stool. Of course, among the Adangme and the Akan the stool is only the symbol of power, not power itself. The okumo's real authority derived from the djemeli, the Anikaka Council, and his close relationship with the priestess of Nana Kloweki. But the story of the loss of the okumo's stool is a significant indicator of the okumo's diminishing authority over Matse Saki.

Following Matse Saki's attempted revolt, Matse Atwiri (Atsere) of Nyewe clan, a Denkyira Krobo immigrant, led a bloodless coup to become the Konor of Bose and, equally important, the first paramount chief among both Krobo chiefdoms.[17] Although the exact manner in which Atwiri came to power is disputed, there is general agreement that he gained control over the chieftaincy by paying off Saki's debts. He called himself konor and renamed Bose, which he called Yilo (*No Yilo Lumo*—the governor to the land). The ascendancy of Atwiri ended the okumo's secular authority over the Bose/Yilo Krobo.

The first decades of the eighteenth century marked the height of Akan, especially Asante, expansion. Every aspect of southern Ghanaian society was affected by expanding Akan states, especially in the area of trade and political organizations. The Adangme and the Krobo were no exception. According to Hugo Huber, "chieftancy, military leadership, and the stool rites which are attached to it have been introduced from *Denkyera, Akwamu* and perhaps other Akan groups."[18] The Bose/Yilo Krobo were especially receptive to the Akan chieftaincy system because of their predominantly Akan background and because four of the six sub-tribes had no djemeli. The adoption of Akan regalia of rulership—paramount chiefs, royal stools, palanquins, gold staffs, umbrellas, Akan drums, and accompanying rituals—was relatively easy for them.[19] Finally, Atwiri usurped only the okumo's secular authority; he did not challenge the entire priesthood nor consider himself to be the okumo's successor. Moreover, the Yilo continued to uphold the preeminence of the major Krobo deities and their priests the djemeli.

The creation of the Yilo Krobo permanently altered the alignment of the old seven Dose Krobo subtribes. A portion of the Djebiam-Ogome clan resettled in Bose. Additionally, for reasons not clear, by mid-eighteenth century the Bonya left Dose and joined the Bose settlement.[20] Both the Bonya and the Ogome continued their political-religious ties with the Dose Krobo through their membership in the djemeli, and their matse and wono (clan priests) continued to be enstooled by the okumo.[21] The subtribes of Ogome and Bonya are now the only Yilo who have priests among the djemeli. It is important to note the continued

53

importance of Nana Kloweki and the Dipo ceremony and the presence of djemeli within the Yilo chiefdom insured the continued influence of the okumo over the Yilo Krobo. The Yilo were therefore not completely politically independent of the old Dose Krobo theocracy.

Yilo Krobo tradition insists that the Yilo were the original settlers of Klo-yo. To support their claim, the Yilo point out that their konorship is the older. The latter point is correct, but it does not prove the former. The Yilo were able to establish a konor earlier because they were *not* connected to the existing system of rulership. The Yilo stool is the older, but it is not a continuation of traditional rulership by priestly kings. It is a separate institution.

The Second Konor

The stealing of the okumo's stool by Matse Saki, the creation of the first konorship by Atwiri, and the political formation of the Yilo Krobo point to a general decline of the secular authority of the okumo, the Anikaka Council, and the djemeli, and concomitantly to a growing split between the secular and the sacred spheres. These factors notwithstanding, external political and economic changes in the mid-eighteenth century directly influenced the Dose Krobo to invest increasing secular authority in a non-priest. Warfare with surrounding peoples was endemic after 1700. Krobo priests, however, could not leave the Krobo Mountain nor engage in bloodshed. Hence military figures, such as Matse Saki, Matse Atwiri, or even Matse Odonkor Azu, emerged as protectors of the mountain and the farms below, and as the Krobo expanded into surrounding lands, it was the military figures who defended the farms.[22]

As Krobo territory gradually expanded after the 1730s, an increasing number of Krobo established farms north of the mountain. This was not political expansion as such, but expansion by individuals and families, who cleared the forest, planted crops, and constructed simple huts without the day-to-day guidance and supervision of the theocratic oligarchy on the Krobo Mountain. According to Hugo Huber: "More and more of the priests' political influence and of their judicial activities were henceforth transferred to the chiefs and subchiefs who became not only military leaders but also the heads of clans and sub-tribes."[23]

Territorial expansion in the mid-eighteenth century initiated a precipitous decline in the old system of priestly rule and a shift to a new system of secular rule among the Dose Krobo. The new farms along the Akuapem foothills rapidly replaced the ancient settlements as the economic center of the state, whereas religious activity remained on the mountain.

The Huza

Krobo territorial colonization began in the middle to late eighteenth century, and accelerated in the nineteenth.[24] This territorial expansion was made possible by the evolution or creation of a new and unique system of land tenure: the huza system.[25] (The economic aspects of the huza are discussed in chapter 5.)

Scholars who have studied the huza system generally agree that it "revolutionized Krobo social life and Krobo politics."[26] Because of the prohibitions against contacts beyond the mountain, none of the priestly rulers could assist in the purchasing of huzas; in consequence, the huza developed its own organizational and governmental structure, independent of both the old theocratic oligarchy and existing social systems. A huza is a tract of land purchased by a group of people, not necessarily of the same kin group, who share a common interest in purchasing land. The head of the huza is the *huzatse* (literally, father of the huza). His authority is territorial, confined to all affairs related to a specific huza. The huzatse is assisted by one or more *dadematse* (cutlass-chief—the cutlass being an essential farming tool for bush clearance), depending on the size of the huza. Huza farmers, like all Krobo, belong to several familial groups, and owe allegiance to the head of each: the matse, the asafo-tse, and the we-nokotoma. In addition, "as inhabitants of the huza and in matters that concern the huza they (and only they) are under the dadematse and the huzatse." Organizationally, therefore, the huza holds a unique position as one of the few West African examples of spontaneous local "native government on a territorial basis," rather than kin basis.[27]

Originally, that is, during the late eighteenth century, the huzatse tended to be a person of no special status, an ordinary person. However, with the spread of the huza system, tracts often measured more than 600 acres and the huza members often numbered over fifty. As a result, the huzatse chosen became increasingly a "big man—a captain" or, before the creation of a paramount chief among the Manya Krobo, a matse.[28] The preference for a big man showed an attempt by the huza members to safeguard their investments, as they generally believed that an ordinary Krobo farmer would not command much respect in negotiations with the neighboring Akan kings from whom land was purchased. In return for the big man's negotiation in the purchase of the huza he would be given (dashed) a parcel of land for himself. Some of the more prominent huzatse, therefore, accumulated many huzas by virtue of their role as huzatse and by outright purchase on their own. Furthermore, the huzatse of a large huza tract could be responsible for a number of huza families, which then might constitute a separate huza village. In one relatively small huza tract of 550 acres, Field observed that the huza huts covered an area four or five miles long.[29] A successful huzatse repeated the process of creating another huza of several hundred acres, and if he was already a big man, that is, a matse or an asafo-tse, his authority expanded both territorially and tribally.

These huza villages along the Akuapem foothills were under the authority of the respective matse. However, at their new homes, the Dose Krobo huza farmers found themselves geographically separated from their ancient settlements on the mountain, and from the djemeli, the okumo, and the Anikaka Council. The distances between the huza and the mountain varied, but by the end of the nineteenth century could be as much as thirty miles over mountainous terrain. The Krobo Mountain retained its importance as the center of Dose and Yilo Krobo culture and religious activities. Naming ceremonies for the firstborn, marriages, funerals, the Dipo ceremony, male circumcision, the celebration of Nadu (the Dose Krobo's god of war, rain, wealth, and productivity), *Ngma-Yem* (millet harvest festival/luna new year), and other annual festivals and ceremonies were still performed on the mountain, and people made the pilgrimage back for these occasions.

The rise in importance of the huza by the first decades of the nineteenth century openly challenged the authority of the okumo, and by the middle of the century had contributed to the destruction of the okumo and the theocratic oligarchy as a political focus. "As the priests concerned themselves more with the religious life of the people," Konor Azzu Mate Kole noted, "more power was given to the clan heads and heads of family groups"—many of whom were huzatse.[30] By the beginnings of the era of legitimate trade in the 1820s, the seeds had been sown for a serious clash between these clan and family heads and the okumo.

Early nineteenth-century huza farmers enjoyed unprecedented economic growth that in turn brought them a measure of independence. The introduction of palm oil as a cash export crop in the 1820s hastened the demise of the okumo's power. The Europeans' increasing demand for palm oil for their machines and for soap and candles further stimulated the Krobo to purchase huza farms. Unlike cocoa, which was alien to the region, palm oil was an indigenous West African food and a staple in the Krobo diet, with a wide range of uses. Moreover, oil palm trees grew abundantly in the Akuapem Mountains, the area already being colonized by the huza farmers in the late eighteenth century. The Krobo farmers also enjoyed a lucrative market for crops of American origin, such as maize, cassava, sweet potatoes, and red peppers, which had come to Africa as by-products of the Atlantic slave trade. They also had rice, bananas, and plantains, which had arrived in West Africa from Asia via East Africa. Farm profits went primarily for the purchase of more huzas. The old theocratic oligarchy was powerless to stop the movement away from the mountain.

The palm oil export trade also encouraged commercial activity at Kpong, Akuse, and Amedica, and at Odumase and Somanya along the Senchi-Dodowa-Accra footpath, primarily to the benefit of the Manya Krobo, because these villages, except for Somanya, were part of Dose Krobo.[31] Sometime during the early nineteenth century, the Dose Krobo changed their name to *Manya* (village), reflecting a major demographic shift in the group's population.[32] The Manya Krobo were divided into two distinct communities: the ancient settlement on the Krobo Mountain and its adjacent lands; and the huza farms and villages lining the base of the Akuapem foothills. Kpong, Akuse, and Amedica along the west bank of the Volta River became part of the Manya Krobo by the 1840s.[33] These villages were important for two reasons: they marked the southern boundary with the Ewe, and they gave the Krobo direct access to the coast via the Volta. Kpong, the oldest village, was initially settled by the Akuapem in the eighteenth century. In the nineteenth century Kpong was inhabited by Ewe and by various Akan and Adangme groups. Increasingly the Krobo, especially the Manya, dominated the political and cultural affairs of Kpong, so much so that Sakite, konor of the Manya Krobo, appointed the chief of Kpong, as well as those of Akuse and Amedica.

The Emergence of Military Leaders

Concurrent with the rise of the huza was the development of another set of forces working against the authority of the theocratic oligarchy. The Akan wars, the slave trade, and, on occasion, conflict between the Krobo and the chiefdoms from which they purchased land produced another new group of leaders: military protectors of the Manya Krobo huza farms and villages.[34] The names of most of these early military leaders have not survived. We can, however, reconstruct the type of individuals these leaders must have been. In all likelihood, some were huzatse, others were either matse or asafo-tse. Indeed, some of the more powerful military leaders were both huzatse and matse or asafo-tse.

Very little is known of these forerunners of the konor of the Manya Krobo (Appendix B). While some of the more prominent warriors are remembered as "kings" or "regents," both are unlikely terms.[35] The Akan term *adontehene* (commander of the center column) also appears. The original term for a war chief created by the okumo, "konor," is conspicuously absent from the titles of late eighteenth-century war chiefs, possibly because its original meaning had been changed by the formation of the Yilo paramount chiefdom under a permanent, peacetime authority who was also called a "konor." The eighteenth-century war leaders had few if any priestly connections. Furthermore, it is doubtful that any of these kings, regents, or adontehene served as the chief of all Manya Krobo villages; it is more likely that certain powerful war leaders were the military representatives of segments or regions of the Manya Krobo.

Who were some of these shadowy figures? By the beginning of the nineteenth century, traditions identify Ba Dua (Ba Asare II) as king of the Manya Krobo and Osei Tutu Boako, matse of Dje-biam-Nam, as adontehene. Both of their names suggest an Akan ancestry. Krobo historians Thomas Odonkor and Noa Azu indicate that Ba Dua and the adontehene were victorious against the Asante in 1811 and 1816. It was Ba Dua's successor, Muala Okumsra (Okumstra), and the adontehene who led the Krobo forces in the combined African and European attack against the Asante at Akantamansu (1826).[36]

Unlike that of the okumo, the military leader's influence depended on personality, personal wealth, and lineage. He appears not to have had any ritual authority. Consider, for example, Matse Osei Tutu Boafo, said to have been appointed adontehene by Ba Dua. His paternal grandmother was from Lomodze, the royal clan of the influential Manya subtribe, and his mother was from the Memlese clan, the royal clan of the Dom subtribe. His first wife, Lako, was the sister of Muala Okumsra, listed together with Ba Dua as one of the last Akeweno rulers; their children were Mate Kole, Opate (Mpate), Tei, Patautuo, Koyo, and Odonkor (Azu).[37] Adontehene Boafo acquired military spoils and prestige as leader of the Manya Krobo forces in their victories over the Asante in 1811, in 1816, and in 1826 at Akantamansu.

When Boafo died around 1830, he left vacant two stools: that of the matse of Djebiam-Nam and that of the adontehene. The young Odonkor Azu was elected matse of Djebiam-Nam and inherited a number of huzas. He was already chief linguist to Muala Okrumsra and was thoroughly familiar with the neighboring Akan chiefdoms and the Danes at Christiansborg. As for the adontehene's stool, its occupant is unclear.[38] Evidence strongly suggests that no single individual after Boafo occupied both the adontehene's and the matse's stools, and therefore that secular authority was not yet invested in one office or controlled by one person.

Noa Azu claimed that Ba Dua and Muala Okrumsra were reputedly the last Akweno rulers.[39] If correct, this claim suggests that there had been similar rulers before Ba Dua and confirms that the evolution of increased political authority among certain matse was well under way by the late eighteenth century. It further suggests a formal connection between the Akweno rulers and the okumo, who was also associated with the Akweno subtribe. (In earlier times, when kin groups were small, the first Dom immigrants were made part of the Akweno and were collectively "Dom Akweno" or "Suotenya.")[40] More specifically, Ba Dua and Muala Okrumsra may have been the last matse delegated or appointed by the okumo to rule over the huza farms and villages. The appointment of Saki over the Bose/Yilo Krobo established the precedent for such an appointment by the okumo. Konor Azzu Mate Kole, recalling the traditions of this era, noted that

> when it became necessary to separate the purely religious observances from the political and military functions, which must be performed by persons with supreme power, the sacred emblem of authority used by priests was enshrined in the chief's stool.[41]

The entire Manya Krobo governmental structure changed during the era of the remarkably able Odonkor Azu (c. 1835-1867).[42] By a combination of personal influence, wealth, and family ties, he seized the political stage when he stepped into the political vacuum created by the death of Muala Okumsra. His radical restructuring of rulership among the Manya Krobo resulted in the establishment of a society ruled by a paramount chief—the konor.

The process by which Odonkor Azu became the first paramount ruler is partially known. At this juncture in Manya Krobo history, there was no established method of selecting a paramount chief and, in formal sense, no secular paramount chiefly office. First, Odonkor Azu apparently gained control of the matse stool of Dom. According to Djebiam-Nam tradition, Muala Okumsra owed Odonkor Azu a considerable sum because of the debt incurred in the 1836 Dum War against the Danes. It is not likely that Odonkor Azu actually purchased the Dom stool; a more plausible scenario would be that he influenced the selection process by contributing to the funeral of Muala Okrumsra, and by bestowing gifts on the Dom's royal clan, Dom-Memlese. This clan was also his mother's, as she was Muala Okrumsra's sister. Lineage is important here, although it alone would not account for his ascendancy.

The change in dynasty was possible because of a major shift in the basis of political power among the Manya Krobo.[43] The old theocracy's authority depended on ritual and religious control over the major deities and ceremonies of the society. By comparison, the konor's authority was based on the political and economic needs of an expanding population, and was closely linked to the production of palm oil for export and to increased contact with Akan and European strangers. Odonkor Azu's constituency was a mirror of his own background: huza farmers, involved in cultivating palm oil for export, with no familial connection with the djemeli.

It is unanimously agreed that Odonkor Azu was the first paramount chief of the Manya Krobo. However, he is listed as the fifteenth ruler of the Manya Krobo in genealogies constructed in the late nineteenth century (Table 4.2). This is not a contradiction. The first twelve rulers, who were okumos, were followed in the late eighteenth and early nineteenth century by a number of Akweno rulers (kings or regents). The listing of Odonkor Azu as the fifteenth ruler is an obvious attempt by the historians of Djebiam-Nam to present Odonkor Azu's konorship as a continuation of and not a radical break with past rule. Like Atwiri among the Yilo, Odonkor Azu did not claim to be the okumo's successor in matters religious, but an extension of the okumo's secular authority.

By the end of the century, the konor of the Manya Krobo did exercise some de facto secular authority over the religious community of both chiefdoms. The earliest Dose Krobo subtribes, those from which the djemeli were selected, were under the konor of the Manya Krobo. Also, two Yilo subtribes, Ogome (formerly part of Djebiam-Ogome) and Bonya, indirectly came under the konor of the Manya Krobo; that is, the matse of these two Yilo subtribes were enstooled by the Okumo, who was selected from among the Akweno, who in turn were under the konor of Manya Krobo.

The tradition-bound okumo and djemeli were powerless to stop the rise of a paramount chief. Odonkor Azu had not violated any specific religious or ritual prohibitions. In vain the okumo opposed any formal recognition of the konorship until 1892, when the okumo failed in their attempts to block the selection of Emmanuel Mate Kole as konor by asserting that they were the traditional paramount rulers of the Krobo. The konor's growing preeminence in secular matters relegated the okumo to a paramountcy in religious matters only.

61

Europeans and the Manya Krobo Konorship

The region's colonial officials viewed the konorship differently. Before the 1830s, Europeans apparently knew little about the Crobbo. This situation began to change during and after the 1835-1836 Dum War. By the reign of konors Odonkor Azu of Manya and Ologo Patu of Yilo (c. 1836-1869), Europeans referred to the two chiefdoms in geographical terms: Eastern (Manya) and Western (Yilo). Because all the Krobo's neighbors had paramount chiefs, the Danes, and later the British, incorrectly assumed that each Krobo chiefdom had a paramount chief. They also incorrectly assumed that both Krobo chiefdoms had the same political and religious structure and the same history. If in the 1830s Ologo Patu was the konor of the Western Krobo, then Odonkor Azu, the most prominent Manya Krobo matse, must be the konor of the Eastern Krobo. Thus, British and Danish assumptions bolstered the authority of both men, especially Odonkor Azu.

Odonkor Azu, who considered himself paramount ruler, was probably not considered konor by his people until the early 1860s, near the end of his over thirty years of rule. Although the traditions of his own subtribe, Djebiam-Nam, insist that he was konor, this title is not confirmed by other traditions, and there are no references to the ceremony that enstooled him as konor. Moreover, as late as 1892, Djebiam-Nam's claim to the konorship was challenged, as will be discussed below. It is likely that many, if not most, Manya Krobo viewed Odonkor Azu as essentially primus inter pares of the matse (clan chiefs), in much the same way as the okumo was the spokesman for the djemeli. Margaret Field, who studied Krobo society in considerable detail in the 1930s and 1940s, shared this opinion:

> This Odonkor Azu was a remarkably able man, and while he was acting as Krobo representative, the Danes in the Gold Coast gave place to the British, and the *British assumed him to be the Krobo chief*. In time his own people acquiesced in this [and] enstooled him on Late Okute's stool.[44] (emphasis mine)

Field's observations are supported by the reports of Danish Governor Fredrick Siegfred Mørch, who in 1836 communicated to

Odonkor Azu his pleasure that the latter was the new paramount chief of the Manya Krobo.[45]

The British, after they took over "Danish Guinea" in 1850, echoed the Danish perceptions of the Krobo. At the initial meeting between Britain's acting governor and the paramount chiefs of the eastern region, Samuel Bannerman noted the attendance of the "King of Krobo [Odonkor Azu] and all his chiefs."[46] Eight years later, when the Krobo were locked in the bitter and bloody 1858 Krobo Rebellion against the British, Governor Henry Bird considered Odonkor Azu to be the paramount chief of both Krobo chiefdoms.[47] As a result, Odonkor Azu had become de facto the konor of all Krobo, at least for people who did not know Krobo history. From the late 1850s to the end of colonial rule, the British pursued policies toward the Krobo that directly influenced the selection of konors. One such policy was to accept that each Krobo chiefdom had royal clans—Nyewe for the Yilo and Djebiam-Nam for the Manya. Such a policy effectively ended the Ogome's claim to the Yilo konorship and any serious challenge to Djebiam-Nam's rule over the Manya.

Inside Manya Krobo it was Odonkor Azu's son and successor Sakite (1867-1892) who consolidated his father's political gains and permanently established the office of konor. He also continued and expanded the huza system,[48] supported the Basel missionaries, whom Odonkor Azu had invited to Odumase in 1856 to establish mission schools, and reestablished cordial relations with British colonial officals.[49] New mission stations and schools were established primarily among the Manya, but there were a few mission substations in Yilo Krobo. Sakite's power was further enhanced by his successful military exploits in the 1873-1874 Asante War (chapter 7). As a result, throughout his twenty-five year reign Sakite's counsel and support were in high demand by the region's Africans and Europeans.[50]

Under Sakite the trade in palm oil expanded, and with it the importance among the Manya Krobo of Odumase and Manyaponguno along the Akuapem foothills and Kpong, Akuse, and Amedica on the Volta. Somanya, along the foothills between the Manya and Yilo Krobo boundaries, was the only Yilo Krobo commercial center of any importance. In 1880, in recognition of the commercial importance of Kroboland and Konor Sakite, the British created the Volta District and selected Odumase to be the district headquarters.[51] During his long reign, Sakite constructed an elaborate (by Krobo standards) court and residence at Odumase modeled after his Akan neighbors.[52] Missionaries and mission-trained artisans did the actual construction. Sakite, colonial officials, and missionaries made Odumase and Kroboland one of the new centers of export trade and missionary activity for the eastern region. And yet, much to the disappointment of colonial officials and missionaries, Sakite never converted. Instead he travelled a narrow path between the Europeans on one side and the traditional forces, that is the okumo, and the Anikaka Council, on the other. Odumase became the Manya Krobo secular capital and the Krobo Mountain became its religious capital. Sakite supported mission education and European style houses and dress; he did not oppose the Dipo ceremonies but did support the British and missionaries in banning human sacrifices to war deities, and burials on the mountain. He was the last konor to maintain such a precarious balance between European values and traditional Krobo values.

During the reign of Sakite, the Yilo konors Sasraku (1869-1874) and Akrobetto I (1874-1906) operated in the shadow of the Manya Krobo konor, whose long and successful reign contrasted markedly with the poor leadership of Ologo Patu and his successors. It should be recalled that Ologo Patu had not supported huza expansion or palm oil production commercially, and in general opposed cooperation with Europeans—traders, colonial officials, or missionaries. And although the disastrous 1858 Krobo Rebellion, the Palm Oil Boycott of 1858-1866, and the 1873-1874 Asante War affected both Krobo states, the Yilo suffered the most; they were ill prepared to pay the heavy indemnity imposed against them, and in the 1873-1874 Asante War the Yilo konor failed actively to support the British (Chapter 6). As a result of these two major events the Yilo entered a political decline from which they have never recovered.

After 1874 the British unwaveringly supported Konor Sakite (chapter 7).[53] When Sakite died, the konorship was well established among the Manya Krobo, although Djebiam-Nam's claim was less secure. Immediately after Sakite's death, there were two major types of claimants to the konorship—supporters of the konorship as established by Odonkor Azu and Sakite and supporters of the tradition of rule established by the okumo. The British entered the

64

fray on the side of Djebiam-Nam, the house of their old friends Odonkor Azu and Sakite. Upon being notified of Sakite's death on 29 February 1892, Sir Brandford Griffith forbade the Manya Krobo to select a successor until he arrived in mid-July. Reluctantly, the Krobo complied, fearing military action against them if they did not. In agreeing to delay the selection process the Manya Krobo implicitly admitted that the British had become the limiting political factor in the selection of the new konor of the Manya Krobo and therefore of all future Krobo paramount chiefs. This radical departure from the past policies of the colonial administrators was brought on in part by the direct administration of the colony after 1874 (the Volta District was created in 1880) and by the Basel missionaries' increasing demands for an end to many traditional religious practices, especially human sacrifice. Indeed, the last time the British had attempted to interfere with the legal selection of a konor, in 1858, the Yilo had refused to depose their konor, Ologo Patu. But at that time the Colonial Office in London had not been politically ready to extend direct, formal control over peoples in the eastern region. By 1892 political matters in London had changed; all of West Africa had been formally colonized during the scramble for Africa in the 1880s.

The Krobo were apparently more concerned about who the next konor of the Manya Krobo would be than about interference from the British, possibly because the British had been indirectly but heavily involved in the affairs of the Krobo since 1858. Essentially two major groups vied for the konorship: those who wanted to continue the policies initiated by Odonkor Azu and expanded by Sakite—huza expansion, commercialization of crops for export, cordial relations with the Basel missionaries and colonial officials—and those who desired a return to limited contact with colonial officials, the expulsion of the Basel missionaries, and a reaffirmation of the secular authority of the okumo and the djemeli.

There were three candidates for Sakite's position: Peter Nyako, son of Odonkor Azu and uncle of Sakite of Djebiam-Nam; the descendants of the okumo from the Akweno subtribe, who were attempting to reestablish the supremacy of the okumo; and Prince Akute of Dom, to whom Sakite allegedly had promised the succession in 1867. Akute, a traditionalist, favored the return to the old ways and to the Krobo Mountain and supported minimal relations with Europeans, especially missionaries. The descendants of the okumo held a similar view, and demanded a return to rule by the old theocratic oligarchy, the Anikaka Council, which they controlled. They were, of course, even more anti-missionary and anti-European than Akute. Peter Nyako represented both the Djebiam-Nam subtribe and the Christian, pro-missionary, pro-European forces. At stake was not merely who was to be the next konor, but which clan was likely to become the royal clan of the Manya Krobo, and whether the Krobo, including the Yilo Krobo, were to seek accommodation with European forces or become hostile to colonial administrators. The selection of Sakite's successor would also constitute an endorsement or a rejection of the political and economic policies established by the Manya Krobo since at least the beginning of the commercialization of palm oil in the late 1820s.

By 1892, some elements of Krobo society had already adopted European practices. European dress, house construction and design, furniture, and the like were common in Kroboland. In political matters, the Europeans had also made an impact—lawyers were used increasingly to settle disputes. In the 1892 succession dispute, for example, Peter Nyako retained the legal services of Accra barristers Edmund Bannerman and James Buckle. Not to be outdone, Prince Akute presented the governor a petition allegedly signed by the six Manya Krobo subchiefs, attesting to the legitimacy of his claim to be konor.

The colonial government and the missionaries obviously favored the candidacy of Peter Nyako or some other Christian. District Commissioner John Williams, stationed at Akuse, reported however that both Akute and Nyako had legitimate claims to the konorship. Although Akute's claim was the more legitimate, he also reported that there were "other equally important factors which must be considered."[54] Specifically, Williams reported that Akute was not fit to rule because of his old age and his character.[55] Age was not the real issue. It was Prince Akute's character that concerned the British: not only was he not a Christian, he strongly supported traditional Krobo religious practices and was, therefore, anti-Christian. For these reasons, Williams concluded in his report to Sir Brandford Griffith, the next konor should be Peter Nyako's candidate, the young catechist and grandson of Odonkor Azu, Emmanuel Mate [Kole,] a man "peculiarly suitable in the prevailing political ambience."[56] The "ambience" was marked by increasing colonial interest in Kroboland and increased missionary for the whole of southern Ghana.

On 19 July 1892, Governor Sir Brandford Griffith summoned all the leading officials of both the Yilo and the Manya to meet in Sakite's west courtyard, where he would announce a number of policies that would affect not just the selection of the next konor but the entire eastern region.[57] As the various Krobo officials descended upon Odumase, the Akan symbols of paramount authority first adopted by Sakite were visible everywhere. Konor Akrobetto "was carried in a hammock by his people." The aged prince was wearing a gray turban-like hat, while a green silk robe covered his body. The six subchiefs of West Krobo "and the six subchiefs of East Krobo" also attended, each "with much splendor and most of them also in a hammock or carried in a chair, accompanied by their speakers and porters of umbrellas, swords, and chairs."[58] The material splendor with which chiefs and other officers presented themselves to the governor indicated the material wealth the Krobo had gained from their huzas, the commercialization of palm oil and other food crops, and trade along the Volta.

Other Africans of the region were in attendance at the invitation of the Governor. The "kings of Christiansborg, Akra, Akropong, and Kyebi [Kibi] appeared also, the latter one with a numerous armed force."[59] The Krobo would soon discover that these officials and warriors had been invited for a political purpose and were not there merely to show respect at the passing of a fellow paramount chief. Their purpose was essentially twofold: to witness and participate in the extension of Britain's authority over the internal affairs of a fellow chiefdom of the Volta District, and if needed, to assist the governor and his one hundred Hausa troops to suppress any Krobo rebellion against the governor's policies.

On July 20, Wednesday, the first people's assembly was held.[60] Again, all the paramount chiefs, subchiefs, major priests and priestesses were in attendance, together with the Hausa troops in dress uniform, with cannons and a Maxim gun. "There might have gathered some thousand people."[61] First, the governor eulogized his old friend, Konor Sakite, and presented the Krobo with a life-sized, hand-painted color portrait. Second, the governor addressed the priests and subchiefs who supported Akutei. When specifically asked, all the subchiefs accused of having signed the petition in support of Akutei denied having done so. In denying having signed such a petition they rejected any formal claim to the konorship.

Sir Brandford Griffith also took the opportunity to address the priests and their supporters on another issue: the practice of human sacrifice in the celebrations of the war gods Nadu and Kotoklo on the sacred Krobo Mountain. These and other barbaric practices, the governor declared, would end immediately. To ensure compliance, the governor decreed that day a new law, forbidding such ceremonies and sacrifices and, more important, directing that the Krobo Mountain be forever abandoned within three days, and all shrines and buildings destroyed. This was the death of the fetish priests and, as Basel missionary Adam Mischitch reported, a development of "the greatest importance for the people and our missionary work."[62] The decree that forbade residence or any use of the Krobo Mountain by Africans also demanded the abandonment of the Shai Hills and the Osudoku Mountains. There would be no more Adangme mountain settlements; this phase of their history ended. The purpose of the armed Hausa troops and the African warriors now became clear to the Krobo and other Africans. Resistance was useless.

While priests, priestesses, and others who had residences on the sacred Krobo Mountain raced against time to recover their valuable belongings from the mountain, the governor moved to the second stage of his apparently well-thought-out plan. On 22 July he held his second people's assembly. In classical British parliamentary fashion, he gave a second reading of his law forbidding the Krobo to live on the Krobo Mountain. Afterward, he announced that the "six chiefs of East Krobo [had] unanimously elected the nephew of the old King Sakite, . . . teacher Emmanuel Mate [Kole was added later], King of East Krobo." (Peter Nyako, because of his advanced years, had deferred to his nephew to ensure a longer reign.) While the Manya Krobo subchiefs may have unanimously elected Emmanuel Mate, it is obvious that the governor influenced their decision. Indeed, even the pro-Emmanuel Mate Basel missionaries reported that Emmanuel was "pushed forward by the government."[63]

On 23 July 1892, at the third people's assembly, Konor Emmanuel Mate was enstooled as paramount chief of the Manya Krobo. At this ceremony, as the governor had planned, "fetish priests were not present." They were preoccupied with salvaging what they could from their ancient stronghold. After they had returned to their villages along the Akuapem foothills, they presented no threat to the new konor, who had in any case been assured that "the English government [would] stay at his side and protect him."[64]

The selection of Emmanuel Mate [Kole] and the decree terminating occupation of Klo-yo ended any remaining political independence the Krobo had enjoyed. Even more important, it ended the traditional process by which the Krobo had selected their rulers from the strongest family and clan. The crowning of Emmanuel Mate [Kole] established Djebiam-Nam as the Manya Krobo's royal clan and marked the end of rule by the okumo, the Anikaka Council, and the djemeli: the theocratic oligarchy.

Britain's ability to implement radical political change among the Krobo depended only in part on the presence of armed troops. The stage for political change had been set by the Krobo themselves, as they had become more and more involved in commercial and cultural relations with Europeans. The Krobo population was sustained by the commercialization of palm oil and other food crops; most Krobo had never lived on the Krobo Mountain, nor had they lived under the secular rule of the okumo or the Anikaka Council. Most Krobo realized that the British, European traders, and missionaries had become a permanent part of the region's political and economic future. Although there were some minor objections to the election of Emmanuel Mate in July 1892, and again in 1896, most of the population were willing to support a konor who was part of the future, provided that such a political leader could enhance their material well-being and at the same time maintain much of Krobo traditional culture. This was the challenge that faced Konor Emmanuel Mate [Kole] and subsequent konors of both the Yilo and the Manya Krobo.

The British and the Yilo Konorship

It is important to note that although the Yilo were de jure politically independent from the Manya, Odumase was de facto the political capital of Kroboland. Hence, after 1880 colonial policies affecting both chiefdoms were established in Odumase, not Sra.

As for the Yilo, the British had not intervened in the selection of Akrobetto in 1874, because Governor Strahan was then just beginning to expand direct control over the region. However, the recognition of Djebiam-Nam as the royal clan of the Manya Krobo led officials to recognize the Yilo's Nyewe clan as that chiefdom's royal clan. In so doing, the British authenticated—doubtless unknowingly—the legitimacy of a group of Krobo who were originally not Adangme but Denkyira Krobo. As in the case of the Manya Krobo, the colonial administration later supported the candidacy of the Christian Godfried Kofi Ologo III (1908-1917), despite objections among the Yilo Krobo, his advanced age, and his ill health.[65] It was important for the British to establish a Christian as konor of the Yilo, as they had in 1892 among the Manya Krobo.

The Yilo konors had been selected from one clan, Nyewe, since the formation of that office in the 1750s. There had, however, been frequent challenges to the Neywe right to select the konor. These challenges, which continued without success into the second decade of the twentieth century, came from one source, the matse of Yilo-Ogome, the clan of Matse Saki. By the time of Godfried Kofi Ologo, the Yilo had begun to follow the succession model established by the Manya Krobo. That is, "all sons of the first, then second, then third wife, etc. could be selected to succeed the previous konor, however, if the person whose turn it is to succeed declines, as did Peter Nyako, he has the right to nominate a successor."[66] (Peter Nyako nominated Emmanuel Mate Kole.)

The Yilo encountered continuous succession disputes from various families within the Nyewe clan. The Yilo selection process is more traditional—that is, the eldest member of a particular Nyewe family is selected—and also less efficient than that of the Manya; it has led to continuous succession disputes and often to very brief reigns. Between 1892 and 1990 there have been only two konors of the Manya Krobo, whereas among the Yilo there have been eight konors and two regents (Appendix A).

The Manya Krobo succession system has undergone two changes—from priestly to secular rule, and from what Henige has termed a collateral to a lineal system.[67] That is, the Manya have changed from priestly rulers of various clans to konors of a specific

70

clan. Among the Yilo Krobo, the system of succession, since the creation of that chiefdom, has been lineal. In part to legitimize the present ruling clan, Manya Krobo tradition has minimized the fact that a change in dynasty took place in the second quarter of the nineteenth century, whereas the Yilo correctly claim that they have had no major change in dynasty since the creation of the Yilo konorship sometime in the eighteenth century.

Colonial officials openly opposed the priesthood, many traditional Krobo practices, and the continued use of the ancient Krobo Mountain for religious and cultural celebrations. They were particularly concerned about slavery, the Dipo ceremony, and human sacrifices, which they viewed as obstacles to the creation of a Westernized Krobo society. Moreover, colonial officials apparently did not recognize the existence or importance of the djemeli or even Nana Kloweki. To colonial officials, priests represented the more conservative elements of Krobo society: they were opponents of colonial rule, Christianity, mission education, and legitimate trade, and supporters of domestic slavery, the slave trade, and human sacrifices. Inasmuch as the abduction of victims for sacrifices and slavery led to frequent conflicts, the priests also contributed to social instability. Colonial officials, then, disliked and distrusted the priests, although it was the Basel missionaries who led the unrestrained attack on them and on the many festivals (chapter 8). In 1892 the British interference in the enstooling of Emmanuel Mate Kole (knighted in 1929) marked the culmination of the work of Odonkor Azu, Sakite, the huza farmers, the missionaries, and the British. There remained a priesthood, the djemeli, but the physical, cultural, and political foundation of the theocratic oligarchy no longer existed (Appendix B).

5

BLOODLESS CONQUEST: THE HUZA, PALM OIL, AND THE KROBO'S RISE TO ECONOMIC PROMINENCE

The prohibition of slavery [1874] and the control of gold mining by the large foreign combines left to the native little else to sell other than his land, until with the increasing economic development of the country, with first palm oil and kernel trade in the later years of the nineteenth century, the planting of cocoa, a still greater impetus was given to the improvident to sell his land to the more far-seeing and industrious man, of which the Krobo is a shining example.

The Stool Lands Boundaries
Settlement (Akwamu) Order
(L.N. 252)

When Emmanuel Mate Kole became konor of the Manya Krobo, both Yilo and Manya Krobo could boast that Kroboland was the center of palm oil production for export for all of the Gold Coast.[1] Collectively the two chiefdoms possessed a territory covering nearly 600 square miles acquired by industrious Krobo farmers during the nineteenth century.[2] This peaceful acquisition of vast strips of land—what Margaret Field called the Krobo's "bloodless conquest"—was made possible by their unique system of land tenure, the huza.[3] As has been explained in chapter 3, the land-hungry Krobo used this system of joint purchase to acquire land from their Akan neighbors, beginning with the Kotrope and the Apirede (Jakiti) in the late eighteenth century.

In the late 1820s, the introduction of palm oil as a cash crop among the Krobo advanced their bloodless conquest by providing both cash and incentives to purchase multiple huzas from their land-rich and numerically small Akan neighbors. By the third decade of the nineteenth century, the area west and north of the Krobo Mountain up to and including the Akuapem foothills had been settled by the Krobo and they began purchasing land in the Akuapem mountains from the Akyem Abuakwa and the Akuapem, as well as from the Juaben and the Akwamu.

Unknowingly, Europeans also assisted in the Krobo's conquest. The Danes and the British colonial officials and traders, and even the Basel missionaries, contributed to the Krobo's territorial expansion by encouraging the commercialization of palm oil. The British and the Basel missionaries, in their respective official reports to London and Switzerland, publicized the Krobo's industriousness in palm oil production and identified Odumase, Kpong, and Akuse as commercial and communication centers for the entire eastern region.

The various nineteenth-century wars, some of which directly involved the Krobo, also served to advance the bloodless conquest. The Dum War of 1835-1836 against the Akuapem and the Danes for the first time clearly identified palm oil as a major cash crop in the eastern region, and the Krobo as one of the major producers, by making payment of the indemnity against the Krobo payable in palm oil. The defeat of the Asante and their allies the Akwamu in 1826, and again in 1873-1874 (the Sagrenti War), opened the entire southeastern region to increased legitimate trade. The Krobo were one of the major beneficiaries of the exodus of the Asante from the region. Finally, the 1858 Krobo Rebellion against the British and its aftermath, the boycott of 1858-1866, clearly established Britain's authority over the Krobo and the eastern region, and also demonstrated the economic importance of the Krobo's control over the cultivation and the production of palm oil for export.

The preceding chapters have attempted to present an understanding of Krobo society before palm oil developed as a cash crop, in order to clarify the change brought about by the commercialization of palm oil, and later cocoa.[4] The traditional Krobo economy, which changed little until the last decades of the eighteenth century, consisted of subsistence farming supplemented by hunting. The Krobo's territorial expansion and population growth during the eighteenth century (chapter 3), and the resulting social changes (chapter 4), in part prepared the Krobo to enter the international economy as agricultural exporters. The driving force behind the Krobo economy both before and after the commercialization of palm oil, however, was not palm oil *per se*, but the unending acquisition of farming land by way of the huza.

The Krobo's Early Exposure to International Trade

The lucrative Atlantic slave trade in this part of West Africa dates from at least the 1600s. By the eighteenth century there were over thirty European trading entrepots along the Ghanaian coast belonging to the British, Danish, Brandenburger, Dutch, Portuguese, and French. The Danes dominated the eastern region (the Danish Guinea Coast), but with only three small islands in the Caribbean—St. Thomas, St. John, and St. Croix[5]—they had limited need of slaves for export. Despite this fact, the Danes had erected a string of trading forts along the coasts of Danish Guinea: Old Ningo (Friedensborg, 1734), Teshi (Augustaborg, 1787), Christiansborg (1657), Keta (Prizenstein, 1784), and Ada (Konigstein, 1784). The British built Ft. Vernon at Prampram in 1780.[6]

The Danes attempted to establish their own plantations in Africa "with African labour," as on the "slave plantations in the Americas."[7] In 1788, Paul Erdmann Isert attempted to establish cotton and tobacco plantations at Malfi, on the Volta River's west bank, and at Prampram on the coast. The scheme failed. Undeterred, Isert founded another plantation along the ridge of the Akuapem Mountains, at about 1200 feet, where the climate was cooler and healthier. For reasons not clear, Isert called his plantation the Republic of Krobo.[8] However, this "most important Danish project" for the cultivation of plantations on the Guinea Coast did not survive Isert's death in January 1789.[9]

The presence of slavers and especially the chronic Akan wars in the late eighteenth century restricted Krobo trading and stifled Krobo economic growth and territorial expansion. However, as noted in chapter 3, these chronic Akan wars precipitated a rapid increase in the Krobo population with the arrival of the Denkyira Krobo and other eighteenth-century Akan refugees to the Krobo Mountain. With a rapidly expanding Krobo population (the number of tribal group rose from seven to twelve between 1700 and 1750), there was an urgent need for more farming land and increased need to trade for food items not found on the dry Accra plains surrounding the Krobo Mountain.

Coincidentally, as the general population increased with the arrival of various Akan refugees in the southeastern part of the Gold Coast, the introduction of new foods from the Americas, a by-product of the Atlantic slave trade, made it possible for the Adangme and others to satisfy their dietary needs. Thus, by the end of the eighteenth century, maize, cassava, sweet potatoes, peppers, and tomatoes were widespread in Kroboland, joining the millet, cow peas, dried fish, wild animals, and palm oil on which the Krobo had previously relied.[10] The new crops from the Americas led to a food surplus that was traded with neighbors or for European goods, especially iron tools and textiles. Thus, by 1800, using local markets and trade with the coast, the Krobo increased their trade with Adangme, Akan, and Ewe. The major items of exchange were millet, maize, dried fish, palm oil, pottery, salt, beads and other jewelry, and a wide range of European goods, including guns, cutlasses, iron goods, and liquor.[11] The desire for many of these goods increased the Krobo's reliance on the commercialization of palm oil, to supply the cash needed to purchase imported items. Although trading had increased by 1800, satisfying many of the Krobo's consumer needs, their need for farming land had not been resolved. The acquisition of land by the Krobo had to wait for the end, or at least decline, of the Akan wars, or more specifically for the defeat of the Asante in the south.

The defeat of the Asante and their allies in 1826 at Akantamansu, near Dodowa (ten miles southwest of Kroboland), ended Asante dominance in the southern part of the Gold Coast and opened the entire southern half of the region to trade in items other than slaves—what the Europeans called legitimate trade.[12] Slave raiding for exportation to the Americas decreased with the defeat of the Asante, the region's major supplier, and because of more effective abolition activities by the British Royal Navy. With slave trading and the Asante less of a threat to the peoples in the eastern region, the Krobo felt more secure in expanding their purchase or occupation of land away from their Krobo Mountain stronghold in the Akuapem foothills.[13] The chief mechanism of this expansion was the huza system.

The Huza System

Although scholars have disagreed on when the huza system originated, they have agreed that it radically changed the Krobo.[14] Cultivating the new foods introduced from the Americas, the huza farmers created an economic surplus. Furthermore, scholars such as Hill, Field, La Anyane, and Benneh have demonstrated that the Manya Krobo dominated huza purchases and palm oil production.[15] This fact accounts for the unequal economic development of the two chiefdoms. While the Manya Krobo did not hold a monopoly on the huza they made more effective use of it than the Yilo or their neighbors the Shai.

The political needs of the huza farmers also led to the radical change in the governmental structure of the Manya Krobo, which culminated in the selection of Odonkor Azu, one of the leading huza farmers of the 1830s, to be the first Manya Krobo konor (chapter 4). The wealth the huza farmers derived from the sale of food and palm oil permitted some Krobo children to obtain a mission education, and the Krobo could then use the resulting knowledge of European culture and language to better market their products at Kpong, Akuse, and Accra (chapter 8). Finally, the commercial success of the Krobo huza farmers led them into greater political and social interaction with their neighbors—for the first time in their history, as equals—and to greater intercourse with Europeans, especially the British.

The involvement of the majority of the Krobo huza farmers in cultivation and production of commodities for export dramatically changed Krobo demography, dispersing the Krobo clans into one set of small huza farms and villages in the Akuapem foothills, and another set of huza farms and villages in the mountains. Of course there was also a portion of the population, especially the old and those associated with the Krobo's majority deities, who remained on or near the Krobo Mountain.

Huza expansion occurred in waves, spreading into distinct geographical regions at different periods.[16] Farmers preferred the valleys and small plateaus and largely ignored the hills; the streams were of the greatest importance, as a source of water and fish, and as a natural boundary between huzas. The largest rivers, such as the Pawmpawm and the Densu, are natural highways. The main rivers needed to be crossed by bridge, ferry, or ford; the smaller streams were natural boundaries, baselines, and landmarks. In the area of Krobo expansion in the Akuapem hills, there are two distinct stream patterns—trellis drainage of the flat-bedded sandstones of the plateau, and dendritic drainage.[17] In the Krobo area, streams are few and generally seasonal. The water supply is second only to defense in importance. For the many huza villages along the foothills, rock cisterns, springs, and riverbeds provided critically needed water. The importance of water to the rise of any village along the base of the Akuapem foothills cannot be over-emphasized. The trading village of Dodowa, along the heavily travelled Accra-Dodowa-Odumase footpath, achieved preeminence solely because of its permanent water supply.[18]

The earliest population movement away from the Krobo mountain was in the region northwest and northeast of the mountain between Trom and Noaso, probably during the last decade of the eighteenth century.[19] The Krobo occupied these lands belonging to the Kotrope and the Apirede during the last decades of the eighteenth century, when the huza system as it is known today was probably not yet completely developed. Indeed, Konor Nene Azzu Mate Kole has suggested that some of these lands were forcibly occupied while others were purchased.[20] While there may have been some minor or occasional disputes over lands taken by the Krobo, especially in the late eighteenth century, there is no evidence of any violent conflicts between the Krobo and any of their neighbors over land.

The second phase of huza expansion occurred with the occupation of Kotrope lands in the Akuapem foothills, probably by 1800.[21] Here the forests were cleared and the first of many permanent huza villages were established. By the reign of Yilo Konor Ologo Patu (c. 1832-1869) and Manya Konor Odonkor Azu (c. 1835-1867), Krobo economic, political, and social life began to be centered in these huza villages. The djemeli disliked this redirecting of Krobo life away from the sacred mountain, but were powerless to reverse the trend. Within a few decades, by the 1850s, each Krobo family and clan had established its own village along a line that paralleled the base of the Akuapem foothills (Appendix C).[22] Today these villages form the center of Krobo life for all twelve Krobo subtribes.

In 1864 Reverend M. Rös provided the earliest European descriptions of the Krobo's system of land tenure and farming.

Their three kinds of settlement patterns led him to conclude that the Krobo were a strange people.

> First of all there are two big mountain towns—Yilo and Maniya [sic] on the majestic Krobo Mountain. . . . Second, the tribe has its numerous villages and farms in the shade of the splendid palm at the foot of the Akuapem Mountains. Where the men work, there are huge plantations; there are those plantations that are located behind the Akuapem mountains west of Odumase. Here, there are wide, magnificent, and very fertile lands that the Krobos buy from the lazy Akuapem. . . . Each Krobo farmer builds a hut in the middle of his fine plantation.[23]

Rös estimated that on one preaching excursion he visited over one hundred farms. Missionaries Jakob Heck and Johannes Zimmermann made similar reports on Krobo farming. Zimmermann in 1867 reports that the "Krobo buy the uncultivated but still cultivable land from the people of Akuapem, who do not cultivate it . . . The Krobos build plantations, especially palm forests. This industriousness gives vigor to the people."[24] Zimmermann estimated that there were at least six hundred huza farming villages. Later that year, 1867, Reverend Karl Aldinger wrote: "Very diligently they [the Krobo] extend the cultivation of oil palm year after year, thus building up oil palm forests."[25]

By 1861 or thereabouts, huza farms extended to the Pawmpawm River to the west and Ajena to the North, from the Begoro and Tafo stools.[26] By 1875 the number of small bush "plantation villages" in the vast hilly and mountainous regions was too great for Kopp to even estimate.[27] It is clear that although missionary accounts do not mention the word *huza* they were observing huza farms and villages. Moreover, it was undoubtedly the huza which permitted land to be purchased in a contiguous pattern, accounting for the expansion of the Krobo into the Akuapem foothills and beyond into the Akuapem Mountains. The huza system evolved in response to basic internal economic needs and in response to the opportunity for territorial expansion that the Krobo found in the last quarter of the eighteenth century. The huza system was not created by the Krobo as a response to the introduction of palm oil as a cash crop and was well established before palm oil or other food crops for export were introduced.

The foothill villages occupied an area of short streams rising in the hills and ending in alluvial fans.[28] Most of this area is Manya Krobo territory. By the middle of the nineteenth century the Krobo villages along the foothills were the economic and population centers, replacing the Krobo Mountain. The cheap, fertile land and the availability of water afforded these foothill villages a degree of urban development and concentration found elsewhere among the Krobo only on the banks of the Volta. (Kpong and Akuse, of course, had no water problems.)

During the second stage of huza expansion, Krobo farmers followed the streams upcountry into the narrow parallel strike valleys.[29] Here the settlements lay along streams, with farms reaching up the hillsides. It was in this region that the characteristic Krobo linear huza settlement first developed. "The measurement of the huza," Field stated, "is interesting and [a] curious lacunae in Native mathematics."[30] Under the huza system, the land was collectively purchased and then immediately subdivided. This Krobo pattern of subdivision—which might more accurately be called the Manya Krobo pattern, as it appeared more frequently in Manya territory—consisted of long strings of farm huts in the river valleys, each standing on its own strip of land stretching away from the stream at right angles; only in a few areas did blocks of land of necessity vary from the ideal rectangular shape.[31] This unique pattern has continued to the present.

The Pawmpawm River, the largest river reached by the Krobo since their expansion into the Akuapem mountains, marked a physical and political boundary for the Krobo. West of the Pawmpawm resided the core of the Begoro. The Krobo continued their peaceful migration into a new area of parallel streams, on a larger scale than those of the strike valleys of the Akuapem foothills. As the settlements extended farther into Akyem territory they entered the area of dendritic drainage, with less regular stream patterns. Here the layouts of the huzas, both of the Krobo and of their imitators the Shai, became much less regular. Huzas often took their names from the stream on which they were based. No corresponding stream-naming pattern is found among the Akuapem.[32]

Finally, beginning by the 1860s, the huzas expanded into the Akuapem mountains and along narrow plateaus as far as the Pawmpawm River to the northwest. The huzas continued to have family residences attached to them, and villages sprang up as markets for the crops cultivated on the Krobo plantations. Major upcountry markets included Bisa, Asesewa, and Apimsu.[33] These huza farms were located a considerable distance from the original huzas and villages along the Akuapem foothills. As a result, upcountry Krobo had limited contact with other centers such as Odumase and Sra. Instead, cultural contact with their nearest Akan neighbors in Begoro, Akyem, and Akwamu increased.

By the 1860s, the eastern region was undergoing a shift away from slave and gold trading to the commercialization of palm oil. The Akyem Abuakwa preferred to continue to rely on slave trading and gold digging and trading, and continued to sell thousands of acres to willing Krobo huza farmers well into the twentieth century, even after slavery had been banned by the British and gold mining had declined. Robert Addo-Fening has documented Akyem Abuakwa land sales to the Krobo and suggested some of the long-term damage this policy did to the Akyem Abuakwa's economy.[34]

By the middle of the nineteenth century, the Krobo's nearest Adangme neighbor, the Shai, also began to expand and take advantage of available land.[35] The Shai did not copy the huza system until the latter part of the century, and they did not enter the lucrative palm oil trade in a significant way until the 1860s. For many Shai who declined to join this expansion, pottery remained their most important source of revenue. The numerically small Shai presented more of an economic challenge to their northwest Akan neighbors, the Akuapem, than to the Krobo.

The Akuapem, the Krobo's northwestern Akan neighbors, became their major competitors for land as palm oil rose in commercial value. Each people attempted to establish a claim over the eastern region in the wake of the defeat of the Asante in 1826. Occasionally conflict erupted, as is evident from the 1835-1836 Akuapem-Krobo War (the Dum War). By 1854, palm oil constituted a major part of the Akuapem economy. However, military strife between the Akuapem, the Akyem Abuakwa, and the Akyem Kotoku in the 1840s and 1850s hindered the Akuapem from presenting a united front against the advancing Krobo huza farmers. And when Akuapem farmers did attempt to commercially cultivate palm oil, their farming plots were dissimilar to the Krobo plantations created by the huzas. Indeed, Hill says the Akuapem model of farms consisted of isolated, often island-like plots.[36] With the entry of the Shai and the Akuapem into the palm oil market, the region was full of farmers seeking to advance their economic standing through the commercialization of palm oil. But the Krobo held the edge; they had control of the best land, access to the major Krobo palm oil markets, and political and economic control of the major markets both inland and along the Volta River.[37]

The export market for palm oil was not the only incentive for the Krobo to accumulate larger and larger farms during the middle of the nineteenth century. Lands adjacent to growing coastal urban centers such as Accra, Osu, Prampram, and Ada could not provide sufficient food for the expanding population. Hence Krobo farmers migrated toward the fertile foothills of the Akuapem mountains to produce food crops for urban consumption.[38]

The Asante War of 1873-1874 interrupted huza expansion, as both Krobo chiefdoms rallied to aid the British against the Asante. In the aftermath of the war, London decided to bring the eastern region under more direct control.[39] Direct Krobo-British contact further increased when the colonial administrative officies were moved from the western region village of Cape Coast to Christiansborg. The eastern region's major commercial centers, Accra, James Town, Ada, Dodowa, Aburi, Akropong, Odumase, and Kpong, became more efficient, for a number of reasons: more and better maintained roads, greater security for travel along the rivers and overland, more consumers of European and American goods, more efficient processing of the palm kernel, and greater proficiency in the English language on the part of some Krobo merchants.

The Preeminence of the Manya Krobo Huza-Farmer

In the early part of the nineteenth century, neither Krobo chiefdom was dominant.[40] Each chiefdom had its areas of dominance. The Manya Krobo exercised politico-religious dominance through their control over the djemeli. In contrast to Manya Konor Odonkor Azu, Konor Ologo Patu exercised more effective political control over his chiefdom, as Yilo secular authority had coalesced by the middle of the eighteenth century. The Yilo were a more centralized society with a well-established konor, who could more easily have directed and encouraged expansion into overseas trade, had he so chosen.

Each konor, no doubt after debate and discussions with influential members of the community, formulated his own policies toward the Europeans and toward the commercialization of palm oil.[41] Yilo Konor Ologo Patu and his two successors, Sasraku (1867-1874) and Akrobetto I (1874-1906), followed rather conservative policies. By contrast, the Manya konors followed the more progressive policies of Odonkor Azu, much of whose support came from huza farmers (see chapter 4). In general, Manya Krobo huza farmers were in the vanguard of political and economic change in their chiefdom. By reinvesting much of their palm oil profits in the purchase of additional huzas, the Manya farmers bolstered their own prestige and assured that of their heirs. The Manya Krobo also gained materially as their towns of Akuse, Kpong, and Amedica became major market centers during the period of palm oil expansion.

A number of geographical factors also favored the Manya Krobo. The Manya Krobo settlement northeast of the mountain occupied the most fertile areas in the Akuapem Mountains. Manya Krobo huza farmers purchased the best watered, best drained land on the river system in the Akuapem Mountains, as a brief geographical study of the migration indicates. Furthermore, the Yilo tended to purchase selected plots or islands (the Akuapem model), in both the nineteenth and twentieth centuries. Equally important was the timing of the large scale huza purchases. In the first half of the nineteenth century the Manya Krobo huza farmers purchased lands from the Kotrope, the Apirede, and the Begoro.[42] Moreover, the location of the Manya Krobo huzas and villages along the Akuapem foothills permitted them more direct and easier access to the major markets such as Kpong and Akuse.

Disputes about huza purchases could and did lead to physical conflict between members of a huza and the seller. After 1874 and 1875, when the British began to exercise more direct control over the eastern region, colonial officials stressed litigation as a way of resolving these land disputes. Among the Krobo, virtually all the major litigation over huza purchases and boundary disputes involved the Manya Krobo.[43]

The first recorded land tenure case, *Begoro v. Apirede (1882)*, occurred during the reigns of konors Sakite and Akrobetto I.[44] It demonstrates the importance of Sakite in the region as well as the territorial expansion of the Manya Krobo. The Begoro alleged that the Apirede had unlawfully sold Begoro lands to the Manya Krobo. Unable to settle the dispute among themselves, the parties agreed to present their case to Konor Sakite for arbitration. After hearing the case, Sakite made the following award:

Begoro v. Apirede

1. The Apiredehene [paramount chief] had illegally sold lands beyond Bisa which legally belonged to the Begoro stool. He was fined £20.

2. Begorohene [paramount chief] Antwi Kwesi agreed to "dash" [give] the Manya Krobo all the disputed land between Bisa and the Pawmpawm River which had unlawfully been sold to the Manya Krobo by the Apirede.

3. The Begorohene agreed to sell to the Manya Krobo any lands east of Bisa which might consequently prove not to have been sold.

4. Whenever any Krobo wished to buy land, the Akyem Abuakwa should sell it to them; however, the Akyem Abuakwa would retain the right to collect snails [an important part of most Akan's diet] wherever found on these lands.

The award reaffirmed the Begoro's and the Apirede's rights to the land in question and clarified—or, more correctly, exalted—the rights of the third party, the Manya Krobo. Sakite's decision in this case was reviewed and upheld in 1893 by Governor Sir Brandford Griffith and in 1923 by Dictrict Commissioner H. S. Newland.[45] The direct result of the 1893 award to the Krobo was to confirm that the region from Pawmpawm River to Bisa belonged to the Krobo.

Thus by 1893 the peaceful penetration of the Krobos had extended their lands from the plain beneath the Krobo Hill northwards as far as the boundaries of the present Afram and Pawmpawm Forest Reserve, a distance of not less than 24 miles as the crow flies.[46]

The origin of the huza or more correctly the beginning of the Krobo territorial expansion was in the second half of the eighteenth century. Marion Johnson suggests there were vacant or more correctly vacated lands northwest and northeast of the Krobo Mountain by the late 1740s. First the previously powerful Akwamu were defeated by the combined forces of the Akyem and the Akuapem in 1733. Soon thereafter, in 1742, before either the Akyem or Akuapem could consolidate their authority over the southeastern region, they were defeated by the new power, the Asante. After 1742 the Akyem and Akuapem were preoccupied with the Asante, and the former allies of the Akwamu—the Kamana, the Begoro (Osino), Apirede, and the Jakite (Kotropoes) in the Akuapem mountains and foothills—fled this area in search of more defensible position in the Akuapem forest or across the Volta. The vacant or vacated lands, according to Johnson, were occupied by the Krobo. Some time after the last quarter of the eighteenth century but before the commercial production of palm in the late 1820s, the huza system evolved.[47]

The huza neither began nor ended with the dominance of palm oil as a commercial crop.[48] As palm oil exports declined in the beginning of the twentieth century, because of the discovery of petroleum as a lubricant and the success of cocoa as a cash crop, the huza and continued huza acquisition remained Krobo preoccupations. Missionary Paul Steiner reported in 1909:

> Their business drives them to always extend their plantations of oil palm, crop and field fruits, and it witnesses their economic interest and far-sightness, that they are always trying to acquire land and cultivate it by buying it from the neighboring tribes.[49]

Nineteenth century accounts of the Krobo's unique system of land tenure by Basel missionaries Aldinger, Heck, Zimmermann, Kopp, Shonfeld, Furer, and Josephans, and studies by twentieth century scholars Hill, Field, La Anyane, Benneh, and Pogucki, associate the pure huza, in which land is purchased in contiguous plots, almost exclusively with the Manya Krobo. No nineteeth century observations mention Yilo Krobo huzas, although they must have existed. The omissions may be due to the fact that on preaching tours the missionaries trekked through many Krobo villages and found the Manya Krobo and their konors more receptive to Christianity than the Yilo.

By the end of the nineteenth century, huza ownership had become the sine qua non of power and prestige among the Manya Krobo, as Field clearly states:

> By far the most striking and important aspect of *huza* farming is that no farmer is content with land on one *huza* only . . . every man who owns land strives, during his working life, to buy enough new land to enable each of his sons to inherit a farm without dividing his own. Thus we find that the typical farmer has responsibilities on two, three or even four separate *huzas*.[50]

The ruling passion of the Manya Krobo, according to Field, is to engage in the commercialization of palm oil, cocoa, and other commodities in order to purchase more huzas.[51]

The introduction of cocoa by the Basel missionaries in the late 1890s on their experimental farms at Aburi, eastern region, initially brought little change among the Krobo.[52] The Manya Krobo maintained their preeminent position because they quickly recognized the potential of cocoa, even replacing some oil palm groves with cocoa.[53] Throughout the early years of cocoa production, until the early 1920s, the Manya Krobo retained their economic dominance. Land became more expensive and scarce, but the Manya, with their capital and the huza method of purchasing large plots, continued to outbid their Yilo, Shai, and Akuapem neighbors.

Yilo Krobo Huza Territorial Expansion

Although during the era of huza expansion the Manya Krobo's growth overshadowed that of the Yilo, the establishment of the Yilo village of Somanya by 1800 suggests that in the late eighteenth century the Yilo may have been more willing to develop permanent villages away from the Krobo Mountain. Similarly, Sra, the village of the Yilo konors, appears to predate Odumase. (Somanya is located less than three miles from the mountain, whereas Odumase is about seven miles away.) Nuaso is the nearest Manya Krobo village to the mountain at about four miles away. The reasons for the Yilo's willingness to leave the mountain may be traced to their ethnic heritage. Four of the six Yilo subtribes were of Akan ancestry, the so-called Denkyira Krobo. Moreover, because these four subtribes had no representation among the djemeli, the ruling theocratic oligarchy, they may have been less attached to the area around the Krobo Mountain.

Somanya was probably the Krobo's first permanent village established along the Akuapem foothills. Advantageously located at the crossroads of the route connecting the Akyem people with the plains and the Accra-Dodowa-Ajena footpath, Somanya expanded rapidly. Unlike nearly every other village, Somanya did not originate as a huza farm or huza village. Indeed, the very success of Somanya and nearby Sra as trading centers may have contributed to the Yilo's continuing reliance on trade rather than on the accumulation of wealth through the acquisition of huza farms. This was the case, for example, of the Akuapem, and to a lesser degree the Akyem Abuakwa; the reliance of both chiefdoms on trade in slaves and gold hindered their interest in, or their ability to adopt, the commercialization of palm oil. Before the rise of Kpong, Akuse, and Amedica in the 1830s, 1840s, and 1850s, Somanya was already the center of Krobo trading. Why, then, should the Yilo put their energies into huza farming and the commercialization of agricultural crops? Given the success of Somanya and their lack of direct access to the Volta, the general Yilo Krobo population in the late eighteenth and early nineteenth centuries may well have considered the huza less necessary to economic gain than did the Manya.

In the 1820s and 1830s, the earliest years of palm oil production for export, Somanya was the center of trading. But the Yilo had a distinct political disadvantage. Their konor, Ologo Patu, remained throughout his long reign (1835-1869) cool to commercialization, despite the fact that oil palm groves surrounded Sra.[54] He resisted the extensive contact with Europeans that would have resulted from the commercialization of palm oil, possibly because he feared the inevitable changes that contact with Europeans would bring. Most Yilo farmers followed Ologo Patu's rather conservative attitude toward the huza until the aftermath of the Krobo Rebellion in 1858 (see chapter 6), when they were fined 4,125 pounds sterling payable in palm oil. From this point forward the Yilo Krobo could no longer ignore the economic benefits of the huza and the international importance of palm oil.

By the late 1850s, however, it was no easy matter for the Yilo to enter this lucrative and competitive market. Established oil palm growers surrounded them—the Akuapem, the Akyem Abuakwa, the Shai, and the Manya Krobo. Moreover, potential Yilo huza purchasers had to compete with their wealthier neighbors—the Manya huza farmers—for the best land. Finally, in the aftermath of the 1858 Rebellion, Ologo Patu, for the remainder of his reign, directed most of his energy to paying the fine and keeping the chiefdom from falling into complete chaos. He never regained his authority. Konor Sasraku (1869-1874) continued the policies of Ologo Patu. Not until the 1880s, under Akrobetto I (1874-1906), did the Yilo Konor and the Yilo huza farmers begin to provide leadership for the general Yilo population in the pursuit of a centralized, consistent, and aggressive huza policy.[55]

Finally, it should be noted that the Manya Krobo's population was considerably larger than the Yilo's; hence, the number of potential land purchasers, including women, was greater. For these reasons, by the end of the nineteenth century Manya Krobo territory far exceeded Yilo territory. The first census of Ghana in 1891, which was not completely accurate, recorded the relative population of the Krobo but not their geographical boundaries.[56] According to the most recent census, 1984, the Manya Krobo owned about 600 square miles, whereas the Yilo chiefdom included slightly less than 300 square miles.[57]

Krobo Markets

Between the fifteenth and the late eighteenth centuries, the Krobo engaged cautiously in local trade with their larger and more powerful Ewe and Akan neighbors. By the late eighteenth century the Krobo had extended their trading activities to their Adangme neighbors with greater confidence and regularity. Krobo men, women, and children head-loaded farm goods to the Shai Hills markets, where they traded for Shai cooking and storage pots and other specialty items.[58] The Shai markets also provided a convenient place to exchange for goods from the interior and the coast, including European ones. The Adangme conducted no slave markets; in fact, the Krobo and other Adangme were frequent victims of slave raiding.

Before the commercialization of palm oil, the main markets were along the coast. The following Klama song recalls this ancient trade:

> In the olden days it was at *Ladoku*
> where they traded with palm oil
> They traded with palm oil at *Nigo*
> They traded with palm oil at *Tema*
> In the olden days at *Ladoku.*[59]

In the old village of Gbugbla (Prampram), the inland Adangme exchanged goods for textiles. This was also true for La, as another Klama song records: "If I go not to *La*, I shall have to wear bark cloth."[60]

Tradition claims that Kukutsunya, at the southwest base of the Mountain, was the Krobo's first permanent market village.[61] Its proximity to the Krobo Mountain suggests that this claim is correct. In the 1860s, missionary reports indicate that it was still one of the main markets. During the early phase of huza expansion in the late eighteenth century, a number of modest roadside selling places emerged along footpaths—Okum-Salonya in the east outside Somanya, Nuaso, Manyakpongno, and finally Agomanya, Odumase, and Ogome.[62] As the population expanded, so did the market villages, moving in a westerly and northerly direction in accordance with the location of huza-farms and villages. Soon afterwards, many of the small Akuapem valleys settled by huza-farmers established local upcountry markets. Guata (Obenyemi), the first upcountry market, was followed by Otrokpe, Apimsu, Bisa, Obawale, Opesika, and Agogo. By the end of the nineteenth century, Asesewa was by all accounts the largest upcountry market. In 1943, Hill described it as colossal.[63]

The major Krobo markets attracted goods and peoples from throughout the eastern region. Markets were also centers of economic and cultural contact, where relatives and friends interacted and where the Krobo discussed colonial rule or local politics, new ideas and commodities. All the Krobo's neighbors were in attendance: the Akuapem, the Akyem, the Akwamu, the Apirede, and the Kotrope from the west; the Ewe (Anlo) from across the Volta; fellow Adangme (Shai and Osudoku, and Ga) from the east; and even northerners (Hausa).[64] The upcountry trade was largely domestic. European trading company representatives were at a minimum at Asesewa and Bisa, but they had large and well-established factories at Somanya and Odumase and at Kpong, Akuse, and Amedica along the Volta. Sra and Odumase, the villages of the Yilo and Manya Krobo Konors, were also important political centers. The nineteenth century was the heyday of the Volta.[65] In an era without good overland roads, railways, or lorries, all goods entered and left the region via the Volta; and above Kpong, Akuse, and Amedica the Volta rapids prevented transport by canoe or, later, by steamer.

For its size the Krobo population established and controlled an impressive number of export market centers. Sometime during the early nineteenth century the Manya Krobo gained control over Kpong, on the west bank of the Volta River.[66] Originally established by the Akuapem in the late eighteenth century as a refuge for escaped slaves and outcasts, by the 1890s Kpong had become a large village composed of Ewe, Akwamu, Akyem, Ga, Adangme, and various northern peoples, especially Hausa. Despite this ethnic diversity, Kpong was culturally and politically a Krobo village. In Kpong, each disparate group segregated itself into a compound. Because of Kpong's easy access to the coast, when it had displaced Somanya as the largest Krobo trading center, Kpong also boasted the largest European population—Danes, British, Swiss, and Germans (Appendix D).[67]

Unlike Africans and Eruropean merchants, Basel missionaries found Kpong revolting. In 1856, Johannes Zimmermann described Kpong as "a rotten town, a free city where runaway slaves and other rabble settled."[68] The "other rabble" included debtors and criminals. The openness of the village made it attractive to many different kinds of people, including not only runaway slaves but slavers. For example, in 1858, Geraldo de Lima burned the town in his quest for slaves.[69]

Kpong traders handled a wide range of goods. Among its most important commodities was salt. Produced by the Ada along the coast, it was transported up the Volta en route to the north. At Kpong, sea salt in block form could be seen "stacked up in long narrow sacks." Other commodities found at Kpong were yams, cassava, maize, maize beer, maize flour, various fruits, kola nuts, and dried fish; and, by the 1860s, cotton.[70] It was also a distribution center for European goods, including iron bars, iron pots, knives, and cutlasses, textiles, furniture, powder and shot, and spirits. By the 1860s, Kpong clearly formed the center of Krobo economic activity and cultural exchange. However, not until Manya Konor Sakite appointed the chief of Kpong in 1871 did it come under the direct influence of the Manya konor. Kpong remained the commercial center of the region, later known as the Volta District, well into the middle of the twentieth century.[71]

The continued increase in trade and the burning of Kpong in 1858 led to the rise of Akuse and Amedica, which were separated by a lagoon. After Kpong's reconstruction, in the late 1860s, Akuse remained the second most important of the three major Krobo villages along the west bank of the Volta.

> Akuse . . . [along with] Amedika, is of great importance for commerce and traffic on the Volta, because it is the most distant place from the coast which can be reached by bigger boats. . . . Akuse-Amedika is therefore the storage place for the products of the Krobo country being taken to the coast for shipment. There settled a number of native sellers, among them some Christians as well as several European merchants.[72]

Both Kpong and Akuse were frequently flooded during the rainy season and became havens for mosquitoes. Amedica, the third Krobo trading entrepot along the Volta, was located inland by about two miles, and escaped the floods. Basel missionaries called it "the port of Akuse which is the entrepot of the palm oil trade."[73] More than Kpong, Akuse and Amedica were devoted to the trade in palm products.

In former times the markets operated through simple exchange or payment in cowries. By the middle of the nineteenth century, cowries continued to be used in small-scale trading but were rapidly being displaced in larger transactions by British, American, Spanish, Dutch, and French coins.

The rise of market villages led to a more economically varied Krobo society. The markets offered opportunities for porters, carpenters, brick and stone masons, clerks, and tailors, trained by the Basel missionaries. Though still basically a farming people, the Krobo began to include wage earners, many of whom held huzas but added cash to the land wealth by working in urban centers. Also, farmers began using part of their palm oil profits to purchase European luxury items, such as furniture, mirrors, clothing, and spirits.

Women and the Huza

Prior to the territorial expansion of the Krobo and the cultivation of palm oil and other foods for sale, most farming was conducted by men and boys. The huza and the commercialization of food crops changed the traditional economic relationship between men and women and provided greater economic opportunities for women. Before the huza, only during such emergencies as war, when men were away fighting, did "the women take their place in the fields and at home."[74] The acquisition and management of multiple huzas necessitated an unexpected and rapid change in the division of labor. By the time Zimmermann had arrived in Kroboland, that is in the 1860s, since "men and women were busy in the same way, the hardest work does not lie on the shoulders of women like other tribes."[75]

The ownership of huzas was limited by the structure of the Krobo family system. Huzas were owned by an individual, a Krobo man, who was the head of a house (we). In Krobo, *Yo yi we* (a woman does not own or rule a house); that is, a women bears children for a particular man's house, either her husband's or father's. Only if there are no male children in her late husband's nearer kin group may a wife assume compelete control over land until the children are adults.[76] However, a man, father or husband, may **give** his daughter or wife land or other property, which cannot be taken back upon his death. Thus, there is **limited** huza owership by women, and considerable control of some other huzas inherited through women, although this is a patrilineal system.

91

Whereas men controlled the huzas, women generally controlled the non-export trade. Women assumed the primary role as traders by default, that is, most men devoted their time, energy, and material resources, including cash, to their many huzas. The symbol of power and prestige in the society was the huza. For their part women quickly took advantage of the economic opportunities afforded them. In the past, women made and sold pottery which was used to carry and store goods; they also made soap, cosmetics and beads, all of which were important items in the daily lives of the Krobo.

Assisted by children or perhaps slaves, women sold a wide range of food and non-food items at road-selling-places (blconya-dzwa). The food sold had been cultivated on their own small farming plots which were part of the numerous huzas belonging to male relatives or grown on land rented from huza farmers. Their clients were farmers who purchased prepared dishes made from maize (blefo), plantain (manaa), yellow yam (bie), millet (ngma) along with poultry, goat or sheep which they owned and had raised. Some women also engaged in trading along the Volta and to the coast to secure fish and tobacco for resale to "double their profit." "Young girls, single and married women," also sold their goods in their modest stores or hawked goods carried on large wooden plates (sowe or sewe) in the towns and larger villages, especially along the Akuapem foothills; other women sold goods at their homes.[77] The profits earned by these women were theirs, which they used for their personal needs which included the purchase of additional goods for sale, and of personal items (clothing). And by the end of the century, these market women used an increased share of their profits to pay for the mission education of some of their children, that is, children born to them before they married who were not their husband's, or girls.[78] Additionally, many women also conducted trade with and for their husbands, fathers, or even brothers, with whom they shared the profits.[79]

Maize and palm kernel oil brought direct profits to women. Maize was processed and sold by women, millet, the traditional Krobo crop, was processed and sold by men.[80] By the 1850s maize, harvested twice a year, was possibly second in commercial importance to palm oil. The processing of palm oil was a family or even a community task. Palm oil profits belonged to men, and the profits from the oil extracted from the inner hard kernel belonged to women. This division of the fruits of the oil palm tree probably had its origin in the early years of the commercialization of palm oil, in that the palm tree is not indigenous to the Krobo Mountain, and therefore its cultivation and harvest were not established until probably the early nineteenth century. Kernel oil reached its highest output in the 1860s, providing additional revenue for women.[81]

Labor System

Although a number of scholars have studied isolated aspects of the Krobo's commercialization of palm oil and cocoa, there have been no studies of the Krobo's labor system in the nineteenth century. Hill wrote extensively about migrant labor from the neighboring peoples among the Krobo and other cocoa farmers in the twentieth century, but little or no evidence suggests the presence of migrant labor among the huza farmers on the palm oil plantations of the nineteenth century.

Given the region's widespread use of slaves and the Krobo's extensive and intensive cultivation of palm oil and other foods on their plantations, the question arises whether the Krobo used slaves as a primary or secondary labor source. Inez Sutton suggests that huza farmers who engaged in the commercialization of palm oil did use slave labor.[82] Basel missionary reports agree, but make it clear that slavery was not the primary source of huza farming labor. "On the new-broken land the slaves are working all the year by mastering the rampant bush, thus gaining a rich crop for their head of the family. But not only slaves, free and rich people also are working a longer or shorter time on these remote planta-tions."[83] The presence of slaves, both for export and for internal use, is well established in the southeastern region of the Gold Coast in the nineteenth century. Virtually all the Krobo's non-Adangme neighbors engaged in slaving and had large numbers of domestic slaves. Slave trading was a major source of wealth for the Akyem Abuakwa, the Akyem Kotoku, the Akwamu, the Ewe, and the Akuapem.

Contemporary accounts of slavery among the Krobo and other Adangme are limited almost exclusively to the observations of the Basel missionaries, who were committed to the complete eradication of slavery and would therefore not seek to minimize any form of slavery among the Krobo. Between 1864 and 1867, missionaries Zimmermann, Aldinger, and Heck wrote a number of detailed reports describing various aspects of Krobo society: the mountain dwellings, the crops produced, and the nature of the Krobo people. These were the first European accounts of the Krobo. In 1867, Zimmermann reported on slavery among the Krobo as follows:

> In Kroboland, slavery is not so repugnant as in other places. Human flesh and blood is not the main currency, but palm oil and other products of the country. The main reason for the shocking slave trade is thus absent. The slave is part of the family, his master eats and drinks with him; he works with him on one plantation. Our missionaries hardly hear about the maltreatment of a slave.[84]

Aldinger, in another report filed in the same year, noted that "the chiefs also work with their slaves."[85] Slaves, along with other non-slave members of the Krobo community, assisted in clearing fields and prepare palm oil, yam, maize, and other crops for markets. However, there is no indication that slaves constituted the major component of the huza farmer's labor. The fact that domestic slaves were important but not critical to the Krobo economy is evidenced by the low impact the ending of domestic slavery had in that society. One of the allegations of slavery among the Krobo after domestic slavery was prohibited by the British in 1875 dates from 1889. In that year the British government in an attempt to assess slavery in the Protectorate and at Salaga in the north employed the services of Thomas Odonkor. The Christain chief of Kpong alleged that "there were large numbers of Hausa, Fulah, Moshi [Mossi], and especially Grushi, slaves held by the Aquamoos, Krepis and Kroboes."[86] District commissioner Firminger reported finding no evidence of slaves among the Krobo, which might only indicate the absence of any widespread use of slaves at this time.

It is very significant that Basel missionaries and colonial officials, both strong opponents of slavery, make few references to slavery among the Krobo. There are actually no references among colonial documents to slavery among the Krobo farmers. Beginning in the 1860s, scores of Basel missionaries moved back and forth across Kroboland with great frequency. To missionaries, the suppression of slavery was second in importance only to the eradication of polygamy; yet the missionaries do not mention slave labor among the Krobo, although they reported slavery among the Akuapem and the Akyem Abuakwa with great regularity and force.

Throughout the nineteenth century, most of the Krobo's labor was performed by relatives, that is, family and clan members. Neighbors often shared the work involved in harvesting and processing palm oil. The finished products were head-carried by porters to market centers such as Bisa, Apimsu, Odumase, or Somanya along the foothills. However, no evidence suggests that the porters were special workers or slaves; they could well have been huza owners or their relatives. We do know that as the Krobo economy expanded during the last quarter of the nineteenth century some Adangme and Ga people migrated to Kroboland to take advantage of the economic opportunities brought by the palm oil boom. Many of these new immigrants became part of the wage labor force in Kpong and Akuse; others worked in the upcountry markets; still others probably worked with and for huza farmers to clear land and process food and palm oil.

There were however, some restrictions on the social mobility of slaves. "Slaves and fallen girls" were excluded from participation in the *Dipo* ceremony, thus denying them full membership in Krobo society. Additionally, "strangers, slaves, and those who died a violent death" could not be buried on the sacred Krobo Mountain.[87] Thus not only slaves but other outsiders were excluded from the highest levels of Krobo society. Moreover, the term "slave" [Odonkor] did not necessarily carry a negative status; for example the first konor of Manya Krobo was Odonkor Azu, and the term reappears in the name of the first Christian chief of Kpong, Thomas Odonkor.

The Krobo had domestic slaves. These domestic slaves were not associated with any one ethnic group, nor do they appear to have been secured in warfare. Therefore, they were probably purchased from neighboring peoples: Akan, Adangme, and Ewe. Domestic slaves seem to have had considerable opportunities for upward mobility, because there are no distinct groups in Krobo society that trace their heritage to slavery. Domestic slaves apparently married or in other ways completely integrated into the larger Krobo society. One account describes the Yilo village of Kpemo as composed of former slaves and poor farmers, but this village does not seem to have been segregated from other Krobo villages.[88] The Krobo, after all, were always characterized by heterogeneity.

It is doubtful that the Krobo had any particular philosophical aversion to slave labor. Before the commercialization of palm oil, the subsistence level economy of the Krobo could not have made much use of slaves either as status symbols or as a labor source. After commercialization, slaves simply were neither cheap nor, apparently, necessary for the working of the huza farms or the production of palm oil. Apparently there was slave trading going on at Kpong, as Sutton has noted. There is less convincing evidence, however, that these slaves were used in any significant numbers in Kroboland. Goods sold in Kpong were purchased by people from throughout the region, not just from Kroboland.

Although slavery was not crucial tot he economic well-being of the Krobo, some slaves had from time to time an unfortunate role in certain religious ceremonies. Unlike their Akan neighbors, the Krobo did not kill slaves in celebrations of the death of high priests or paramount chiefs, but rather in the celebrations of the war gods *Nadu* and *Kotoklo*.[89] Another distinction in the killing of these slaves was that among the Krobo the deaths were acts of individuals, not of the society as a whole. Slaves or strangers (little or no distinction was made between them) were often used for this purpose. These sacrifices were not domestic slaves but people kidnapped for the purpose. The killing of a domestic slave for sacrifice in 1891 precipitated Governor Griffith's order for the Krobo Mountain to be abandoned.[90]

Population

Before the eighteenth century, the Krobo were a small and ethnically relatively homogeneous group of Adangme-speaking

96

people. During the first decades of the eighteenth century a small number of people of Akan ancestry were added to the Krobo population. By the last quarter of the eighteenth century, the Krobo population began to increase dramatically in size, given an earlier influx of war refugees, and the new opportunities of expanding lands. By the time of Reverend Jacob Riis's first outside account in the mid-1830s, the huza system was well established and the Krobo population was divided between farms and the original mountain dwellings. Distracted by the uniqueness of the dwellings on the Krobo Mountain, Riis and most subsequent missionaries failed to observe accurately the size of the Krobo population.

During the reign of Konor Sakite (1867-1892), the Krobo expanded territorially, and the population of the lands also became more ethnically diverse, as peoples from surrounding communities were attracted to Kroboland seeking economic opportunities. The major Krobo villages along the Volta (Kpong, Akuse, and Amedica) already included people from a wide range of ethnic backgrounds. During the 1860s, 1870s, and 1880s, the Adangme and Ga population also increased in the major Krobo villages along the Akuapem range (Somanya, Sra, Odumase, Nuaso, and Manyapoungo). The new Adangme and Ga artisans, merchants, and traders had languages and backgrounds similar to those of the Krobo. As in centuries past on the Krobo Mountain, many of these immigrants soon became de facto Krobo themselves.

An 1867 Basel mission report estimated the populations of Sra and Odumase at about 500. Except for this rough approximation, there are no figures on the size of the Krobo population until 1881. In 1881, when Basel missionary Christaller estimated the population of Kroboland he unknowingly included the recent Ga and Adangme immigrants (Table 5.1).[91] By the reign of Konor Emmanuel Mate Kole, the Krobo were no longer considered one of the smallest chiefdoms in the region, but were equal in numbers to the Akyem Abuakwa and their long-time rival the Akuapem.

By 1891, the Manya Krobo chiefdom was nearly twice the size of the Yilo chiefdom.[92] The largest Krobo villages, as well as the most important ones (both administratively and commercially), were within the territory of the Manya Krobo (Table 5.2). For example, in 1891, Odumase, the village of the Manya Krobo

97

konors, had a population of almost 2000, whereas Sra, its Yilo counterpart, had a population of around 1700; Kpong had almost 3500 people, while the largest Yilo trading village, Somanya, had only slightly more than 600. No Yilo town or village could boast a population of more than 2000 (Table 5.2). In contrast, the Manya had one village of slightly less than 7000, four villages of 3000 or more, and six villages with more than 1000 inhabitants.[93] Manya Krobo villages were not only the most important among the Krobo, but also among the largest and most important in the entire Volta District (Table 5.3). The apparent causes of this differential are the Yilo's late entry into the business of purchasing huza; their preference for trade, not farming, which in the long run brought less profit; and the fact that the Manya started earlier to attract incomers to their villages, many of whom became part of the Manya Krobo.

Table 5.1

POPULATION OF THE KROBO AND THEIR NEIGHBORS

	Christaller (1881)	Basel Missionaries (1890)	Census (1891)
Krobo	30-40,000	c. 45,000	45,482
Akuapem	40,000	c. 55,000	57,586
Akyem Abuakwa	50,000	c. 18,000	33,585
Shai	10,000	c. 10,000	8,690
Akwamu	----	c. 6,000	11,062

The success of the bloodless conquest was evidenced by the relative wealth and size of the Krobo population by the end of the nineteenth century. Although continual territorial expansion and the resulting economic growth did not bring the Krobo into violent conflict with their neighbors, it did bring the Krobo into conflict with the British.

Table 5.2
LARGEST KROBO VILLAGES 1891

Manya (Total Pop. 28,000)		Yilo (Total Pop. 17,000)	
Agbom	6,939	Mekepeti	1,957
Kpong	3,435	Madami	1,940
Susui	3,163	Sra	1,695
Dorm	3,115	Nodow	1,542
Piengua	2,985	Piem	1,466
Odumase	1,991	Bunase	1,355
Akuse	1,442	Odarve	998
Manyakpongno	1,339	Lamisanya	988
Afiduasi	1,078	Tesanya	981
Asakore	1,017	Akole	664
		Somanya	604

Table 5.3
VILLAGE POPULATION IN VOLTA DISTRICT 1891

Aburi	10,393
Akropong	9,013
Mampong	5,832
Kpong	3,435
Odumase	1,991
Sra	1,695
Akuse	1,442
Somanya	604
Nsawam	700
Dodowa	113

6

THE KROBO REBELLION AND BOYCOTT
1858-1866

No other single event or series of events in the nineteenth century affected Krobo-British relations as deeply as did the 1858 Krobo Rebellion and Boycott.[1] It marked the turning point in Krobo political and commercial relations with the British as well as the end of Krobo reliance on the previously almost impenetrable Krobo Mountain. The role in the rebellion of konors Ologo Patu and Odonkor Azu and their respective clan military leaders made it almost impossible for either chiefdom to return to rule by a theocratic oligarchy. Finally, the attempt to pay the large indemnity imposed by the British tied the Krobo economy permanently and inextricably to the commercial production of palm oil, which in turn greatly facilitated the continued rapid purchasing of huzas.

The Krobo's success in the palm oil trade had led to conflict with their major purchasers, the British. After 1850, when Danish Guinea became the Gold Coast Colony and Protectorate, the British, unlike the Danes, became directly involved in Krobo internal affairs. Among the Krobo, reaction to British presence was divided: Odonkor Azu welcomed the British, but Ologo Patu did not. The latter's resentment of the British increased with the imposition of the now infamous Poll Tax of 1851 which evoked widespread, violent opposition throughout the colony and protectorate.[2] All opposition was crushed by September 1854, and the poll tax scheme finally was abandoned in 1861.

The poll tax fiasco worsened Krobo-British relations, while two other incidents helped to precipitate the Krobo Rebellion. The first was the 1856 Asibe War. Tete Atia, a subject of Ologo Patu, sought British protection and resolution of a dispute between himself and Ologo Patu. James Bannerman, civil commandant for the eastern region, promptly summoned Ologo Patu to appear before him at Christiansborg Castle. The konor refused. Basel missionaries recorded a vivid account of what happened next: "The Commander, Samuel Bannermann, sent him lead bullets and corn to choose between war and peace. The negro prince chose lead."[3]

What began as a civil matter between the konor and one of his subjects had developed into a public rejection of British authority over the Yilo. However, when faced with a small contingent of the Gold Coast Artillery Corps (GCAC) outside Sra, in April 1856, Ologo Patu surrendered, apparently unwilling to take military action against the British, whether because of lack of support or lack of preparedness. He was fined 3,000 cowries. The Asibe War, in reality a dispute, directly challenged Britain's claim of a protectorate over the Krobo and brought home to the Krobo the meaning of a British presence in the eastern region. It also set the stage for real military conflict two years later between the Krobo and the British.

In late August 1858 Odonkor Azu accused Ologo Patu of interfering in the affairs of the Manya Krobo. What followed is known to the Krobo as the *Hoc Ta* (Saturday War) and to the British as the Krobo Rebellion, or Freeman's War.[4] This war was important in the annals of both groups: it marked the end of effective Krobo political independence and clearly demonstrated Britain's willingness to establish a permanent presence in the eastern region of Ghana, by force if necessary.

According to the British, the rebellion originated in the actions of the "influential, turbulent, and refractory Chief of Western Crobo [Ologo Patu] and Noy his son," who rejected Britain's claim of overrule and the accommodation policies of Odonkor Azu.[5] The colonial government accused Ologo Patu of (1) engaging in the slave trade; (2) inciting Matse Tenu to rebel against the lawful authority of his paramount chief, Konor Odonkor Azu (note this *de jure* recognition of Odonkor Azu's paramount rule); and (3) demonstrating a general disrespect for and violation of British laws against slavery and human sacrifice, and thus causing civil disruptions in the entire eastern region.[6] While the British regarded all these charges as serious, they were especially concerned about Ologo Patu's challenge to their own authority and rather less concerned about his disruption of internal Krobo affairs, except when such disruptions threatened the flow of palm oil.

Since the early 1850s, colonial officials and Basel missionaries had considered Odonkor Azu progressive, that is, supportive of the commercialization of palm oil production, accommodating to colonial officials, and receptive to missionary activity. Ologo Patu was believed by Europeans to be the antithesis of Odonkor Azu. The British justified their intervention in the dispute on two grounds: that it would demonstrate their resolve to establish a Pax Britannica in the region and that it would support the konorship of the progressive Odonkor Azu, their ally, who had in fact requested British support in restoring peace.[7] Behind these justifications lay a concern with the continued export of palm oil from Kroboland.

The colonial officials' first attempt to bring Ologo Patu to Christiansborg in 1858 failed. A small military force under Reverend Thomas Birch Freeman, civil commandant for Accra and the eastern region, received a severe verbal rebuff at Sra. The British were treated "with contempt and threatened with force by Tenu, Patto [Ologo Patu], and Noy and their aiders and abettors."[8] The Sra incident raised the seriousness of the Krobo Rebellion for the British to a new and critical level. By his actions Ologo Patu had brought into question Britain's claim of protectorship. Governor Bird's response was unequivocal: "These rebellious persons must be made to submit and respect British authority. These rebels should be brought to trial for their *grave and treasonable offenses*" [emphasis in original].[9]

Bird moved swiftly. On 3 September 1858, he convened at Christiansborg a special meeting of the Executive Council, the Colony's administrative body, which unanimously passed two resolutions.[10] The first stated that "to insure justice, insurgent chiefs of Crobboe should submit to humane and equitable jurisdiction and be *reduced to submission* and compelled to obey decrees of courts and justice" [emphasis in original].[11] The second resolution called upon "all disposable forces of the Gold Coast Artillery Corps, guns, (2 howitzers, 5 rockets)" and all friendly tribes including the "Eastern [Manya] Crobboe" to join in the suppression of the rebellion.[12] The attack on the Krobo, however, was to be restrained; Krobo property was not to be destroyed. The governor was apparently concerned that wholesale destruction of

Krobo property might result in a long-term interruption of the valuable palm oil trade.

For the British forces, the Krobo Rebellion had a festive air about it—a nice little war. On 9 September, Freeman led a force of about 2,500, including a number of African merchant volunteers, from James Town and Cape Coast to rendezvous with other forces under Captain Cochrane just north of the Shai Hills on the Accra plains. James Bannerman led the volunteers, who included Robert Hutchison, mayor of Cape Coast, R. J. Ghartey, Robert and John Hansen, William Lutterodt, J. E. Richter, and L. Hesse. Their interest in the rebellion was personal: Bannerman, Hansen, and Hutchison were all major exporters of oil. Supporting the military action against the Krobo would reaffirm their commitment to Britain's right to rule the region and might further increase their share of palm oil exports.[13] The Akyem Abuakwa, the Akyem Kotoko, the Akuapem, the Shai, and the Ga (Accras) also hoped for material rewards from the British for their support; the Akuapem were more interested in settling some old grievances with the Krobo. Whatever their reasons, Bird welcomed their support in reaffirming British authority in the eastern protectorate. Supplies were issued on Monday, 13 September; military preparations continued. The colonial force now numbered about 4,000. "This was an extremely exciting day."[14]

A dramatic and unexpected turn of events preempted the attack scheduled for 6 A.M., 18 September. Faced with the choice of siding with the British or with their Yilo brothers, the Manya Krobo forces refused to follow the leadership of Odonkor Azu and joined Ologo Patu and the Yilo Krobo. The festive air of the expedition suddenly grew serious. Cochrane attempted to regain the military advantage by a counterattack against the mountain, but failed. The Krobo owed their military success to the strength of their position, their knowledge of the terrain, and a combined fighting force of Yilo and Manya Krobo warriors. For his part, Cochrane was hindered by the desertion of the Osu, the Shai, the Accras (Ga), and the Akwamu. In the rout that followed, Cochrane was forced to abandon some ammunition and guns.[15]

While the British reassembled their forces and planned strategy at Abonsi, the Manya Krobo, without the Yilo, also assembled to address the issue of Odonkor Azu's leadership. *Dormdsunao*, a special place on the Manya side of the mountain where all essential matters dealing with war were discussed, was the site of the meeting. Matse Tenu and Ba, of the Akweno and Dom subtribes, both of whom coveted the konorship, led the verbal attacks against Konor Odonkor Azu for his refusal to lead them against the British. For three days and nights of spirited discussions, Odonkor Azu faced the greatest challenge to his rule over the Manya Krobo. During these meetings "the tumult on the mountain home had no bounds. Shouts, war dances and abuses to the King [Odonkor Azu] were the prominent objects to be seen and heard by any spectator."[16] According to Thomas Odonkor, a nephew and supporter of Odonkor Azu, the konor's opponents accused him of two specific capital crimes: siding with the British against fellow Krobo, the Yilo; and refusing to lead the Manya Krobo warriors into battle once they had decided not to side with the British.

Odonkor Azu also received unqualified support at the meeting from his chief captain, Padiator, who according to Thomas Odonkor's colorful account, challenged Odonkro Azu's accusers, notably Chief Tenu, in the following manner:

> I swear! I swear! I swear! by all the elders who are gone before us, that before you kill Odonkor Azu my King, you shall have to kill me first! On hearing this the rebels became quiet as if they had received a thunderbolt.[17]

Padiator's example inspired "another Captain Tetomotse, then another and another," to swear allegiance to Odonkor Azu, until the meeting was dissolved.[18] Odonkor Azu's opponents had no choice but to drop their allegations for one clear reason: civil war, in the midst of a war with the British, was too high a price to pay even for the konorship of the Manya Krobo. By no actions of his own, therefore, Odonkor Azu narrowly escaped destoolment and probably death.[19]

After the Dormdsunao meeting, although they were willing to continue fighting, both the Yilo and the Manya Krobo faced a shortage of powder. Moreover, despite their initial success against the overwhelming forces sent over them, the Krobo feared that the British would not retreat. On the contrary, Cochrane would return with even greater resolve to destroy the Krobo, perhaps with an even larger force. Considering this reality, the Manya Krobo chose to minimize their losses and sued for peace.

Peter Nyako, Odonkor Azu's recently converted Christian son, headed the peace delegation. He was accompanied by Noa Ague Azu, another recently converted Christian son, Akuki, the konor's daughter, "a maiden of about 20 years," and Mapoyo, the konor's chief linguist.[20] They carried a white flag and the Union Jack given to Odonkor Azu by acting governor James Bannerman in 1850. On Monday morning, 13 October, the konor, his captains, and the subchiefs of the Manya Krobo descended from the Krobo Mountain and surrendered at Mueyo. After some interrogation by Cochrane and Brownell, it was determined that the Krobo forces numbered about 1,130.

Ologo Patu, however, had not surrendered. Cochrane sent him a message suggesting that if he was determined to continue hostilities he should permit the women, children, and old men to leave the mountain. Two days later on 15 October, Ologo Patu sent a message to Odonkor Azu, now at Odumase, that he still did not recognize Cochrane's authority. To demonstrate his resolve against Ologo Patu, Cochrane continued preparations to attack the western, or Yilo, side of the mountain. Eventually the Yilo konor surrendered, but only after three attempts to delay the inevitable.

After the rebellion, the British were determined to make an example of the Krobo for the benefit of other African peoples in the Eastern Region who might be considering rebelling against British authority. What began as a request for assistance by one Krobo paramount chief against the other had ended in a general rebellion against British authority by all the Krobo. The punishment imposed upon the Krobo was severe.

The trial of Ologo Patu and Odonkor Azu began almost immediately after the war ended. It was held at Mueyo Hill (Saddle Hill), less than two miles southeast of the mountain. When the court convened on 31 October 1858, Chief Justice R. D. Ross was the presiding magistrate.[21] In attendance with the Krobo, whose weapons had been taken away, were the African merchants and the African chiefs and their warriors who had marched in the defeat of British forces. Colonial officials now held center stage, with virtually the whole of the Gold Coast Colony and the Protectorate watching. This was the eastern region's first experience with the

British justice system; not only the Krobo, but also the British colonial rulers were on trial.

In the case of *The Queen v. Odonkor Assu*, the government accused the konor of (1) unlawfully neglecting to join Her Majesty's forces, which had been sent at his request, (2) permitting certain captains and people "to rebelliously and traitorously" fight against Britain's forces, causing the death of several men, and (3) neglecting to inform the British of certain captains' intent to support Ologo Patu. The konor was not without his supporters, who reminded the court that Odonkor Azu himself had supported Britain's efforts against Konor Ologo Patu, and that Odonkor Azu's conduct generally "*was so satisfactory* he had shown a desire to introduce Christianity and civilisation among his people" (emphasis in original).[22] Odonkor Azu had the support of Basel missionaries Aldinger and Zimmermann, who were stationed in Odumase. Unimpressed by this evidence, Chief Justice Ross severely criticized the konor for his action of 18 September, namely for being unable to control the Manya Krobo warriors who attacked the British forces, and, in good colonial tradition, attributed the konor's actions to his "timidity and want of judgment and determination."[23] Odonkor Azu was judged guilty; however, his punishment was distinctly different from that allotted to any of the other defendants. In the Court's view, it was the rebellious Manya Krobo captains who had caused Britain's humiliating defeat, not the konor, whose role was accessorial. As a result, Odonkor Azu was not personally fined, but only made responsible for the collection of the fine assessed against his captains. But there was more. To insure that the Manya Krobo people and the konor fulfilled their obligations in paying the indemnity, Odonkor Azu was to be imprisoned until the full Manya Krobo fine was paid.

In the case of *The Queen v. Ologo Pato*, the colonial government, as expected, was particularly harsh. Konor Ologo Patu was charged with (1) starting the Krobo Rebellion by his support of Matse Tenu, (2) refusing to appear at Christiansborg when ordered to do so by a civil summons issued against him, and (3) causing, by his rebellious actions, the deaths of three members of the Gold Coast Artillery Corps. The court found him guilty on all charges and passed three harsh penalties: (1) he was to pay a fine of 1,875 pounds sterling; (2) he was to be imprisoned in

Christiansborg until the fine was paid; and (3) he was to be destooled. All the other defendants were found guilty of abetting and assisting Konor Ologo Patu in an act of rebellion against the "lawful authority of HMG" that resulted in "death and injury to many."[24] The colonial government, acting through the court backed by military power, clearly attempted to exact punishing damages against both konors, but especially Ologo Patu.

Each of the twelve subchiefs was made to leave hostages to insure payment of the fine. These were indeed harsh penalties, but some Krobo were relieved that they were not forced to abandon the Krobo Mountain, nor was the mountain occupied at this time.

Table 6.1

THE KROBO FINE

	Cowries	Pounds Sterling
Manya	0	0
Odonkor Azu	6,000	750
Tanu	24,000	3,000
Chiefs and Captains Sub Total	30,000	3,750
Yilo	15,000	1,875
Ologo Patu	20,000	2,500
Chiefs and Captains Sub Total	35,000	4,375
Total	65,000	8,125

The amount levied against the Krobo suggests that the colonial officials were determined not only to punish the Krobo but, at the same time, to gain a British monopoly of their palm oil, at a time when Danish, French, German, and American merchants were also purchasing Krobo palm oil (Table 6.1). The indemnity was more than the total revenue collected during any year from the poll tax. Viewed another way, it was twice the annual grant allocated by Parliament for the administration of the Gold Coast

Colony and Protectorate. This was a considerable amount for a small nonindustrial society to pay in the mid-nineteenth century. Moreover, the fine was assessed against specific individuals, so that each Krobo chiefdom had to devise its own methods of collecting oil or currency from the rest of the population. The harshness of the fine did not, however, destroy the Krobo's political and economic autonomy, and it did not destroy either konor, as the colonial officials had hoped. Instead, it united the Krobo as never before against the British and their agents, British traders.

The Krobo Rebellion: Phase II

Following the pattern established by the Danes in the 1836 Dum War, the British made the 1858 Krobo rebellion's indemnity payable in palm oil. As an additional punitive measure, they set the price to be paid for the Krobo's oil at about half its market value, and announced that they would charge interest. The Krobo initiated their own answer to the severity of the fine, in the form of the Krobo Boycott of 1859-1866.[25]

Freda Wolfson, the first scholar to study the boycott, stated the Krobo did not pay the 8,125 pounds sterling fine equivalent to 195,000 gallons or 600 tons of palm oil. In fact, however, the Krobo paid the principal but not the interest nor the additional expenses assessed by the major surety, Richard Hutchison.[26] Hutchison, a wealthy African merchant, mayor of Cape Coast, and one of the volunteers, was also the chief agent of Messrs. Frank and Andrew Swanzy, the trading company granted the right to collect the fine.[27]

Colonial officials had no apparent warning of the impending Krobo boycott against payment. Governor Bird reported to the Secretary of the Colonies in December 1858 that the fine would be paid in six months, however, at best the fine would be paid in about two years.[28] Both the government and the Swanzy company anticipated quick payment, given the imprisonment of the Krobo konors, which they expected would make any organized, sustained, peaceful resistance such as a boycott impossible. But neither the colonial nor the company officials reckoned with the Krobo resolve to maintain their economic independence.

The first sign that obtaining payment might prove difficult was the escape of Ologo Patu and Odonkor Azu, aided by the daring efforts of Sakite, Odonkor Azu's son, and others. The two konors were never recaptured, apparently because the governor was not willing to spend the necessary money. Still, payment of the fine at first went well. In January 1859, Hutchison paid the British slightly more than 70 percent of the total.[29] The balance now owing was £2,383 8s. 2d. However, the governor was beginning to express some reservations about the wisdom of having farmed out the collection of the fine. In April 1860, Governor Edward B. Andrews noted that the actual value of the produce obtained from the Krobo was far greater than the £5,741 19s. 10d. paid to the government by Hutchison, who had purchased the oil at 10d. per gallon—one-half its market value.[30] Also, the excessive interest and expenses attached to the original indemnity displeased the governor.[31] The collection agents had claimed approximately "50 percent to expenses because so many peculiar circumstances [were] being connected with this business."[32] In early 1861, Andrews reported to the War Office that Hutchison's profit on his investment was about 25,000 pounds sterling.[33] The War Office took no action on this matter. Hutchison's aggressive and excessive collection practices caused a resurgence of Krobo anti-British feelings. In December 1861, several government cotton storage buildings at Kpong were destroyed by arsonists, probably Krobo, and some officials began to fear that the anti-British feeling might spread to the Akyem and the Akuapem.[34] Fiscal injustice would continue, Andrews maintained, because the fine had been farmed out to unscrupulous sureties (Hutchison and Addo) and "because the unfortunate debtors can neither read nor write."[35] The Krobo, who were astute traders, knew well that they were not being treated fairly.

Although a definitive record of all the palm oil sold by the Krobo to the British is not possible, the case of Chief Tenu may be instructive. Tenu, who vehemently opposed Odonkor Azu's claim to be konor and was a major belligerent in the rebellion, opposed paying the fine. Charles de Ruvignes, civil commandant for the eastern region, considered Tenu the leader of what he called "passive-resistance," and warned that "Tenu must be dealt with, as he is a perfect fire-brand in Crobboe and excites the people to mischief."[36]

Tenu only remained a strong opponent of colonial rule, but his refusal to continue to pay the fine was not without other causes. He was fined 6,000 heads of cowries, or about 750 pounds sterling—an outrageous sum. Hutchison refused payment in cowries, and payment in oil was pegged at 10d. per gallon, or about five-eighths of the existing market rate of 1s. to 1s. 4d. per gallon. By the admission of de Ruvignes, "Tenu [had] already paid approximately 4,000 gallons [of oil]." Even at 10d. per gallon, 4,000 gallons of oil amounted to £1,666 7s.; and the real market value of Tenu's oil was about £2,333 3s. Governor Andrews, appears to have been aware of such overpayment by Tenu and others, as he reported to the colonial office that the overpayment of the fine by the Krobo might be as high as "200 percent."[37]

The boycott gained momentum as the years passed. In 1861-1862, when the government made a feeble effort to force continued payment by blockading the shipment of Krobo oil down the Volta to the coast, the blockade failed. Rather than sell at such low prices, the Krobo shipped their oil overland, where it was sold to British merchants other than those associated with the Swanzy company and to French, German, American, and Danish merchants. The Krobo also devised another way of bypassing the selling of oil; large quantities were stored in tanks dug in the earth.[38] In 1863, the Asante War of that year and the smallpox epidemic in the eastern region dominated the interests of colonial officials. Nevertheless, payment had become a "matter of honor for the authorities."[39] In April 1865, even the presence of 12,000 troops stationed in the eastern region in the aftermath of the 1863-1864 Asante War, who could have been used against the Krobo, failed to force an agreement. After seven years, the Krobo boycott was a clear success; Swanzy and its agents had not been paid the inflated charges they demanded, world oil demand was up, and there was easy access to markets. Recognizing these factors, the sureties conceded defeat and accepted a government settlement in April 1866.[40] The whole affair had been a Pyrrhic victory for the British and a moral victory for the Krobo.

Information on the effects of the boycott on daily life is sketchy, except for 1860. Carl Aldinger reported in his "Quartalsbrercht" of April 1860, "The effects of the Krobo war last year still keep down our small, industrious people. The wound which has been inflicted on them has not healed. It is still a bad time."[41] The pressure of payment produced a crisis of leadership as early as 1859. Fearing reimprisonment and possible deportation, both chiefs were willing to pay their contribution as soon as possible, and they took care to encourage their subjects and partly to force them. The people thought about payment differently. A great part of them did not want to pay any more which led to quarreling.[42]

What emerged was a crisis of leadership, with many Yilo and Manya Krobo rejecting the advice of their konors to make a prompt payment of the fine. On several occasions, missionaries reported that the Krobo were close to a civil war over this issue of payment, but "Prince Odonko Azu contributed most to keeping the peace." In the same report, however, Odonkor Azu was reported to have "little or no influence on his district."[43] Apparently the Manya Krobo lacked strong central leadership from their konor during the early years of the boycott.

Payment of the fine also positioned Ologo Patu against his people, at least those who opposed payment of the indemnity. Ologo Patu had sworn to turn over to British officials anybody who refused to pay his share. "The consequence was that two Yilo shot themselves on June 1. . . . one was wealthy and did not want to pay; the other had been sick and could not pay."[44]

The Basel Missionary Society's interest in the effects the boycott had on the Krobo, especially Odonkor Azu, was purely selfish. In 1856, Odonkor Azu had broken with tradition to invite the society to establish a permanent mission in Odumase, and construction of a chapel had begun in 1859. Any significant loss of authority and prestige on his part would adversely affect the missionaries' own tenuous presence.

The boycott also led to renewed friction between the Krobo and the Akwamu and Akuapem. Supported by de Ruvignes, Hutchison proposed to farm out the oil payment scheme further to the Akwamu and the Akuapem, two traditional enemies of the Krobo.[45] It was hoped that the Akwamu, the Akuapem, or both would pay Hutchison in oil and would in turn either collect oil from the Krobo or confiscate their land. The Krobo land, Hutchison reasoned, was more valuable than the payment of the fine. The benefits to Hutchison and the colonial officials were obvious, but the scheme was apparently never implemented.

Politically, the boycott demonstrated the Krobo's resolve to insist upon equitable treatment, and the colonial government's resolve to enforce its decisions, despite irregularities in the conduct of its agents. The failure of the rebellion clearly established British supremacy over the Krobo. Economically, the boycott established palm oil as the chiefdoms' cash export crop, because both Krobo chiefdoms increased their cultivation and production of palm oil to pay the indemnity. Finally, the drive to collect oil generated a need to accumulate additional oil-producing farms, and hence contributed directly to further Krobo territorial expansion.[46]

On another level, the Krobo were embarking on a new era. Odonkor Azu's prerebellion political and economic policies had begun to pay dividends for the Krobo generally and for the Manya and himself specifically. With the increased presence of British officials in Kroboland, especially at Odumase, Sra, and Kpong, came an increased importance of literacy in English. The Basel missionaries, who had arrived in Odumase in 1856, two years before the rebellion, became important foci of communication among colonial officials, European traders, and the Krobo.

In the early years of the boycott, both konors lost prestige and authority among their people because neither the accommodation policies of Odonkor Azu nor the anti-European policies of Ologo Patu had been able to maintain Krobo society as in the past. Odonkor Azu's actions in the rebellion particularly weakened his position. Three months after the troops withdrew from the Krobo Mountain and shortly after Odonkor Azu had escaped from prison, according to Aldinger, "the people hardly listened to him and did not count on his word."[47]

But by the end of his reign, Odonkor Azu had apparently regained much of his influence and authority. The imposition of a fine payable in palm oil placed a particular burden on the oil-producing huza farmers; but it simultaneously confirmed them as the economic foundation of Krobo society. The palm oil farmers had been among the strongest supporters of Odonkor Azu during his early years of rule, in the 1840s and early 1850s. On balance, the boycott contributed in no small way to a renewed growth of their economic-*cum*-political importance, and by extension, to that of their spokesman, Konor Odonkor Azu.

In comparison, the boycott era left the Yilo in a relatively weakened position. Before the 1850s, neither Konor Ologo Patu nor the general Yilo population accumulated huza farms or became systematically involved in the overseas trade in palm oil. Hence, when faced with demands for oil for payment of the indemnity, the Yilo had considerable difficulty responding.

Before the rebellion, neither Krobo polity was preeminent; each konor had his share of personal influence, with Ologo Patu having perhaps a slight edge.[48] By the end of the boycott the opposite was becoming true. Although Odonkor Azu's support for the British during the 1858 Rebellion may have been mistaken, his aggressive pursuit of palm oil commercialization and his policy of accommodation with missionaries by inviting the Basel Mission Society to establish a station in Odumase in 1856 (Chapter 8) produced long-term benefits for his people. Because missionaries were stationed in Odumase, it became a communication center for other African peoples, colonial officials, European and African traders, and of course missionaries. Krobo oil exports increased the importance of Kpong, Akuse, and Amedica, the major trading entrepots in the region, all of which were in Manya Krobo territory. The Yilo town of Somanya, which had previously enjoyed preeminence, was surpassed in importance by several Manya towns. Odonkor Azu's personal fortunes suffered less than that of the Yilo konor. He managed to survive serious challenges to his rule, emerging shaken but politically more astute and more secure than Ologo Patu or any of the other Manya Krobo clan chiefs. Moreover, he was not personally fined; there is no reason not to believe that he managed to save a significant portion of his oil for personal use, particularly as he was already a major palm oil huza farmer.

How does one explain the close attention given by the British to Krobo affairs in the eastern region? First, the Krobo dominated both the cultivation and the production of palm oil, unlike the Efik at Old Calabar, who merely traded in it. In 1849 and 1850, British administrator Fitspatrick identified Kroboland as the Gold Coast's main center of palm oil cultivation and production. Moreover, as early as the 1830s, British merchants dominated the palm oil trade among the Krobo. Control of the Krobo palm oil may not have been vital to colonial interest in the region, but it was vital to the commercial interest of British traders. Furthermore at the time of the rebellion, the price of oil was at its highest.[49] Consider Governor Bird's description of the Krobo, in one of his earliest dispatches after the 1858 Rebellion, as "cowardly" and "very rich."[50] The Krobo were not cowardly, but compared to their neighbors, they were very rich, or, more correctly, potentially very rich. The wealth to be derived from the export of palm oil is made evident by the fact that French and Spanish palm oil agents offered to take over the collection of the palm oil indemnity.[51]

Finally, in addition to maintaining the flow of oil exports to the United Kingdom, Britain had to impress upon the Krobo, especially the Yilo, that the colonial government, not the konors, held ultimate sovereignty over the Krobo. There are no Krobo-British treaties; the 1858 Rebellion defined the political relationship between the two groups, but left no formal documented definitions of that relationship. The case of the Krobo thus exemplifies the informal expansion of the British Empire accomplished by action of colonial officials on the spot.

Their military defeat notwithstanding, the Krobo emerged a people more unified socially and more aware of political and economic affairs outside their own small chiefdom. The Krobo Rebellion marked a turning point in their political and economic history, especially in their relationship with Europeans—colonial officials, traders, and missionaries. After 1858, the Krobo were both less politically independent and more deeply linked to the wider world economy. At the same time, their involvement in export trade continued to encourage their territorial expansion into the Akuapem hills and made them an increasingly important factor in the political and economic calculations of the British and of their African neighbors.

7

KONOR SAKITE AND THE SAGRENTI
WAR OF 1873-1874

Inside the main hall of the residence of the konor of the Manya Krobo hangs a life-sized color portrait of Konor Sakite (1867-1892) given to the Krobo people by Governor Sir Brandford Griffith.[1] This was an unusual gift from the British colonial government. It is representative of the unusual position occupied by Sakite during his long reign and suggestive of his important and consistent service to the colonial government during and after the 1873-1874 Asante War and of his invaluable assistance in the administration of the Volta District.

The long reign of Odonkor Azu's son and successor Sakite was marked by major changes in southern Ghana, including Kroboland. When Sakite began his reign in 1867, Britain's commitment to rule the Gold Coast was still unclear; by his death in 1892 the entire Gold Coast, including the northern territories, had come under the direct colonial rule of the British. The Krobo had emerged from the difficult years of the 1858 rebellion and boycott committed to continued production of palm oil for export, and during Sakite's reign their territorial expansion accelerated in an unprecedented manner. In 1867, Krobo loyalty to Britain was suspect; under Sakite's leadership, the Krobo, especially the Manya, became the colonial government's most loyal African ally in the eastern region. Finally, by 1892, colonial administrative, missionary, educational, and commercial activities in the Volta District, which had been created by the British in 1880 and included the Akuapem, the Shai and the Krobo, were centered among the Manya Krobo. Although much of the material prosperity the Krobo enjoyed was directly tied to their own industriousness as palm oil farmers, another key factor which contributed to the preeminence

5

of huza farmers, especially those of Manya Krobo, was the leadership of Konor Sakite.

The Early Years of Sakite's Rule

The death of Odonkor Azu produced only a mild succession dispute.[2] This fact was important because among the Manya Krobo the concept of the konorship had been established, but not, as yet, the method of selecting a konor's successor. (The Yilo had established a succession system decades earlier.) Three groups of claimants sought to succeed the konor. The first group, led by enemies of Odonkor Azu, felt that the latter's personal influence had not established a new governing system, and that authority should therefore revert to the old theocratic oligarchy headed by the okumo. This group had few backers apart from Odonkor Azu's arch rivals Matse Ba and Tenu. Another group of possible candidates were the Christian sons of Odonkor Azu—Akute, Noa Azu, and Peter Nyako. They represented those who wanted to break with the traditional system of rulership based on non-Christian political, cultural, and religious values. No Christian candidate had a chance of being selected konor because Christianity as yet had no broad support among the huza farmers or any other group, nor was the colonial government willing to support them at this time.[3] Simply stated, the Manya Krobo would not have accepted a Christian candidate. Sakite, the matse of Djebiam-Nam, and Lawe (later Nathaniel) Dua, matse of Dom, headed the last group of candidates. Competition for the konorship was greatest between Sakite and Lawe.

Precisely how Sakite became konor is not recorded. Djebiam-Nam traditions state that "the elders of Nam and Odumase [clans] assembled at the house of Lawe Dua (Nathaniel Lawe), a son of Koy Patautuo, and empowered him to select a new king."[4] What is known about the candidacy of Lawe Dua, matse of Dom, does, however, indicate that some negotiation went on: in a compromise agreement, Lawe Dua was to succeed Sakite.[5] The fact that Odonkor Azu's office was seriously pursued by several candidates from outside the Djebiam-Nam subtribe strongly suggests that his office by the time of his death was indeed perceived as a paramount chiefship, not merely primus inter pares among the matse.

The selection of Sakite was not merely a compromise. He had excellent credentials for the role. Among other things, he was the favored son of Odonkor Azu. Furthermore, he had been given the important reponsibility of making Odonkor Azu's funeral arrangements; he was a daring leader who had led the rescue of the konors from Christiansborg in 1858; and he was a major and successful huza farmer. Although not a Christian, he supported the Christian community, and he was a political realist who accepted the fact of European presence in the region (Table 7.1). The selection of Sakite began the process by which the Djebiam-Nam became the royal clan of the Manya Krobo, and ended the long political hold of the old theocratic oligarchy of the Okumo and the djemeli.

In 1867, the year Sakite became konor, the Anlo War erupted between an alliance of Ada, Krepi, and Accra peoples and the Akwamu and Anlo chiefdoms. At issue was the continued independence of the Ada, Krepi, and Accra chiefdoms from the Akwamu, and the control of the Volta trade in African and European goods. The Akwamu, who were allies of the Asante, were attempting to regain the preeminent position they had held in the region before their defeat by the Akyem Abuakwa and others in 1730. The Akwamu, the Asante, and to a lesser extent the Akyem Abuakwa all wanted to reestablish and control trading in slaves and firearms in the middle and lower Volta. If they succeeded, the Krobo economy would suffer.

The revival of slave trading along the Volta by notorious Portuguese slaver Geraldo de Lima caused a further decline in Krobo trade, especially along the Volta. In March 1867, this Afro-Brazilian conducted a series of raids along the Volta, staying clear of the British Royal Navy, which was attempting to end all slave exporting activity in West Africa. De Lima pillaged and destroyed villages along the middle Volta, including Akuse, Kpong, and Auschare.[6] By themselves the Krobo were no match for de Lima's professionals; they therefore joined the Ada and others against the Akwamu, not to end slave raiding per se but to insure that they remained in control of all trading along the Volta. The British, as one would expect, provided military support for the anti-slave trade forces.

Table 7.1

ODONKOR AZU'S FAMILY

Wives	Children
1. Soyo	Tetnua, Mateko, Koko, Teinigo, Nah
2. Koyo	Koleki, Opam Teiagboyibo
3. Adsowa	**Akute, Noah Akuno Aguae***
4. Kodo	Nyumu, Awesiki, Tetboloyo, Abeyo
5. Dsabakwa	Sakite, **Nyako***
6. Kokoyumu	Lawe, Ata
7. Kokotsu	Mate
8. Ama	Koleki, Kolekuo, Kpabitey
9. Ayemie	Debo, Tetsayo
10. Ogayo	Anmokuo, Nyako
11. Domeyo	Osom, Mateko
12. Mansa	Yo
13. Pesianu	Odikro

* Christians.

Source: Noa A. Azu, "Adangbe (Adangme) History." *Gold Coast Review* 3 (1927): 89-116. Interview with Konor Azzu Mate Kole, 22 November 1973.

Control of the Volta was central to the resurgence of the Akwamu. The Asante supported Akwamu territorial ambitions because both these Akan states favored the continued flow of guns into Asante territory and hoped to revive the declining export of slaves. The Asante also hoped to regain political ground lost in the eastern region as a result of their defeat at Dodowa in 1826. Consequently, when the Akwamu began to falter against the united opposition, the Asante entered the war.

118

In late March, Gyaasewahene Ado Bofo of Kumase crossed the Pra River, the boundary between the Asante Empire and the British Colony and Protectorate established as a result of the 1826 Asante-British War, and headed toward the Akwamu chiefdom. The presence of the Asante rekindled Britain's fears of renewed Asante activity south of the Pra River, which in turn might lead to increased trade in slaves and arms. Captain Richard Simpson traveled from Accra to Dzelukofe, the Anlo capital, in an attempt to negotiate an end to the conflict. His mission having failed, colonial officials then sought a military solution and created a southern alliance of Ada, Ga, Akuapem, and Krobo forces, all of whom were enemies of the Asante and the Akwamu and feared the return of the Asante in the southeastern region. For his part, Sakite successfully defended Akuse, Kpong, and Amedica from further attacks.[7] Events in Kumase, not in the field, determined the outcome of the conflict. When Asantehene Kwaku Dua (c. 1795-1867) died, in late 1867, the Asante recalled Gyaasewahene Ado Bofo to Kumase. Between 1867 and 1873, an uneasy calm returned to the region.

Sakite used this period of relative peace to consolidate his political power by addressing certain pressing internal problems. He consolidated huza territory purchased under Odonkor Azu in the Akuapem foothills and established direct control over Kpong, Akuse, and Amedica by appointing the chiefs of these villages. Sakite also devoted time and personal resources to the elaboration of his court, which included the introduction of gold staffs and drumming.[8]

By Sakite's time, a string of permanent Krobo huza villages ran along the Akuapem foothills. Each of the twelve Krobo sub-tribes established its own villages (Appendix C). Sakite's village of Odumase was among the oldest, having been established by Odonkor Azu at least by the 1820s. Still, Sakite, as konor, needed to distinguish his village from those of the other Manya Krobo chiefs. He decided, in a break with tradition, to build a royal residence at Odumase. No previous Krobo ruler, including Odonkor Azu and Ologo Patu, had established his primary residence away from the mountain.

With the new residence came a new court and new symbols of paramount authority—umbrellas, gold staffs, and palanquins modeled after Akan equivalents—another dramatic break with

119

tradition. The Krobo and other Adangme considered the various larger and politically more centralized Akan chiefdoms as their enemies; for Sakite to copy Akan symbols of paramount secular authority, attests to the widespread recognition accorded such items throughout Ghana, even among the Adangme.[9] Tradition prohibited the Adangme and Krobo from using gold in objects of power such as staffs, and in rings and other adornments of symbolic power. On the ancient Krobo Mountain, before the arrival of the Denkyira Krobo, before the huza, and before the agricultural revolution, the priestly rulers could not wear or use any objects made of gold.

Sakite was neither a priest nor a descendant of the old theocratic oligarchy. More important, by the time of his reign, Krobo society had changed dramatically; most people no longer lived on the mountain but on huza farms and villages, and were engaged not in subsistence farming but in surplus food production and the exportation of palm oil to Europeans. To the Krobo of the mid-nineteenth century, gold, silver coins, and other ornaments were new symbols of wealth and power. The Krobo of the 1870s had changed in other ways also. They were more numerous and more ethnically diverse, and they had spread over a larger and more varied physical environment. They were engaged in many different occupations, although farming was still the foundation of their economy. They were relatively wealthy, were becoming more urbanized, and were increasingly influenced by European values, in religion, house construction, household furnishings, clothing, and language.[10]

The traditional restrictions on residences and symbols of power associated with the priestly rulers, (that is, the djemeli and the Okumo), Sakite probably reasoned, did not apply to him as a secular ruler. Moreover Sakite admired the imposing position the neighboring Akan chiefs occupied in their large courts, surrounded by staffs of gold and accompanied in public by drumming. Sakite acquired talking drums (*Nkrawiri*) from the Omahene of Akropong. To insure their correct use, he appointed Osiekum Totime of Adome (Akyem Abuakwa) as "Atumpani" specialist. As his chief advisor on matters of ceremony, including the use of gold staffs, palanquins, and clan umbrellas, he appointed Agobonosi, a former hostage of the Akwamu. Truly, "Sakite had fallen deep into the ways of the Akan."[11] Politically, however, Sakite distrusted the

Akan; these courtly changes were designed not to facilitate alliances with Akan peoples but rather to increase his own acceptance and prestige as the paramount chief of the Krobo, both by outsiders and by his competitors among the Manya Krobo.

In early 1873, more demanding matters claimed Sakite's attention. In mid-January, the Asante again threatened Kroboland, when they crossed the Pra River to join their Akwamu and Anlo allies. Their objective was to reestablish control over the entire southern part of Ghana. The author generally agrees with A. Akoshua Aidoo that it was essentially a conflict between two competing imperial forces—the Asante and the British—over control of the southern Gold Coast.[12]

The Sagrenti War

The Sagrenti War, as the Africans call it after Sir Garnet Wolseley, also known as the Asante War of 1873-1874, ended forever the Asante's dominance over the southern half of Ghana. The defeat of the Asante established the British as undisputed political rulers over southern Ghana, a position that they systematically exploited after 1874. These and other aspects of the war are still being discussed by a number of scholars.[13]

Despite the voluminous material on various aspects of the 1873-1874 Asante War, scholars have neglected the role of the "Eastern Tribes," including the Krobo, who were crucial to the defeat of the Asante. Although there is considerable material on Wolseley, the commanding officer of the British forces, the commander of the eastern tribes, Sir John Hawley Glover, has received little attention.

For the Krobo and other Africans of southeastern Gold Coast who fought the Asante, the war was essentially a war against Asante domination. Participation in the Sagrenti War offered the Krobo a number of opportunities. It would protect their flourishing economy and the territorial gains made since the late eighteenth century. It would protect the hundreds of their huza farms and villages that were scattered throughout the Akuapem and Akyem Abuakwa region from attack by Asante warriors, and would protect their villages along the Akuapem foothills, such as Odumase and Somanya as well as secure the Volta trade routes once and for all from the Akwamu and the Anlo, allies of the

Asante. The Sagrenti War was for the Krobo both a repetition of and a sequel to the 1826 Asante War, when they fought with Europeans and other Africans against the Asante to safeguard their own interests. In 1873-1874, they were fighting to sustain the economic and political gains they had made since then.

In January 1873, Batamahene Amakwatia and Gyaasewahene Ado Bofo, two of the highest officials in the Asante Empire, led a large Asante force across the Pra River. Thus the war technically had begun. Colonial officials were quick to realize the strategic importance of the eastern region, especially control of the Volta River. With their allies, the Akwamu and the Anlo, the Asante could control the Volta and its vital trade with the interior (especially in guns and powder), and could attack any British force on its right flank. The colonial officials' position was succinctly stated in the *Cape Coast Standard*: "Nothing could be done without the active co-operation of the tribes of the eastern districts."[14] The British commitment to securing the Volta from Asante control arose from concern not for the safety of the Africans in the eastern region, but for the success of the campaign generally and the security of the British at Accra. This motivation prompted the British to solicit the support of the Ga, the Akyem (Abuakwa and Kotoko), the Krobo, and the other Adangme-speaking peoples.

The War Office selected Commander Glover of the Royal Navy to command the eastern tribes. He seemed an ideal candidate. Recently retired as administrator of Lagos Colony, he had taken part in the 1871 expedition along the Volta.[15] On 6 August 1873, he was appointed Special Commissioner for the eastern region. Initially Glover was responsible for maintaining control over the vital Volta River trade. Specifically, he was to insure by military action that the Akwamu and the Anlo did not assist the Asante nor gain control of the flow of firearms in the region.[16]

The important selection of a general commander for the war against the Asante fell to another branch of the British government. In late September 1873, the Earl of Kimberley, Secretary of State for the Colonies, who had overall responsibility for the colony, appointed Wolseley to be the military and civil commander of the Asante expedition. The fact that Wolseley and Glover were from different branches of the military, each selected by different branches of the government, with opposing styles of conducting a campaign, would cause considerable friction between the two during the coming months.

Glover was thus placed under Wolseley, but throughout, Glover, with nearly twenty years of military experience in West Africa, was personally senior to Wolseley and was in addition a member of the Senior Service, the Navy, while Wolseley was a professional army officer. Glover had worked closely with the Yoruba and Hausa-speaking people of Nigeria, while Wolseley had no previous African experience and virtually no confidence in the loyalty or abilities of the Africans in the campaign, or for that matter of Africans generally. More pertinent to our dicussion here, however, is the effect of the less than cordial relationship between Glover and Wolseley on later Krobo-British relations.

Understandably, the ambitious Wolseley had one objective, the quick defeat of the Asante. In July 1873, he instructed Glover to use the "tribes of the eastern district of the Protectorate in order to cause a diversion in the rear of the Asantee army, and at the same time threaten Commassie."[17] Wolseley's strategy thus made many of the chiefdoms in the eastern region, especially the Krobo, the Akyem Kotoko, and the Akyem Abuakwa, an indispensable part of his elaborate campaign against Kumase. Glover, in contrast, understood that his expedition had not one but two objectives: first, to gain control of the Volta, and second, to assist Wolseley in the march to Kumase, which was to be a joint effort beginning from the Pra River on 15 January 1874. Wolseley could not have disagreed more. As commander-general of the forces and governor of the Cape Coast, Wolseley insisted that Glover's only purpose was to assist him in his march toward Kumase.

As Special Commissioner to the African Chiefs of the Eastern Region, Glover set out to accomplish the two main objects with which he had been charged by the War Office. His first objective was to secure African military support; his second, to establish bases along the Volta and at Ada, both to supply Wolseley's columns attacking the Asante in the interior and to keep the Akwamu and Anlo from attacking Wolseley's flank.[18] Glover needed the explicit support of the region's paramount chiefs if he was to achieve his first military objective. In order to obtain that support, he held meetings from 20 to 26 September at Akropong, the capital of the Akyem Abuakwa, with Akuapemhene Asa Krofa, Manche

Dosu of Ada, and konors Sakite and Sasraku (Ologo Patu's successor, 1867-1874).

With varying degrees of enthusiasm, all the African kings supported Glover's plan of attacking the Akwamu and Anlo.[19] Fear of the Asante and uncertainty over Britain's commitment to defeating that power made the African chiefs less willing to commit themselves to any direct attack beyond the Pra River, their southern Asante boundary. To help the paramount chiefs overcome their apprehension, Glover thought it necessary to reward them for their support in advance from War Office funds. Powder and shot, rum, and silver coins were sent to the paramount chiefs.[20] Wolseley opposed Glover's attempts to buy or reward the Africans' support, perhaps out of general contempt for the African peoples, or perhaps because he did not need to worry about the performance of warriors in his column because his combatants were Europeans. Glover's payment to the paramount chiefs directly affected Wolseley's recruitment of porters. Wolseley had identified the Akyem of Kotoku and Abuakwa as sources for his porters. However, the Akyem chose to accept Glover's generous gifts and to provide porters instead for the Volta expedition. It should also be noted that, for the Akyem, joining Wolseley meant participating in the march to Kumase, a much more dangerous expedition than protecting the Volta with Glover. Wolseley, to be sure, did not share the Akyem's concerns. He was furious that Glover had undercut his recruitment of the Akyem.

On 12 October 1873, Glover held a meeting in Accra to discuss the details of the campaign. Attending this "Grand Meeting of the Friendly Chiefs of the Eastern District" were all the major leaders of the region, including the "King of Western [Yilo] and the King of Eastern [Manya] Croboe," and the "principal merchants of Accra."[21] When the "Grand Meeting" had ended, the African kings had promised Glover about 44,000 warriors and noncombatants. The Krobo offered 7,000 men, most of whom were to be porters.[22] This number must have been about one-third to one-half of the adult male population. Aware that most of the peoples of the eastern region feared the Asante, Glover recruited combatants from among the West Africans he knew best—the Yoruba and the Hausa.[23] In a fortnight, by 28 October, all forces were to rendezvous with him at Fort Adda.

Sakite's Troubles and Triumphs

Sakite's involvement in the Sagrenti War has been the subject of some debate.[24] To understand the events immediately prior to the Volta expedition it is necessary to go back to 1870. Since the 1870 Anlo War, some Cape Coast officials had questioned Sakite's loyalty. Although the British were not directly involved in the war, they carefully monitored the flow of arms up the Volta. This concern had prompted Accra Administrator H. T. Ussher to send Captain Ross, the military commander for the eastern region, to Odumase to question "Sakkitay and his Chiefs" about their trade dealings with the Akwamu, particularly the allegation that Sakite maintained "communications with the Asante and the Akwamu, and supplied them powder &c." Sakite denied any collusion with the Asante or Akwamu, and the government never produced any evidence to sustain its allegations. Given the history of hostilities between the Krobo and the Akwamu, any kind of friendly agreement between the two seems unlikely. Despite the absence of any evidence of Sakite's guilt, Ussher suggested that the konor should prove his loyalty to the government—specifically, that he should "encourage his people to increase the flow of palm oil down the Volta."[25] Britain's economic interest and Sakite's loyalty were apparently Ussher's real concern.

Once the 1873 War began, it was not long before some of the most prominent paramount chiefs of the eastern region challenged Sakite's commitment to the campaign. On 14 October, shortly after the oath-taking ceremony at the Grand Meeting, a meeting was held at Ussher Fort (*Kinka Mono*). Without warning, Akuapemhene Asa Krofo, Akyemhene Amoaku Atta, Manches Tackie and Solomon of Accra and James Town accused Konor Sakite of supplying the Akwamu with gunpowder and of "other acts of friendship and assistance to the Asantee, and Aquamoos" in the 1870 Anlo War.[26] Though surprised and angered by these unsettling charges, Sakite was not permitted to answer the allegations. Presuming him to be guilty, his accusers demanded that he swear to be on good behavior in the future.[27] The enraged Sakite left the meeting, and outside the fort his accusers physically attacked him. The fortuitous arrival of deputy commissioners Tucksfield Goldworthy and H. F. Blissett saved Sakite. Later, Captain Sartorious and ten Hausa troops escorted Sakite to James Fort until the matter could be

125

resolved. On 20 October Sakite's enemies requested that Glover imprison him for the duration of the Volta portion of the campaign.[28]

At the time, Glover, who did not know Sakite personally, did not consider the konor's personal support important but feared that the Sakite affair might adversely affect the expedition by turning the Krobo people against him and the British. He needed the support of the chiefs from all the larger and more powerful states, including the Akyem Abuakwa, the Akuapem, the Ga, and the Krobo. Glover knew from his expedition along the Volta in 1871 that certain villages were key points in the distribution of equipment and supplies from the Volta into the interior. Kpong and Akuse were to be the main embarking and debarking points for supplies, and the Basel mission chapel at Odumase, Sakite's village, was to be the storage depot for military goods. Finally, aware of the importance of the Manya Krobo in the export of palm oil to Britain, Glover did not wish to implement any policy that would adversely affect either the future flow of palm oil or Manya Krobo relations with the British. If Sakite the man was expendable, the Krobo's palm oil after the war and certain villages during the war, namely Odumase, Kpong, and Akuse, were not.

Glover therefore bowed temporarily to the chiefs' wishes and put Sakite under arrest. But he also sent his aide-de-camp, Captain Sartorious, to Odumase and Sra to assure the Krobo people that Sakite was safe. Sartorious explained that Sakite's imprisonment was for his own protection, and that he would be released after the completion of the Volta campaign. Sakite's internment apparently caused no great disruption in Manya Krobo affairs. Notey Odkumado and Adkipa, two of Sakite's trusted war leaders, took charge of the Manya Krobo porters (levies). Peter Nyako and Noa Azu represented Sakite at Odumase, and Abotake, chief of Kpong, represented Sakite before the British at Kpong, Akuse, and Amedica.[29] The commander of all the Krobo, both Manya and Yilo, was Matse Lame of the Ogome subtribe of Yilo; poor health prohibited Yilo Konor Sasraku from assuming the leadership. The presence of two Christians, Peter Nyako and Noa Azu, in the Krobo administration established a precedent for later rule.

By mid-November the military preparations were moving along slightly behind schedule and Glover began inspecting his camps at Akuse, Fort Adda, and Blappah (Table 7.2). But by late

126

November the number of troops had not changed, and Glover began to make inquiries about the causes for the delay. Although a few more troops arrived at camps Blappah and Fort Adda, by December the boastful Accra Manche Tackie had sent only 1,000 of his promised 5,000 men, and Solomon had sent only 100 of his promised 3,000 men.[31] The slowness with which the troops arrived threatened the Volta expedition and made it increasingly improbable that Glover would be able to cross the Pra River along with Wolseley's other forces on January 15.

Glover had no leverage over the African chiefs, for he had already paid for the troops. The lack of commitment to the Volta campaign by many of the chiefdoms adversely affected those few warriors who did arrive at the base camps. The Akuapem, for example, when ordered to fight, refused until the other promised forces had arrived. The Krobo and the Krepi "displayed a similar disinclination" to obey Glover's orders to attack the Anlo.[32] By mid-December, Glover's plight worsened as the Akyem Abuakwa and the Akuapem troops held in reserve at Djebketi deserted upon hearing rumors that the Asante planned to attack their villages.[33] Suddenly, except for the Hausa and Yoruba, Glover had no effective Volta campaign force. As Wolseley prepared for his march from Cape Coast to the Pra River, the Volta remained in the hands of the Akwamu and Anlo.

In a dispatch of 22 December, Glover reported the rapidly deteriorating situation to an angry and unsympathetic Wolseley. It would take him about forty days, Glover said, to secure the Volta by defeating the Akwamu and Anlo forces, and he requested to be excused from the joint attack previously agreed upon.[34] Wolseley's reply left no doubt about Glover's role and the Volta expedition. Wolseley could not attack the Asante from the central region and leave his right flank open to a counterattack by the Juaben and Akwamu. On 23 December, he dispatched to Glover a "preemptory order," in which he commanded that Glover should

> *immediately* upon the receipt of this letter move the Houssas and any other disciplined troops under your command, by the shortest route to the point indicated by you in your dispatch of 14th ultimo [November] . . . . *You will therefore make this your one object.* If necessary to its attainment, you will break off all

operations on the east bank of the Volta, which have no direct bearing on the main issue. . . .[35] [emphasis added]

With no choice left, Glover prepared to leave the Volta and reorganize his meager forces at Odumase. To cover the withdrawal, Captain Sartorious attacked the Anlo villages of Adedomy and Sophie with a force of 50 Hausa, 100 Yoruba, 50 Akuapem, 50 Krepi, 8 native Christians, and 50 Krobo.[36]

Table 7.2

COMPOSITION OF BLAPPAH CAMP
BY MID-NOVEMBER 1873

Chief	Number of Men
Adumarun ("Campaign Charlie")	1,000
Boarfor Ansah ("The Demon")	500
Chief Lavie (Lamie) [Krobo][30]	500
Osudoku Chiefs	200
Kwafo (Krepi)	1,000
Shai	600
TOTAL	3,800

Source: C.O. 96/102 Wolseley to the Earl of Kimberly, 18 December 1873, Inc. 4; Brakenburg, *Ashanti War*, p. 395.

Enter Sakite

It was now apparent to Glover that he could not rely on the chiefs of the Akyem Abuakwa, the Akuapem, and the Accras of James Town and Christiansborg. Still, he desperately needed the support of a loyal and reliable African chief and porters, now more than before. Thinking that the imprisoned Sakite might possibly be that chief, and the Krobo the porters, Glover released the konor on

Christmas Eve. It was the right move. Sakite joined Glover at Blappah, apparently welcoming this opportunity to discredit his accusers by honoring his promise to provide levies for the campaign. From this point to the conclusion of the march against Juaben, the Krobo were the main porters for the expedition. Two days later, on 26 December, Glover, Sartorious, the Yoruba and Hausa troops, a small contingent of Akyem Abuakwa, and the Krobo, the latter led by Sakite, began to withdraw from the Volta in order to begin their move north toward the Pra River.[37] The importance of the Hausa-Yoruba troops notwithstanding, Glover later wrote that the success of the expedition now depended

> on three native chiefs: the chief of the Kroboes
> [Sakite]—quite the best personally, and commanding
> some good tribesmen, too; the second, the chief of the
> Akwapims; the third, the chief of the Eastern Akims. . .
> It was fated happily that these three, at least, should
> not fail him.[38]

From Amedica, Glover, Sartorious, and Sakite marched to Odumase, the konor's village, and planned their strategy for the march to the Pra River and beyond toward Juaben. Sartorius commanded a vanguard of Hausa and Yoruba troops. The Krobo and a smaller contingent of Akuapem and Akyem Abuakwa under their respective kings provided the porters. Given the distance, the terrain, and the tight time schedule, these porters were crucial to the success of the expedition. Initially, Glover had promised to pay the porters 10d. per day, but that was before the defections of the Akyem and others. The Krobo porters, realizing their importance to the campaign and the constraints under which Glover was operating, now demanded 3s. per day, a considerable sum. Glover agreed and at the conclusion of the expedition, each Krobo porter received in addition a bonus of one Snider rifle, valued at about 13 pounds sterling.[39]

Wolseley's plan for the defeat of the Asante was daring, if not foolish. It called for a four-column attack directed against Kumase, the capital. This attack, over almost ninety miles, had to be completed before the heavy late February rains. Wolseley was in charge of the main column, the only column composed entirely of British troops, including reserves. The three other columns were

129

to divert Asante forces and their allies away from Wolseley. Captain Glover led the right or eastern column, Captain William F. Butler commanded the column from Akyem Kotoko toward Kumase, and Captain Richard Dalrymple commanded the west column from Cape Coast.[40] All four columns were to begin their assault from the Pra River on 15 January.

After reorganizing his forces, Glover reached the Pra on schedule. With Sartorious in the vanguard, Glover, Sakite, and some 2,000 troops crossed the Pra into Asante territory on 15 January.[41] In addition to the 800 Hausa and Yoruba combatants, there were 600 Akyem Abuakwa under Akyemhene Amoako Ata and Begorohene Antwi Kasi. The 600 Krobo—a significant showing for a chiefdom only a fraction the size of the Akyem Abuakwa—were under Konor Sakite.[42]

The first in a series of skirmishes occurred on 22 January. At Konongo-Odumase, in a brief encounter with some Juaben, Glover's forces carried the day. On 2 February, Glover again fought with the Juaben, just twenty miles from Kumase, and prevented them from joining forces against Wolseley. Wolseley's strategy to divert the Juaben forces away from his own column and Kumase was working. By the end of the first week in February, Glover had penetrated deep into Juaben territory, actually flanking Kumase on the east as Wolseley had originally planned. He halted the column and sent Sartorious to Wolseley at Camp Fomena, to report his location. Sartorious' arrival in Wolseley's camp was anticlimactic. Eight days earlier, on 12 February 1874, Wolseley had entered, attacked, looted, and burned the deserted Kumase. The war was over; or more correctly, Wolseley had achieved his main objective, though many of the Asante's allies had not surrendered.

Wolseley ordered Glover to withdraw all his troops immediately behind the river Pra, and to march back to Accra.[43] Although the Asante had signed a peace treaty, their allies along the Volta, the Akwamu and the Anlo, had not. Leaving the Volta campaign still unresolved, Wolseley divided the items captured from Kumase among his closest lieutenants and departed for London, where he and his men received a hero's welcome from Queen Victoria. The 1873-1874 Asante War marked the beginning of Wolseley's meteoric rise to international prominence.[44] Not surprisingly, Wolseley did not invite Glover along with the other British officers to the victory celebrations in London, despite the fact that his column was the only one except Wolseley's to achieve its major objective. Glover's actions of 22 December had made him persona non grata with Wolseley. It was not until 1876 that his role in the war was recognized and he too was awarded the Most Distinguished Order of St. Michael and St. George (KCMG).[45]

Glover did not, however, neglect to recognize the efforts of his subordinates. In his final report to the Secretary of State, Glover praised his deputy commissioners, especially Captain Sartorious, and three African kings. Sakite received special recognition as the "only chief who was always able, willing, and ready to obey the orders he received. . ."[46] Glover held most of the other paramount chiefs in contempt and was determined that kings Tackie, Solomon, Amoaku Ata, and Asara should not share in the glory of the Asante's defeat.

After the Sagrenti War the Gold Coast changed dramatically. The legendary power of the Asante ended. A heavy indemnity payable in gold was assessed against the Asante Kingdom, and although Kumase was rebuilt and the "Golden Stool," the symbol of the empire, escaped the clutches of the colonial government, the Asante never regained their old supremacy. The Asante had control over southern Ghana—permanently lost to the British—and a British resident was assigned to Kumase.

Sakite's decision to support Glover and the British in the Sagrenti War proved politically and materially advantageous. As payment for his services to Her Majesty's Government, the colonial government offered him Juaben land, in the center of the Asante Kingdom. He declined this generous offer because Juaben was too far from Kroboland. However, Sakite, along with twenty-three other chiefs of the eastern region, did accept a special medal commemorating the war. Important as a token of appreciation and symbol of friendship between certain African kings and the British, this medal cannot compare with a unique award received by Sakite that has been the subject of some controversy.

Manya Krobo traditions maintain that Sakite was nominated for the KCMG, a claim denied by the London keepers of this award. The KCMG carried with it knighthood, and only Wolseley and Glover verifiably received this coveted and prestigious award.[47] However, Sakite did publicly receive an intricately engraved silver sword, and a large engraved silver medallion hung on a long silver chain, and was apparently told, possibly by some government official, that they were part of the KCMG regalia. Both Heskitt Bell, a minor colonial official of Lagos Colony, and Governor Griffith confirm that Sakite did publicly wear and display a special decorative sword and medallion, which he considered to be a gift from Queen Victoria.[48] Officially, neither official discounted Sakite's claim or offered another explanation. These regalia are still present in the treasury of the Manya Krobo today.[49] The silver sword and medallion, whatever their origin, set Sakite apart from his fellow kings, especially the konor of the Yilo Krobo.

Sakite's military exploits and loyalty to Glover led directly to closer relations with colonial officials, at a crucial time in the expansion of British rule over southeastern Ghana. In 1874, Governor George C. Strahan, a strong supporter of British expansion in West Africa generally and Ghana in particular, solicited Sakite's assistance in extending British authority in the eastern region and in ending the last traces of hostilities in the region. Sakite agreed, and by the end of June 1874, he had been instrumental in negotiating three major agreements for the British. On 15 June 1874, in Odumase, the Akwamuhene signed a peace treaty with the British.[50] Three days later, again in Odumase, Sakite was instrumental in concluding a treaty of protection between the Akyem Abuakwa and the British. The British-Anlo Treaty, signed on 22 June at the Anlo capital of "Jellah Coffee" (Jelukpe), ended the last vestiges of hostilities in the Volta region caused by the Sagrenti War.[51] From this point forward, colonial officials considered him their most loyal ally in maintaining colonial authority throughout the eastern region.

British support and confidence in Sakite rendered him by 1875 the de facto paramount chief of all Krobo. Jakob Kopp, a Basel Missionary stationed in Odumase in 1875, wrote that because of the war with Asante, Sakite, the chief of Odumase was not "only well known but also honoured; nobody asked for Noie [Sasraku], the former chief of Sra [Yilo]."[52] Odumase became the most important administrative town in the region. Kpong, Akuse, and Amedica, already important commercial centers, expanded even more rapidly and became centers of communication, mission education, and, later, colonial administration. The Krobo population and territory grew in both size and ethnic diversity, as neighboring peoples, Adangme and non-Adangme alike, increasingly migrated to these important centers.

Exit the Yilo Konors

The events of the Sagrenti War also once and for all shifted the balance of power between the two Krobo polities. Manya Krobo had led in huza expansion and palm oil production for export already before the war, but politically, the Yilo konor and the Manya konor had remained independent of each other and their polities relatively equal in power. But unlike Sakite, Yilo Konor Noi Sasraku did not experience a rise in status as a result of the war. It was not that Glover made any effort to elevate Konor Sakite over Sasraku; and in fact, during Sakite's imprisonment, Sasraku could have emerged as the leader of the Krobo. Nor were Sakite's achievements made at the expense of the Yilo konor. Glover, aware that there were two Krobo chiefdoms, makes no reference to Sakite as *the* leader of the Krobo. Konor Sasraku simply did not take advantage of the political and economic opportunities that accompanied the conflict. Some Yilo Krobo did participate in the Volta campaign, but not in the important march toward Kumase: Matse Lamie, of the Ogome subtribe, for example, is mentioned in the campaign documents. Sasraku disappears from the political scene after the Grand Meeting, in Accra. He is not mentioned in Glover's final reports nor in his subsequent memoirs, nor is Sasraku one of the twenty-five paramount chiefs who received the special commemorative medal given to the loyal African chiefs who served Her Majesty's Government in the war.

The reason for Sasraku's absence is not clear. It may in part reflect the older Yilo Krobo policy of avoiding involvement with the British, which dated from the time of Ologo Patu (c. 1835-1869), or it may be due simply to his ill health, for according to Basel Mission reports, Sasraku died on 17 March 1874 after a protracted illness.[53] The later Yilo did offer an explanation, albeit dubious, for Sasraku's lack of involvement. Konor Akrobetto I (1874-1907) stated that a ritual prohibition against the Yilo's and the Manya's jointly engaging in the spilling of blood accounted for the absence of the Yilo from the Sagrenti War. But this reason is improbable; in the Dum War of 1836 and the Krobo Rebellion of 1858 such a prohibition does not seem to have applied.

Whatever the reasons for Sasraku's lack of involvement in the Sagrenti War, that conflict marked the beginning of the political decline of the Yilo konors, not only because of their inaction, but more important because of the successes achieved by the Manya konor and the Manya Krobo. Before the war, Sasraku's village of Sra and Sakite's village of Odumase were of equal importance. After the war, outsiders and Krobo alike considered Odumase as the capital of both Krobo chiefdoms. While the Yilo knew that Odumase was not the de jure capital of Kroboland, they also knew that Sra, although politically separate, was no longer equal in stature and importance to Odumase. The dominant position achieved by the Krobo, and the Manya Krobo especially, resulted in no small measure from Sakite's military and political successes in dealing with the colonial government.

8

THE BASEL MISSIONARY SOCIETY

> Although by 1914 the Christian community in Odumase
> and its seventeen outstations numbered 1,646 the basic
> situation remained the same, much hearing of the Gospel
> with little response. We have noted how this pattern was
> set from the beginning by the Konor, Nene Odonkor Azu,
> who died in 1867 still unbaptised. Another factor in the
> situation was the Huza system of land tenure . . . .
> Furthermore the worship of the war god 'Nadu' was very
> strong, while the Dipo custom by which adolescent girls
> were initiated made it almost impossible for the Mission
> girls' schools to function.[1]

European missionary activity in the Gold Coast began as early
as the fifteenth century.[2] Portuguese priests made their presence
felt at one of their earliest permanent West African stations, El
Mina, constructed in 1482. At the middle of the seventeenth
century, as the slave trade flourished, there were Portuguese
Augustinians along the coast at El Mina, Efutu, and Komenda; by
1637 the French Catholic Capuchins had established a post at
Assini; in 1688 representatives of the English Society for the
Propagation of the Gospel were stationed at Cape Coast Castle;
and by 1700, Dutch Moravian missionaries established stations at
El Mina, Cape Coast, and Accra. These diverse groups of
missionaries attended to the spiritual needs of the European
community and children of African and European parents. Beyond
this small group, virtually no attempt was made to convert the
general population. Consequently few Ghanaians converted to
Christianity. Ghanaian converts, however, included some notable
persons: Philip Quaque, an ordained minister of the Society for the
Propagation of the Gospel at Cape Coast Castle;[3] William Amo of

Axim, who gained a doctorate at Wittenberg in Germany;[4] Jacob Capitein, who studied in Holland and gave discourses in Latin, including one titled "Slavery and Religious Freedom are not incompatible;"[5] Frederick Pederson Svane, who graduated in arts and philosophy at Copenhagen and latinized his name to Fredericus Petri Svane Africanus; and Christian Jacob Protten, a Moravian convert, who studied at Copenhagen and Herrnhut.[6] The achievements of these Gold Coast Christians notwithstanding, no missionary group made any significant effort to move beyond the castles and trading posts along the coast until the late eighteenth century.

The Atlantic slave trade was not considered an obstacle to conversion. Thomas Thompson, a minister of the Propagation of the Gospel and Philip Quaque's mentor, published a pamphlet in 1772 in defense of the slave trade while at the same time recognizing the value of maintaining many African beliefs and practices, especially their language. Other missionaries and ministers along the west African coast in the eighteenth and nineteenth centuries held similar views. Neither specific religious groups nor any European power had any interest in general conversion.

A new era of mission activity began in the nineteenth century with the decline in the Atlantic slave trade, increased interest in encouraging legitimate trade, and a desire to establish mission stations in the southern region. The three pioneering missionary societies in the nineteenth century were the Wesleyans of Britain, the Basel Missionary Society with mostly German and some Swiss personnel, and the Bremen Missionary Society from north Germany.[7] Each occupied a specific region, the Wesleyans the central coastal region under the political authority of the British, the Basel Missionaries the eastern region under the Danes, and the Bremen Society the trans-Volta region, at first also under the Danes but later, in the 1880s, under Germany. Each of these missionary groups sought to convert the African to Christianity; the creation of a mission-educated African elite of teachers, catechists, and clerks was considered essential.

British missionaries approached the education of the African differently from their Swiss and German counterparts. The Wesleyans taught in English and placed only minor emphasis on practical skills such as better farming methods.[8] The Basel and

Bremen Missionaries, however, taught in the vernacular. By the last decade of the nineteenth century, the teaching of the famous Black American educator Booker T. Washington reinforced the Basel Missionaries' policy of placing strong emphasis on economic independence for Africans.[9] Accordingly, in the Basel mission schools academic subjects were as important as the teaching of practical skills such as tailoring, sewing, bricklaying, carpentry and more efficient farming methods, which would help insure the African Christian's economic independence. Another important departure from the British was the commitment of German and Swiss missionaries to teach in the local language. Everywhere German and Swiss missionaries established schools this policy was implemented. In the 1880s, when Togo came under the political control of Germany, the Bremen mission schools were forced to teach in German, although they also continued to teach in Ewe, the predominant local language.

Reverend Andreas Riis and his successors based Basel mission education on three main principles. First, to create and sustain an African Christian community the missionaires needed Africans trained as teachers and cathechists. Second, the Africans should be literate in their particular languages. Beginning with Riis' work in Akuapem, the society consistently strove to realize this ideal. By 1880 there were forty-five mission schools with an enrollment of 1200 pupils, the language of instruction being Ga or Twi.[10] Reverends Johannes Zimmermann and C. W. Locher transliterated Ga into a written form: a Ga "primmar" (1853), a grammar book (1857), a dictionary and catechism (1865), and complete Ga translation of the Bible (1866).[11] Third, the conversion and education of African women was as important as that of men if an African Christian community was to be established. For the 1830s, these were unique if not radical ideas. Other missionary groups and the government did not adopt these progressive policies until the 1920s. Governor George Guggisberg, who more than any other British colonial official helped establish the educational system in the Gold Coast, commented that "nothing is more detrimental to the progess of this race then the old system of educated husbands and illiterate wives."[12] Four years after the first school was opened in Akropong (eastern region) in 1843, a girls' school with similar curriculum was opened to fulfill this commitment to women's education. By 1918, when the society was expelled from the Gold

137

Coast, the ratio of boys' to girls' schools in Akuapem, the site of the Society's first established mission schools, was almost equal. The ratio was considerably less at their other schools. These numbers are made more relevant when compared to the Wesleyans who had a 7:1 (boys:girls) ratio.[13]

The Basel missionaries, along with all other mission groups and the government, were in agreement on one basic position: they strongly believed that there were two worlds—one African, the other Christian. Thus, except for language, all aspects of the African's culture—art, music, political and religious institutions—must be destroyed to make way for Christianity. "Hence the traditional forms of training for citizenship (the Dipo custom among the Krobos) were regarded as 'bulwarks of Satan,' and schoolchildren were trained to be citizens of minority Christian communities rather than of the community as a whole."[14] Basel missionaries therefore lived separated from the indigenous population in so-called "Salem" [self-segregated Christian] villages.[15]

Basel missions stayed in the Gold Coast for slightly less than a century. The first four members of the Basel mission arrived in Christiansborg on 18 December 1828.[16] At Osu, the African village adjacent to Christiansborg, they established their first school for mulattoes. Both the school and the attempt to convert the mulattoes failed. A large segment of the European community hindered the missionaries' efforts by mocking the missionaries' attempts to learn Ga. Additionally, the nominally Christian Europeans provided no example for potential converts: some Europeans continued trading in slaves for export and generally lived an unchristian life that included drunkenness and unchristian living arrangements and relations with African women.

The hostile European community at Christiansborg eventually drove the missionaries away. However, the planned relocation at Ningo, along the eastern shore, never materialized. Of the first five missionaries who arrived in April, only Johannes Henke, a Swiss, remained alive in June. Karl F. Salbach, Gottlieb Holzwarth, both Germans, and Johannes Gottlob Schmidt, a Swiss, were dead. Henke died in November, 1831. Undeterred, the Basel society sent three more missionaries, Andreas Riis and Peter Petersen Jager, who were Danes, and Christian Frederick Heinze, a doctor from Saxony. They landed in Christiansborg in March 1832, rented a house in Osu, and began learning Twi with the intention of working among the Akuapem. However, by mid-July 1832 both Heinze and Jager were dead. Riis survived a critical illness only because of the treatment by a native herbalist and a long period of rest on the inland plantation of George Lutterodt, a prominent trader and friend of the missionaries.[17]

In 1835, with the generous material assistance of Lutterodt, Riis established the society's first permanent inland station at Akropong. Akropong offered Riis a distance from the destructive alcohol-consuming European community at Christiansborg, a cooler mountain climate, and a location in the midst of the African population. The Akuapem Omanhene, Ado Dankua, warmly received Riis and permitted him to erect his own house. In November 1837 Johannes Murdter, Andreas Strang, and Anna Walters, his bride-to-be, joined Riis. Murdter died the next year. Riis failed to gain a convert and the first Akuapem mission schools were not established until 1843. Colonial politics followed him inland also. Because the Danish governor Mørch considered Riis pro-British rather than pro-Danish, the governor instructed Omenhene Adum, Ado Dankua's successor, not to cooperate with him. Another problem facing Riis was the widespread existence of slavery, which remained an integral part of the Akuapem economy, both for export and domestic use.

The Basel Missionaries and the Krobo

On the eve of the arrival of the Basel missionaries in the mid-1830s, the Krobo were in the process of radical internal political and economic changes. At the center of Krobo social history at that time lay the expanding huza system and increasing commercial production of palm oil for export. Related to these developments was the secularization of political authority, especially among the Manya Krobo, as the konor's influence came to rest increasingly on his followers' and his own socio-economic status.

In 1836 Riis had a fortuitous meeting with the Krobo; he assisted the Danish governor in negotiating a settlement in the 1835-1836 Dum (Akuapem-Krobo) War.[18] In addition to providing the Governor with information about the Akuapem who claimed authority over the Krobo, Riis administered medical assistance to many injured Krobo in the aftermath of their brief battle with the

Akuapem-Danish forces. His personal concern for their physical well-being earned him the respect and gratitude of Odonkor Azu and the general Krobo population.

Encouraged by his brief encounter with Konor Odonkor Azu, Riis briefly revisited *Klo-yo* in late April 1836 and again in 1838, this time accompanied by Murdter.[19] However, neither Odonkor Azu nor the Krobo were receptive to conversion to Christianity. The Krobo were not yet willing to accept the establishment of a permanent station or any close cultural alliance with missionaries or other Europeans, for that matter. During the next ten years the Basel missionaries concentrated their efforts in Akuapem and Akyem Abuakwa. After a brief visit to Kumasi in early 1840, Riis returned to Basel and reported to the Home Board, the missionary society's governing body. Despite four years in the Akropong, there were no conversions.

Three years later, in 1843, Riis returned to the Gold Coast accompanied by several missionaries and their families, including some Jamaicans, who the society thought could better withstand West Africa's tropical climate.[20] In that year the first mission school was established. Because schools were usually the same buildings as the chapel, "Christians were referred to as 'school-people', *sukuufo*."[21]

In order for the missionaries to communicate effectively to the Akan and Ga-Adangme people, they had to learn their languages. Accordingly, in 1859 Johannes Gottlieb Christaller published the Four Gospels and the Acts translated into Twi. Christaller's other translations included the Bible (1871), a grammar (1875), and a dictionary (1880). Between 1850 and 1870, assisted by the use of Ga and Twi in written form, mission schools, and a more steady flow of missionaries, evangelical activity spread to the main villages of Akuapem, Ga, and Krobo. Eight main stations were established in Christiansobrg, Abokobi, Aburi, Akropong, Kibi, Anum, Ada, and Odumase-Krobo.[22]

By the early 1850s, relations between the Krobo and the missionaries increased. According to Yilo tradition, for example, Konor Ologo Patu permitted one of his sons to convert sometime before 1856.[23] The son's unexpected death was blamed on the Yilo's flirtation with Christianity by those opposed to missionaries. As a result, the tradition claims, the missionaries were expelled. Basel Missionary Society records do not support this Yilo tradition and it may therefore be a belated attempt to explain why the Yilo rejected early conversion to Christianity.

Odumase, the village of the konor of the Manya Krobo, was the site of the first Basel Missionary Society mission in 1856. Reverend Jakob Auer, the first Basel missionary assigned to Odumase, reported that "the king of Odumase has a liking for the Gospel."[24] He was only partially correct. Just as the Basel missionaries planned to use the Krobo for the spread of their religion, Odonkor Azu planned to use the missionary factor to serve his own political and economic needs. Missionaries provided Odonkor Azu with potential political and economic allies at a time when his claim to the konorship was not without challenges. Understandably, therefore, his support of Christian missions came at the expense of some alienation from the more conservative or traditional members of the Manya Krobo. But it should be noted that these elements had not supported his leadership even prior to the arrival of the missionaries. Having missionaries in Kroboland also helped to strengthen Odonkor Azu's hand in dealing with the British and with European traders. Two years later, in 1858, Reverends Johannes Laissle, Carl Aldinger, Jacob Stanhauser, and Johannes Zimmermann established a permanent mission station at Odumase. Stanhauser died the following year. Zimmermann remained longer than any missionary; he left in 1876 in ill health and died the following year in Switzerland. As was their practice, several African catechists accompanied the European Basel missionaries, including Carl Christian Reindorf, Paul Mohenu, Adolf Brandt, Carl Quist, and Obobi.

In 1858 Konor Odonkor Azu and the Omahene of Akropong were the only African paramount rulers to have literate advisors, European or African. By the time of his death in 1867, there existed a small Christian community of ninety, a girls' boarding school with twelve pupils taught by one of Zimmermann's daughters, twenty-three children in a day school, and substations of Odumase at Sra and Ada along the coast. Partly because Manya Krobo had become the center of missionary activity by the 1880s, most colonial officials considered it the "Capital of Krobo-country."[25]

In 1858, two years after the missionaries' arrival, Odonkor Azu extended his commitment to the missionary presence by giving Zimmermann and Michael Stanhauser three of his sons for conversion: Akutei Azu, the first Krobo Christian actually baptized, in 1857; Akutei's brother Noa Akunor Aguae Azu; and his half brother Nyako.[26] At Akropong, they were trained as teacher-catechists. Much to the disappointment of the the missionaries, Odonkor Azu himself never converted. Even so, he remained friendly and accessible to the missionaries, especially to Zimmermann.

The konor's three Christian sons served both the Christian and the Krobo communities. Noa Azu, the most prominent of all the earliest Krobo converts, wrote the *Adangbe (Adangme) History* and recorded 2,024 Adangme proverbs and historical songs; collectively these works are a major source on Krobo history prior to and during the nineteenth century.[27] Peter Nyako and Noa Azu served their borther Knor Sakite as interpreters and advisors during the Sagrenti War and during negotiations with the Akwamu, the Akyem Abuakwa, and the Ese. Christian Akutei (Tei) Azu, like his brothers, attended the primary and secondary schools at Abokobi; he served throughout the Ga-District of the Basel Mission Society, including Ada and Kpong, as teacher-catechist. Emmanuel Mate Kole (1892-1939), the sone of Peter Nyako and the grandson of Odonkor Azu, became the first Christian konor. His son, Fred (Azzu) Mate Kole, also a Christian, succeeded him (1939-present). Officially, all were officers of the Basel Missionary Society, but to the Krobo they were more than that, of course.

Despite the conversion of Odonkor Azu's three sons, only a few other Krobo followed their example. Many of the more influential converts were also related to the konor's family. Not the least of these were Enoch Azu, grandson of Odonkor Azu and a teacher-catechist who translated the Bible into Adangme; Princess Ester Naki Sackitey, granddaughter of Odonkor Azu and the first European-trained midwife; Matetse Lawrerngwa, grandson of Odonkor Azu and father of another more famous Krobo, Thomas Harrison Odonkor, who wrote *The Rise of the Krobo* and was chief of Kpong during Konor Sakite's reign; and Michael T. Kofi, grandson of Odonkor Azu, an evangelist at Sra, Odumase, Dofo Adenklebi, and Akole, who was educated to be a teacher, and posted at Christiansborg, Dodowa, Abokobi, Ada Foah, and Bawaleshi. Three of Abraham Nyako Azu's daughers, Darley Sikpi, Angmorkwo, and Angmomle, were also among the earliest Krobo Christians.[28] Thus, from the beginning, members of the konor's

142

family formed the foundation of the Krobo Christian community, even though the konor himself did not convert.

The Yilo konor's position toward the missionaries was less receptive, often hostile. Okepsi, the first Yilo mission station, was like all subsequent stations, a substation of Odumase. There was not a single Yilo Krobo teacher-catechist when the Society's missionaries were expelled in 1915. Indeed, virtually all primary and all secondary mission schools were in Manya Krobo villages. Additionally, in 1892 the Manya Krobo enstooled the first Christian konor, whereas the first Christian Yilo Konor was not elected until 1906. Thus the coming of Christianity and missionary education tended to intensify existing differences between the Manya and Yilo Krobo, and to reinforce the perception of many non-Krobo that Manya Krobo was the "capital" of missionary activity in Krobo.

In the tradition of his father Odonkor Azu, Sakite made effective political use of the missionary connection. A long list of missionaries attended his court as unofficial political and economic advisers (Appendix E). They translated British colonial government dispatches from the District Commissioner at Christiansborg and practiced European medicine. To be sure, these advisors also vied with the konor's traditional advisory staff.

The partnership served the needs of both the missionaries and the konor. Reverend Jacob Kopp made this point clear in 1874, when he compared the courts of the Manya Konor Sakite and Yilo Konor Akrobetto:

> [Sakite] has people at hand when he was to read a letter from the English government and to answer it, while the chief of Sra [Akrobetto] has to send a deputy to Odumase each time to have such a letter read.[29]

As translators and interpreters of official government documents, missionaries became, at the least, de facto agents of colonial rule. Undoubtedly missionaries also used their position to interpret not only the language but the intent of colonial directives to their own benefit. After the Krobo converts such as Noa Azu and Peter Nyako obtained sufficient Western education to assist the konors in European matters, the direct influence of the European missionaries over the konors probably declined.

Conversion and Resistance

Within Krobo society there was significant opposition to the missionaries' operations, led by the priesthood [the djemeli]. Missionaries often found themselves greeted with the cry "You disturb our town, our village!"[30] The priests and their number of supporters fought the changes introduced by missionaries. Although weakened by the huza expansion and the resultant decentralization of the population and by the rise of the secular authority of the konors, the priesthood still exercised considerable cultural influence over most Krobo. The Krobo Mountain remained their cultural and religious center, although the pattern of residence and livelihood had shifted away from that ancestral home. By constant attacks against human sacrifices, female initiation in the Dipo ceremony, polygamy, burial on the Krobo Mountain, and the use of domestic slaves, missionaries incurred the continued wrath of the priesthood and their supporters.

The old theocracy, the djemeli, actively worked against the missionaries and proclaimed a number of specific measures designed to reinforce older habits of life and thereby impede missionary activity.[31]

1. No oven should be constructed in any house (traditionally cooking was conducted outside the house);
2. No corn loaf should be eaten (maize was used, but not eaten in this form);
3. No dough or kenkey should be made and eaten (again, maize dough was associated with Christian diet);
4. No goats should be domesticated (kept as non-ritual meat sources; traditionally goats were primarily used in sacrifices in the Dipo festival for the atonements between men and the gods);
5. No mud, that is permanent, walls should be used to construct a building on the plains (tradition prohibited the building of permanent structures outside Klo-yo);
6. Girls who had not passed through the rites of womanhood (Dipo) must not be baptized or sent to school;
7. No manual labor would be undertaken on Thursday, the day of the goddess Kloweki;

8. No Krobo should observe Sunday or Christian holidays; and
9. Converts should be declared dead.

These sanctions proved effective obstacles to conversion. Priest-messengers (*labiabi*) confiscated goats, destroyed compound walls and kitchen ovens, and harassed school children and children of converts, especially girls. Apart from the members of Odonkor Azu's family, few Krobo became Christians and those who did instantly became outcasts on the fringes of society; they were often declared dead by their families and were ritually and symbolically buried.[32]

From the earliest years, that is the early 1860s, the Manya and to a lesser extent the Yilo population generally supported its own priesthood. Nevertheless, a small number of people did become Christians. Although the actual rates of conversion were erratic, by 1875 there were about 100 converts (47 men, 34 women, mostly from Ada, and 17 boys).[33] The next four years were better. In 1879, twenty years after the establishment of a permanent mission station in Odumase, there were 279 Krobo Christians and 87 students. Until 1889 the mission averaged an estimated 24 adult conversions per year. By 1889 there were 566 Krobo Christians and 215 pupils.[34] Basel records do not mention Krobo Christians outside Odumase. Missionaries considered Kpong and Akuse "difficult stations" because of the "strong fluctuations of people"[35]. Indeed, the population of Kpong and Akuse was a mixture of various ethnic groups drawn to the two trading towns by the possibilities of rapid material gain.

During the 1890s the rate of Krobo conversion slowed.[36] After ten years the Christian community had grown by a mere fifty-seven members, to an average of nine baptisms a year, for a total of 617 adults and 292 school children. In 1893, of the 1000 baptisms reported by the Basel Missionary Society throughout the Gold Coast, just 166 came from the Ga District, which included Christiansborg, Ada, Abokobi, and Odumase.[37] In 1895, the Krobo Christian community reputedly numbered "some few hundred," and consisted of those people who had be "subjected to the influence of evangelisation for a long time."[38] This pattern continued the following year; of 831 baptisms in 1896, 132 were from the Ga District.[39] Nor was any change reported in 1897, except that a new outstation was established at Okpesi (Yilo Krobo) among the "Krobo plantations."[40] Only ten Krobo converted in 1898. And although dismissals and low conversion rates were common throughout the eastern region during this era, Basel missionaries reported that "the pagan world shows the strongest opposition in the Odumase area, in Krobo land."[41]

The cause of this increasing Krobo opposition to conversion was the resurgence of the Dipo ceremony as the priests recovered from their expulsion from the Krobo Mountain in 1892. To circumvent a government ban on the practice of the Dipo ceremony, a new name for the ritual was introduced: *Boleum*.[42] Additionally, the church's dismissal of Konor Emmanuel Mate Kole in 1894 for taking additional wives and failing to oppose many of the Krobo's ceremonies and festivals, including Dipo and *Nyam*, the harvest celebration, lent support to the revival of many of the more traditional elements in the society.[43]

By 1898 the Basel missionaries could boast of little progress among the Krobo or other peoples in the eastern region.[44] Consistently disappointed by the lack of conversions and dismissals of many who had converted, the missionaries underwent a reversal of feelings toward the Krobo. In the 1870s and 1880s, the Krobo people were considered the most promising of people in the eastern region. Now, in the 1890s, Basel missionaries were particularly disappointed with the actions of Konor Mate Kole, "formerly a Christian now expelled."[45] Of the general population, the disappointed Kolle reported:

> The longer I live with these people the more I have to admit how rotten this society is. I am fully convinced that the Krobos are the most licentious and most sensual tribe on the Coast.[46]

The Krobo Christian community was anything but stable, as were other Basel Missionary communities in the eastern region. For the year 1899, the number of people who converted to the Basel missionaries' form of Christianity remained the same as in the previous two years. However, the number expelled rose to an all-time high: "445 people, more than 2½ percent of our Christians, were expelled in one year alone." The Akyem had the highest number of expulsions, with 118. The reasons given for this phenomenon were the youthfulness of many converts, the sensual nature of the people, and their worldliness—"they devote themselves to business and commerce and acquisition of fortunes." The missionaries considered all "Black Christians," including the Krobo, to be morally weak. Additionally, the European missionaries blamed the native assistants for not providing proper examples for the Krobo community.[47]

Missionaries often attributed their difficulties among the Krobo to one cause: the huza, not polygamy. To visit the hundreds of huza farms and villages which dotted the Akyem foothills and mountains, missionaries had to travel great distances. Many farmers, who had purchased plots far from outstations, frequently remained near their western and northern plantations at places like Dawa and Adumase, which were outside the reach of the ministers at Odumase and Okepsi.[48] Moreover, when the farmers did return to their main villages such as Odumase, Somanya, and Sra, it was primarily to participate in traditional, not Christian, ceremonies.

Ironically, while the relative wealth of the Krobo attracted missionaries to their villages, this same prosperity also hindered extensive conversion. Many Krobo used their mission education to enlarge their fortunes in the expanding cash economy; the promised eternal rewards of the Christian faith apparently held little interest. Few educated Krobo wanted to be teachers; instead, they were attracted by the cash economy, urban living, and the opportunity to become part of a prestigious new class of Africans. Most educated Krobo wanted to be merchants or clerks in the larger European or African firms stationed at Odumase, Kpong, Akuse, Amedica, Abokobi, or Aburi. Moreover, the "great and difficult" distances between Krobo farmers in the forests of the Akuapem mountains and European ministers stationed in the larger urban villages forced the missionaries to rely on the work of itinerant African catechists.[49] The Krobo created "house churches," that is, ordinary houses used as churches but without the explicit sanctions of the Basel Missionaries, in their villages or huzas and plantations, for neighbors and their families.[50] The huza had actually helped determine the social nature of Krobo Christianity, which centered on small huza-based rural communities. European missionaries and the appointed "Native" catechists were not part of the Krobo's house churches. The house churches, therefore,

147

represented the beginning of an independent Christian Krobo religious institution.

The rate of conversion remained slow throughout the 1880s and 1890s, with Christiansborg continuing to show the greatest increases in the Ga District. Some of the outstations of Odumase, such as Tando, Jibomang, and Akoli, experienced a net decline in church membership; however, membership increased in Kpong, Okpesi, and Obuadase. With the explicit support of the chief of the Manya subtribe, Manyapoungno erected a chapel with a school and a "double teacher's house;" the local population paid for the erection of these structures.[51]

During the 1890s, the Society reported that "suspensions were balanced by the equal number of readmissions." Konor Emmanuel Mate Kole's third wife, of course without forswearing polygamy, was among the list of new converts. (The conversion of a third wife of anyone, even the konor's, demonstrates some of the difficulties the Society had in gaining women converts in this polygamous society.) By 1899 the total number of Krobo Christians was listed as 649 adults and 272 students, with twenty-seven "pagans" attending baptismal schooling.[52] Without apparent objections, the number of "pagans" involved in the mission education process gradually increased, especially in the early 1900s.

The missionaries did achieve some notable successes in the late 1880s and 1890s. Especially gratifying to them was the conversion of some priests and priestesses. The most noted of these was Noa Azu, the son of Odonkor Azu; in 1887, in Sra, another priest converted, an unnamed man estimated to be about sixty years old. Kopp, in Odumase, also converted a fetish priest, who was renamed Abraham.[53] The missionaries recorded similar successes among Akuapem people, where in Abobobi they converted a former priest, renamed Paulo Mohenu, who had become a workman. The most celebrated Christian among the Yilo Krobo was Paulo Fino of Kpemo, a wealthy man and a former "fetish priest." Among the priestesses who converted were *Onyamedom* (God's grace) and Biako, renamed Christian Onyamedom, who was about sixty years old in 1887.[54] Although the actual number of priests and priestesses who converted was small, any conversion of traditional religious leaders to Christianity had an impact on the community much greater than any number or conversions from any other segment of Krobo society.

In the structure of the administration of mission stations, Sra was merely another outstation of Odumase. Sra, the Yilo Krobo capital, was considered by the missionaries as subordinate to Odumase of the Manya Krobo; such thinking was probably at least in part a response to the hostile reception by Yilo konors Ologo Patu and Sasraku, and a way of rewarding Manya konors Odonkor Azu and Sakite, in that Odumase was his village. It is indeed ironic that Manya Krobo is the center of both traditional Krobo religion and Western Christianity.

Sra's first chapel took twenty years to complete (1879-1899), because of the lack of support by the Yilo konors and the Yilo people. After the appointment of Winfried Tekpenor Odjidja, a Manya Krobo from Agromanya and a member of the royal family of Manya Krobo, as catechist and teacher in 1897 conversions among the Yilo increased. Shortly after taking over the Okepsi mission in 1898, he was responsible for the conversion of fifteen people at Kpemo, near Sra.[55] However, no other Yilo conversions were reported that year or the next, with only three souls readmitted in 1899.

The relative lack of Basel missionary successes in Yilo Krobo was due to several factors. First, the hostility or indifference of Yilo leadership; second, unlike the contiguous Manya Krobo huzas, the Yilo huzas frequently tended to be in isolated plots; third, the number of missionaries was always small, hence they concentrated their efforts in the areas of greatest promise and larger population centers, both of which were usually in Manya Krobo. One effect of these factors was that there were no Yilo teachers or catechists until well into the twentieth century. Unlike Odumase, there was no core Christian community in Sra or any other Yilo town, and no European missionaries, only a "bad [African] catechist."[56] As late as 1898 when the Christian community in Odumase was well established, its Sra counterpart was not considered to be serious. Due to the Yilo Krobo's general lack of personal and material support for mission education, it was not until the 1920s, after the Basel Missionary Society had left the Gold Coast (1914), that a mission school was constructed in Sra.

The Yilo's hostile policies toward missionaries changed during the reign of Akrobetto I (1877-1906). One contributing

149

factor to this shift was the konor's recognition of the missionaries' influence in non-religious spheres. Although Basel missionaries were delighted to accept Konor Akrobetto's invitation to establish direct ties between them, they were also aware of the reasons for this rather radical change:

> He [Akrobetto] is an intelligent, calculating man, not a fanatic like his predecessor [Sasraku] . . . he now realizes, together with his elders, how far the chief of Odumase has proceeded under the influence of the mission.[57]

Akrobett'ss actions came too late. Odumase remained the center of mission activity well after the Basel Missionaries left in 1914.

The rejection of Christianity was not caused by a declining economy; the economy was booming in the 1880s and 1890s. Abundant rains and high prices for palm oil and palm kernels brought increasing wealth to the Krobo farmers and merchants, and a protion of these profits supported mission activities. In 1899, for example, the church raised more than 1000 marks from church events, 80 marks from church dues, and 250 marks from school fees.[58]

The Dipo Ceremony and Polygamy as Obstacles

The Dipo ceremony and polygamy made the conversion of girls and women extremely difficult.[59] Polygamy, Kopp reported was "the main obstacle in converting . . . for the first condition to be taken into the Christian Community is the dismissal of extra wives."[60] Less was known about the Dipo ceremony in the missionaries' earliest years in Kroboland. Michael Rös, the first missionary to observe some of the public aspects of the Dipo ceremony in 1864, and Zimmermann, who described the ceremony in 1867, both recognized the Dipo ceremony as an essential part of the Krobo ethos.

It is instructive to note that although Odonkor Azu gave three of his sons to missionaries he gave none of his daughters. The first women who became Christians were few in number, generally older than their male counterparts, and often distant members of Odonkor Azu's family. It was not until 1888, thirty years after the conversion of Noa Azu and his brothers, that Konor Sakite permitted two of his daughters to be converted, after they elected not to undergo the Dipo ceremony. Sakite's actions prompted Kopp to report that the Dipo problem and declined in importance.

> Since King Sakite allowed his two daghters to make their choice—either to go to the Krobo Hill to make *Otufu* (*Dipo*) or go to the mission school and be baptized (they opted for the latter), we have overcome the *Otufu* problem.[61]

But Kopp's exultation was premature. Few, if any, women followed Sakite's lead. Moreover, Sakite had not opposed the Dipo ceremony; he merely attempted to present himself as progressive.

Educational opportunity and not Christian beliefs was the attraction for women. Accordingly, a girls' school was established in 1874 in the chapel at Odumase. Mission school training offered economic mobility by teaching marketable skills in sewing and midwifery. Women with mission school backgrounds, however, were generally attractive as wives only to other Christians; even many Christian men actually preferred non-Christian wives. The case of Konor Emmanuel Mate Kole, a Christian, who took additional non-Christian wives, is the most obvious example.

Although missionaries had attempted to establish an entirely new way of life for the Krobo Christians, a life separate and apart from traditional values, some thirty years after 1858 they had only partially succeeded. By the late 1880s, an increasing number of converts were returning to their old religious practices. It was not that they rejected Christainity completely; they wanted to be part of both worlds. One Krobo reportedly stated that "the world is so sweet that I want to enjoy it a little more."[62] Konor Emmanuel Mate, once the paragon of a Krobo Christian, exemplified the failure of Christainity to completely change a Krobo's commitment to traditional Krobo values.[63] The konor and other Christians continued to celebrate traditional rites such as Dipo, naming ceremonies for their children, and burial rituals, and to use traditional medicines. Missionary criticism of polygamous marriages by Christians did not go without challenge from the Krobo men. "Sir," said one of them, "if you allow us to marry more women, so they can help us with work on our plantations, then we will become Christians."[64] Kopp noted that "the dismissal of catechists and teachers because they broke marriage vows or committed other lecherous sins was not uncommon. Even a priest had to be dismissed because of such sins."[65] It should be noted that although these wayward individuals had been dismissed from the Church, non-Christians continued to consider people like Konor Emmanuel Mate to be Christians.

The missionaries blamed various sectors of Krobo society for the recent converts' lack of commitment to their new faith. A prime target was of course the konors, especially Emmanuel Mate Kole, who lived a less than model Christian life, and Akrobetto of Yilo Krobo, who was not as receptive to missionaries as he could have been. In 1890, missionaries reported that of the members of the king's family, only a few took their conversions seriously. Most of them lived in open sin. The condition of the small Christian Krobo community did not improve after 1892, when the teacher-catechist Emmanuel Mate became konor. In fact matters worsened. In 1894 he too was expelled from the church for taking additional wives.[66] The konor's priorities were clear and the missionaries quickly acknowledged this fact. In 1895 they reported that Emmanuel Mate Kole's "main aim [as Konor was] to please the government and stimulate the culture of his people."[67]

There had been earlier signs of Emmanuel Mate's refusal to follow strictly the church's orders. As a young Christian, he had major disagreements with the Basel missionaries. While a teacher in the small Krobo village of Tibomoung, he constantly complained about being posted there and demanded to be transferred. When no transfer was forthcoming, he resigned; "but after 14 days he came back on his own accord! Of course, such a man cannot do much."[68] Apparently Emmanuel Mate, one missionary reported, was never completely happy doing the Lord's work. What the missionaries apparently failed to understand was that when he became konor, he would then have to represent all Krobo—both the minority Christian community and the majority non-Christian community also. Not surprisingly, the colonial government understood this political fact, whereas the missionaries rejected such realities.

By the late 1880s, Christians frequently went through a kind of revolving door: expulsion then readmission. "Station Odumase,"

Kopp reported, "is the only Ga-Station and perhaps the only Station at all that had no increase but decrease of six souls. It was a bad year." The expulsion of souls was common throughout Kroboland. Later in the same 1890 report, Kopp noted that 34 souls had returned to their traditional religious beliefs, "15 of them in Odumase alone, one of whom was a presbyter, the first in years! Apart from that, young Christians have shown much disobedience and apathy."[69] Disaffection and lack of loyalty to the church were widespread in the Ga District. Missionaries frequently used ineffective threats of expulsion to keep recent converts in line. They considered the areas around Ada and Odumase to be the "least responsive" to their efforts.

What a dramatic change from the 1870s. Although specific figures for each mission station are not available, a general picture emerges. In 1891, 150 Africans were expelled from the Basel churches. In its most "rewarding year ever," 1893, when 994 were baptized, 237 were expelled.[70] A similar ratio of expulsions to admissions obtained the following year. In 1894, "a good year for missionary work," of the 999 persons baptized, 813 were thought to be really worthy, and "as usual, many had to be excluded."[71] In the first decade of the twentieth century, the problem of fidelity to the missionaries' version of the Christian faith continued to plague the missions. In 1909 there were 838 conversions and 704 expulsions for all stations in the Gold Coast, leaving a real growth of only 134 souls. In the same year, 366 previously expelled Christians were readmitted.[72] A particular group among those dismissed caused the missionaries considerable concern. In the early twentieth century the largest number of expelled African Christians belonged to a "new class" of people—the "scholars"[73] (Appendices E, F, and G).

The Huza and Christianity

In both the Manya and the Yilo chiefdoms, the reluctance among the Krobo populace to convert may have had more to do with political and economic realities than with hostility toward Christianity. For example, in 1867, Zimmermann reported that conversion of the Krobo on their upcountry huzas was impeded by their preoccupation with "planting oil palm and preparing palm oil."[74] In 1884, Kopp, Zimmermann's successor, held a similar view.

153

There was a great deal of absenteeism among the Christians at chapel, "because of their commitment to work on plantations."[75] Zimmermann concluded that "the ways of the European, their textiles, houses, religion, and spirits had little value within [Krobo] society."[76] While both Zimmermann and Kopp applauded the Krobo value system for not placing a high premium on such European commodities as liquor, this same value system also put such traditional practices as Dipo and huza farming ahead of Christian conversion and urban living.

The huza, combined with the commercialization of palm oil and other food crops, brought wealth to the Krobo, a portion of which found its way toward the financing of chapels, schools, salaries, houses for teacher-catechists, and for the education of Krobo children. Church officials were pleased by this. On the other hand, the continual expansion of the huza farms took a large part of the Krobo population farther and farther from the centers of missionary activity, such as Okpesi and Odumase. By the 1880s, huza farms covered over six hundred square miles, hence the task of reaching Krobo farmers became increasingly difficult. Thus, some of the very cultural and economic factors that had been attractive to the missionaries in the 1850s and 1860s were seen as hindrances to control and conversion by the 1880s. Writing in 1909, on the fiftieth anniversary of the Basel Missionary Society's arrival in Kroboland, Paul Steiner reported that

> this way of living [huza farms with hundreds of villages] proved an obstacle to missionary work and especially to a [Christian] community life. [In Krobo] we had to travel to preach from the beginning to the numerous villages and hamlets.[77]

A Basel Missionary Society report two years later was less critical of the huza's impact on conversion in Manya Krobo. "On the East-Krobo [Manya Krobo] plantations we have a strong, well-rooted and religious population of farmers; they still partly belong to the pagan world, but show now more interest in Evangelism than ever before."[78] Perhaps European missionaries had begun to accept the huza and its inevitable effect on Krobo life. The huza farmers were driven by the desire, if not personal need, to continue the acquisition of additional huzas. They had no interest in supporting missionary efforts, or in hindering them, for that matter. It should be recalled that at the beginning of the nineteenth century the Krobo priests had lost authority as the huza farmers expanded away from the Krobo Mountain; now it was the turn of the Christian priests. Huza farmers were simply continuing a process which pre-dated the arrival of missionaries in 1858, a process which had its origins in an attempt to bring economic security to Kroboland. Viewed in this light the missionary's message had little chance of radically changing the impact of the huza on Krobo life.

Mission Medicine as a Tool for Conversion

With conscious manipulation, missionaries used whatever means they could to attract the Africans to their religion; education and medical knowledge were high on their list. Missionaries sought to prove that Christian supernatural powers were superior to the Krobo deities. In the 1892 report, *Why We Missionaries Practice Medicine*, Kopp was very explicit: "The medical mission has undertaken to convert pagans into Christians through its medical practice; it serves as a means justified by the end."[79]

All missionaries from Riis at the battle in 1836 between the Krobo and the Akuapem had practiced European medicine. However, it was not until the 1880s that any medical doctor survived long enough to be effective. In 1886, two European-trained medical doctors arrived in Odumase to serve the needs of both the missionaries and the Africans. The doctors were to engage in "self-help" and to improve "the awful sanitary conditions in which the natives live." The missionaries also felt that their medical knowledge could assist in demonstrating the superiority of Christianity not only against snake bites and a wide range of sicknesses, but also against yellow fever outbreaks like those in May 1911. "If we do not know how to keep the sick we shall be giving back our Christians, one after another."[80] Equally important was the belief that successful treatment of illnesses would help to undermine the credibility of traditional healers.[81]

Mission doctors eagerly seized every opportunity to practice their skills. Their greatest challenges, and the potential for greatest rewards, lay in treating converts, children, and priests. "After I had cured many children," Reverend Matthew Ros reported, "the ice

155

was broken—the mothers brought to me sick children from everywhere." Through medicine, missionaries such as Ros, who had gained a great reputation as a physician among the Krobo people,[82] were able to gain access to young children and their parents, especially the mothers. Krobo priests also asked for medical help, which was not denied. The mere fact that the priests sought healing from missionaries was a clear admission that missionary medicine was superior.

The effectiveness of the medical strategy should not be overstated, Kopp warned. "The number of people treated by the missionary doctor(s) who converted as a result is not great." The important point was the positive initial contact between the missionaries and the people. As Kopp concluded in his report on medical missions: "One should not forget, however, that between the first encounter and the conversion there is a long stretch of time."[83] Mission medicine was merely another tool in the arsenal the missionaries used to convert the Africans.

Mission Education

Mission education was essential for the spreading of the gospel. Africans had to be trained to read and write in their own language. Christians were "school people" *(sukuufo)*—products of the *Erziehungsantalten* or boarding schools, and the *Gemeindeschulen* or day schools. Day schools originated in the practice of taking children into a missionary's household semi-permanently and training them in Western ways, which eventually led to boarding schools where instruction was more complete and the student was isolated from the local, non-Christian community. By 1861, under J. G. Aujer, the middle schools emerged, replacing the boarding schools with a four-year curriculum comprising arithmetic, geometry, geography, history, natural history, the local language, later also English, and Bible study. Greek was added later for seniors. The Seminary headed by Eidmann and Dieterle in 1848 in Akropong had a difficult curriculum which included teaching methods, biblical studies, homiletics, music, church history, Ga or Twi, later English, and how to care for a congregation.[84]

Beginning with the mission education of Odonkor Azu's three sons in the late 1850s, an ever increasing number of Krobo, predominately boys, were separated physically and, what is more important, culturally, from traditional Krobo culture. Mission education took place outside their homes, away from huza farms at primary and secondary boarding schools. Although family, clan, and subtribe relationships continued to be important, gradually another factor unified this group: mission education and the rigors of boarding school life. The mission-educated Krobo who graduated from secondary schools rapidly became a separate class, who were more comfortable in the towns and larger villages than in the small huza villages and farms.

Missionaries, colonial officials, and the Krobo all had different, although not mutually exclusive, ideas about what kind of education was best. The missionaries needed trained teacher-catechists and colonial officials needed literate Africans to assist them in the administration of the Protectorate. The konors, especially of Manya Krobo, hoped to use the acquisition of Western education to increase their ability to consolidate political and territorial expansion and to communicate more effectively and directly with European traders and colonial officials. Similarly, individual Krobo families considered mission education as an investment in the continued advancement of their huzas and related trading enterprises.

The first generation of mission-educated Krobo, those educated between 1860 and the late 1870s, presented no challenge of any kind to the konor or the djemeli. Their numbers were small and colonial rule had not yet been established in Kroboland. People such as Noa Azu and Akutei were stationed in Kroboland and later sent to Akropong, Abokobi, or Aburi.[85] From 1867, with the completion of the first primary school in Odumase, mission education expanded gradually with the addition of other primary schools in Manyapoungno, Kpong, and Somanya, and the first secondary school in Odumase in the 1870s. Mission schools not only served to educate Krobo youths; through their payrolls and their need for food and services, they added to the material wealth of the Krobo villages where the schools were located, increased the size and diversity of these villages, and added a literate sector of the population to places like Odumase, Kpong, and Manyapoungno. The missionaries intended for the first generation of converts to be catechist-teachers. Ga, not English, was the language of instruction, and religion dominated the

157

curriculum. Accordingly the early years of mission education produced such men as Noa Azu, Peter Nyako, and Emmanuel Mate Kole, who did not seek economic and political positions outside the Basel Missionary Society as merchants or clerks with the colonial government.

The second generation, that is, those educated between the 1880s and the first decade of the twentieth century, faced an environment different from the first Christian pioneers. Their numbers were considerably larger. After 1874 colonial rule was firmly estalished in the region, there were several large European and African trading companies stationed in Kroboland, and missionary activity was widespread. All these sectors of Krobo society provided opportunities, personal and economic, for the literate and/or skilled mission-educated individuals, especially men.

Many of the motivations for obtaining mission education changed in the 1880s. By this date there were increasing economic opportunities brought about by the expansion of palm oil and palm kernel production and a general increase in trading activity along the Volta at Kpong, Akuse, Amedica, and Ada. Moreover, in 1880 Odumase became the administrative center of the newly created Volta District. The extension of direct control over the peoples in the Volta District by the British resulted in government employment opportunities as clerks, for those who were literate and knowledgeable in Ga, Adangme, and Twi. With this second generation of Krobo converts, although the need for catechists-teachers grew in pace with the Christian community and mission schools, fewer converts were attracted to this profession, primarily because of economic reasons. Educated converts realized that the salaries and prestige of other employment options within both the Krobo and European community were considerably higher than what one could earn from missionary work. Moreover, mission-trained Krobo who took positions with merchants or with the colonial government could continue many Krobo practices away from the watchful eye of the missionaries.

Like the huza, but for a more select group, mission education offered many Krobo greater economic upward mobility. Charles H. Bartels, a wealthy African trader at Accra, commented that most school leavers, those who had not finished secondary school, wanted to be merchants.[86] Even more to the point, many students had concluded that "the key to all important positions in the government and commercial houses (firms) is through the school, and so there are more candidates for the middle schools that offer higher levels of education."[87]

Other Krobo, however, merely wanted to expand their farming land, using the education to acquire cash and hence additional commercially producing huzas. According to Lochermann, "everybody want[ed] to have a big cocoa plantation and to build a big house; some newly rich Christians [had] acquired a second wife and had to be expelled from our communities."[88] Clearly, many Krobo sought education because they equated it with economic and financial success and not because of its religious message.

The development of an educated Krobo community, albeit small, was a double-edged sword for the missionaries and the Krobo. While deliberately estranging the Krobo from their traditional institutions, mission education ironically also had the potential of leading them away from the Christian community as well. Mission education also increased ethnic and economic diversity, especially in the market towns on the Volta. For missionaries this was not a blessing. Of these market centers it was said that "here paganism and its materialism, frivolity and liberty bloom in those centers and present our mission with different problems." Interestingly, the missionaries noted that another danger to the Krobo lay in "European Cultures," meaning material temptation such as clothing, jewelry, furniture, foods and liquor.[89] Whereas in the past missionaries had to compete with fetish priests, they now had to contend with competition from secular Europeans as well. This was a strange turn of events indeed. Similarly, some of the Krobo Christians refused to accept even the secular authority of their konor, of the respective heads of their families, clans, or subtribes, if these leaders were not Christians.

The second generation of students presented the missionaries with yet another set of unexpected problems—the school leavers and the scholars. Many students did not complete their course of study, often because of financial constraints. Their mission education placed them in a kind of cultural middle community—partly African (traditional) and partly European (Christian). It was difficult for those who left school early to find acceptance in either community as equals. "It is the school-leavers," Reverend Wilhem Dettli reported in 1913, "who give us the most trouble. They do

159

not recognize any authority any more, and do not succumb to any law."[90]

The scholars, as the missionaries disdainfully called these graduates of at least middle schools, rejected the catechist-teacher profession and instead pursued higher paying positions in the government and business community. Probably more important, these young men were extremely proud of their educational achievements and demanded that everybody treat them with deference. The scholars' attitude particularly displeased the missionaries, who reported that these scholars were

> people who went to the higher schools. They are very proud of it, but still they are *nobody special*. . . . They come to church now and then, and demand special treatment and respect for their rank and title. They want to sit with the elders and missionaries on social occasions.[91]

Although the number of scholars is not given, it must have been considerable, as it was reported that they gave the missionaries a lot of trouble. These scholars by virtue of their education and their employment in business and government, were an important component in the Kroboland's increasingly cash-based economy.

> By profession they do all kind of work—secretarial—in all possible places—governmental departments, firms, offices, etc., up to the first clerks. Some of them are real Christians. . . . Most of them do not bring honor to Christianity. Proud, haughty, badly dressed and behaved young people they are. To be one's own master, caring for nobody, greeting no one anymore, dressing after the latest fashion—this is the picture of a perfect educated gentleman?[92]

It was precisely because they occupied virtually all the professional positions that their carefree life caused the missionaries trouble. More than any other factor these scholars offered an alternative life-style to students considering entering the ministry or teaching profession. Finally, some missionaries must have reflected on the irony that the scholars had played a very large part in the creation of mission education. That is, it was the mission school with its introduction to Western education, which among other things stressed the importance of a cash economy, including the accumulation of imported goods, that gave some students the skills, motivation, and confidence to break with traditional values and establish their own community, which was neither completely traditional nor Christian. The scholars also occupied an acknowledged position in Krobo society. Colonial officials and missionaries both noted, with some regret, that it was obvious that "the *scholars* will shape the future of this land and people . . . they are well off, and later in life they will have influence."[93] For these reasons, neither the missionaries nor the colonial officials could ignore the scholars.

In 1887, by an ordinance of that year, the government entered the business of education in a serious manner. Colonial officials created a Board of Education with an inspector and schools were divided into government and assisted [missionary] categories. The curriculum of all schools after 1887 became secularized; they were inspected by the Board; English became a mandatory subject; British texts and tests were required; subsidies were allocated.[94] By the early 1900s, the Basel mission schools had become de facto institutions of the colonial government.[95] Apparently most students did not lament the passing of relative autonomy of the mission schools. In practical terms, the anglicization of the curriculum expanded their economic and political options. Moreover, as the colonial government began to establish itself as the main patron of African education by asserting its political and financial authority, Christianity became less of a prerequisite for mission or Western education. For example, when in 1913, the government opened a new school in Sunyani, northeast of Kroboland along the west bank of the Volta, and posted the following notice in all nearby villages:

> The education given by the government does not make it necessary for you to change your religion, as the missionary schools demand; the boys will attend the school to learn how to read and write, count and all practical things, and nevertheless remain faithful to their religion and traditions.[96]

The Basel Missionary Society, along with other missionary groups, had lost its monopoly over education and with it an important tool for gaining converts.

Western education produced a more stratified society—educated and non-educated, literate and non-literate—while Christianity challenged the religious world of the Krobo. For some, Christianity offered another alternative to traditional religious systems and Islam, which was increasing in the Volta District, because Moslems had settled at Kpong and Akuse during the last quarter of the nineteenth century.

In some communities, including Christiansborg where the European population was largest and the seat of the colonial government, by the first decade of the twentieth century it was fashionable to be baptized.[97] Many African merchants, claimed to be Christians, regardless of whether they were baptized or not, for socio-political reasons—it was good business.

By the late 1880s little work was conducted on Sundays by either Christians or non-Christians. Although missionaries called Sunday a day of worship, the observance of that actually owed more to the fact that colonial authorities and European traders did not work Sunday and schools were closed. Christian holidays, such as Christmas and Easter were also observed by many non-Christian Krobo, but in a traditional manner.

Material Impact of Mission Education

Although the Krobo farmers continued their search for additional huzas, their success in the commercialization of palm oil and other food crops inevitably increased their ability to afford imported goods. In the beginning of the nineteenth century they wanted practical items, such as cotton cloth, cooking accountrements, European-made farming tools, and weapons. By the time of Odonkor Azu, some Krobo including the konor began to wear selected European clothing; Konor Odonkor Azu favored a red jacket and a top hat, according to mission reports in the 1860s. By the last quarter of the century some Krobo had begun to build relatively large houses, partially furnished with European styled furniture, such as beds, dressers, and mirrors. Glasses replaced wooden bowls, and knives and forks appeared in greater regularity, along with various styles of European made shoes, sandals, clothing, and jewelry, imported spirits, imported food items especially, bread, milk, tea, sardines and biscuits. And as the Krobo economy shifted from barter to cash, profits derived from palm oil and later cocoa were used increasingly to purchase large amounts of consumer goods (food and drink) in the celebration of births, marriages, naming ceremonies, marriages, the Dipo ceremony, burials, confirmations, baptisms and even the induction of catechists and teachers. On the eve of the forced departure of the Basel Missionary Society by the British government in 1914, Rev. B. Groh wrote: "Heathenism walks in modern dress, with a different character than even ten years ago."[98]

The Basel missionaries and their African artisans transformed the architectural landscape in Kroboland. Houses began to be constructed of mortared stone, not of mud as before; there were windows with glass, floors of stone or wood, and corrugated tin roofs. Lockable doors appeared for the sake of style, not in response to a rise in theft; kitchens were built inside the house, and walls were whitewashed inside and out. Along with multiple huzas was added the large European styled and furnished house, with of course a son educated by missionaries or government schools. The materials needed to build and furnish a Christian or Western-style house were imported.

The three most impressive structures that combined these innovations were the chapel in Odumase, the school, and Sakite's residence. The chapel was first constructed in the 1860s by mission trained artisans under the direction of Johannes Zimmermann. After a fire, it was rebuilt and enlarged in 1872. Still the center of Krobo Christianity, the chapel is strategically located about fifty yards north of the Manya konor's residence. The Basel mission's first primary school for Krobo boys, constructed in the early 1880s, lay to the west of the chapel.

Of all the buildings constructed by mission-trained artisans using local building materials, Sakite's residence was the most impressive. This Mediterranean-style two-story stone residence also functioned as a place of audience for the more important figures visiting the konor and a court, and its courtyard was where "durbars" (public gatherings) were held. It had four large rooms upstairs, including the main hall, three rooms on the ground floor, and a balcony that ran the full length of the southwest side.

It is evident that Krobo society in the second half of the nineteenth century was developing and changing because of and in response to changes in the regional political environment and economic opportunities. Missionaries were responsible for a significant number of these changes, especially in education, building technology, and the rise of a Christian community. But the key point is how Krobo managed to use the missionary factor to enhance individual fortunes and how major figures (Manya konors) encouraged and used these developments for their own benefit and to the material and political advantage of the Krobo generally. In a radically changing late-nineteenth-century Gold Coast, the Krobo managed to hold to traditional political, religious, and social values. By 1914 this was evident to the Basel missionaries. The conversion of a member of the royal family, the konor, or even women had not changed significantly the Dipo ceremony's importance. It remained the single most important religious ceremony for the Krobo. Krobo life was merely compartmentalized to accommodate both Christian teachings and traditional teachings. When the Basel Missionaries left in 1914 the impact of Christianity was unmistakable. Kroboland was the center of mission education, it had the highest per capita number of students (male and female) of any other group in the Volta District, both its konors were Christians, there were mission-trained artisans throughout Kroboland. Yet the Krobo retained all those elements of their pre-Christian era: the religious ceremonies; the religious importance of the Krobo Mountain, traditional marriage, naming and burial ceremonies, and polygamy. Kroboland was culturally divided, but not to the extent that the divisions were disruptive. Christians and non-Christians co-existed in relative harmony. The missionary factor assisted also in the formal imposition of colonial rule, not only because of the introduction of European (Christian) values, but also by the support of the crowning of one of their own, catechist-teacher Emmanuel Mate Kole, as konor in 1892.

9

CONCLUSION

The evolution of the Krobo from a numerically small, relatively insignificant member of the Adangme-speaking peoples of the eastern region of the Gold Coast is remarkable. The history of the Krobo is both the study of the incorporation into that society of people of disparate backgrounds and how the Krobo used or more correctly manipulated their unique concept of land ownership, the huza, to their political and economic advantage.

There are essentially four main periods or eras of Krobo-Adangme historical development prior to the full imposition of British colonial rule in the last decade of the nineteenth century. These periods are the migration (c. 800 to c. 1400), the period of acculturation and the development of Krobo ethnic identity (c. 1400 to c. 1740), the period of emergence of a secular authority competing with priestly djemeli authority (c. 1750 to the early 1800s), and the nineteenth century, with the emergence of Krobo as an economic-cum-political force.

The first period experienced the migration of groups of Adangme families into the Accra plains and the initial settlement of the Krobo Mountain (*Klo-yo*). The second period is characterized by the arrival of additional Adangme and Ewe in the Krobo settlement, who brought about significant socio-political change in which the distinctive features of Krobo culture were created that set them apart from other Adangme groups. As part of this process the proto-Susui immigrants introduced a powerful new deity, Nana Klowek, through which the Dipo ceremony, the crucial integrative institution of Krobo society, was controlled. This was also the period when the Akweno and the Susui clans gained control of the most influential position within the ruling theocratic oligarchy, namely the Okumoship and the priesthood of Nana Kloweki.

165

The third era began in the early eighteenth century after the first seven clans of the Krobo had been formed—Manya, Bonya, Susi, Akweno, Djebiam, Dom, and Piengua. It was a period of strong Akan influences marked by the arrival of significant numbers of Denkyira and Akyem immigrants. These Denkyira Krobo were segregated from the existing mountain settlements and settled at Bose, later renamed Yilo. Their presence demanded a new system of government which in turn set off the second major period of structural change among the Krobo, in which the older Dose Krobo (Manya) community was able to exert political control over the recent immigrants. The failure of the Dose (Manya) Krobo society and its theocratic based structure fully to control the Bose resulted in the emergence of two politically separate Krobo societies—the Manya and the Yilo. The latter consisted of six subclans: Ogome, Bonya, Nyewe, Buna, Okpe, and Plau. Thus, it was during the third era of early Krobo history that the theocratic oligarchy's authority began to decline as the result of the rise of the konor or paramount chief.

In the late eighteenth century the Krobo began a series of radical and rapid economic changes which were brought about by the adoption of the huza system of land tenure and the commercialization of palm oil for export. Throughout the nineteenth and well into the twentieth century, it was the huza and palm oil, followed by cocoa, that helped to determine the modern Krobo state. Huza farms and villages became the single most identifiable cultural characteristic of the Krobo by the last quarter of the nineteenth century. The peaceful acquisition of huzas increased Krobo contact with surrounding peoples and established new symbiotic economic relations with all their neighbors including Europeans, traders, colonial officials, and missionaries.

Within Krobo society the new economic opportunities of the period also increased the political and economic separation between the Manya and the Yilo, primarily because Manya konors Odonkor Azu and Sakite led in the commercialization of palm oil and other food crops and supported closer ties with Europeans-traders, colonial officials, and missionaries, while the Yilo did not.

Whereas there are many specifics of the evolution of early Krobo society which are not shared by other members of the Adangme language group, one can make a significant number of comparisons. First it should be recalled that the traditions of migration are not Krobo but Adangme. A separate and distinct Krobo history does not begin until the settlement of the Krobo Mountain after the thirteenth or fourteenth centuries. The date of the arrival of the proto-Krobo on their mountain settlement occurred after the settlements at Lolovor on the Accra plains. Even after the Adangme had established permanent settlements beyond the Volta River, non-Adangme peoples continued to have an impact upon Adangme societies. For example, Ewe influences were greatest among the Adangme settlements along the lower Volta and at Ada, whereas the Osudoku (Osu), who at the beginning of the eighteenth century fled to a new location just east of Christiansborg Castle, were strongly influenced by the Ga.

Among all Adangme, the creation of war-chiefs, called "konors" among the Krobo, "banahene" among the Ningo, and "mantse" among most other Adangme, was a response to the increased political and military pressures of the seventeenth and eighteenth centuries, and were indicative of the increased size and stratification of Adangme societies. The creation of paramount chiefs marked the beginning of the shift of authority away from the theocratic oligarchy. The development of these secular institutions followed an established pattern among most of the Adangme. First, Akan refugees and immigrants, usually Akwamu, Denkyira, Akuapem, and Akyem, were either permitted or invited to settle among the Adangme. Second, after a brief period, less than a century, these now-assimilated Akan strangers who provided the initial konors had managed to usurp authority from the various theocratic oligarchical rulers. For reasons which are not clear as yet, this shift from priestly to secular authority did not occur among the Ningo, where the banahene remains subordinate to the priests.

Adangme states along the coast in the seventeenth century experienced an economic revolution, the result of direct trade with Europeans. It was not until the late eighteenth century that this economic revolution began to affect the inland Adangme state of Krobo. By the 1780s, the Krobo began to alter their entire society as they began their peaceful occupation of lands north and north-west of the Krobo Mountain where they established new farms and villages along the Akuapem Mountains and at Kpong, Akuse, and Amedica along the Volta River.

By the end of the nineteenth century the eastern region, especially the Volta district with its capital at Odumase, led in export trade statistics for the Gold Coast. In 1880 when Odumase, the village of the Manya konor, became the administrative center of colonial administration for the Volta district, this not only benefitted the Manya Krobo but enhanced the prestige of all Adangme chiefdoms. And as Kpong, Akuse, Amedica, Bisa, and Asesewa became centers of domestic and export trading activity in the district, all the districts' major European firms such as F. and A. Swanzy and Alex Mill Bros., and W. B. Ocansy, and Tetty Caesar, both Ada men, stationed their agents at Kpong, Akuse, Amedica, Bisa, and Asesewa as well as at Ningo, La, and Prampram. Finally, by the third quarter of the nineteenth century, certain Krobo villages, especially Odumase, became the center of missionary activity for all Adangmeland including the lower Volta. Mission education thrived in Kroboland, attracting other Adangme, Ewe, and Akan peoples. Thereafter, Odumase became the mission education and skills learning center of the Volta district as well as the district's commercial and administrative center. Mission-educated Krobo youths were in a particularly advantageous position to benefit from these new economic opportunities. It is not surprising, therefore, that when Emmanuel Mate Kole became konor of the Manya Krobo in 1892, he was the first mission educated and first Christian paramount chief from the eastern region.

Granted that most if not all Adangme societies experienced a net economic gain during the closing years of the nineteenth century, it was the Manya Krobo who had become the dominant political and economic force among the Krobo and the most important people of the southeastern region. This advantageous position had been achieved in part because the Manya konors had pursued policies which successfully led to mutually profitable ties with Europeans, the commercialization of palm oil and other food crops, and the continued accumulation of huza farms. Equally important, the konors, including Emmanuel Mate Kole, took advantage of the missionary presence to acquire for their people access to the benefits of Western education. Eventually Krobo independence was superseded by British colonial rule, but the Manya Krobo continued to maintain their Western educational and economic advantage over the Yilo Krobo, as well as over other Adangme during the twentieth century.

APPENDICES

Appendix A
RULERS OF THE YILO KROBO
FROM THE EARLY 1700S

S. Odonkor	Padi Akrobetto III/ G.N.A. III	Family
1. Saki	Saki	Ogome
2. Padi Oketeku	Padi Oketeku c. middle and 2nd half of 18th century	Akrobetto
3. Dawute	Dawute	Akrobetto
4. Dawunor Amponsa	Dawunor Amponsa	Akrobetto
5. Narhkitse Atiapa	Narhkitse Atiapa	Akrobetto
6. Ashong Odjam	Ashong Odjam	Akrobetto
7. Ologo Patu	Ologo Patu, c. 1836-1869	Akrobetto
8. Noi Anoba Sasraku	Noi Anoba Sasraku, 1869-1874	Akrobetto
9. Tetteh Akrobetto I	Tetteh Akrobetto I, 1876-1908	Akrobetto
10. Godfried Kofi Ologo III, 1908-1917	Godfried Kofi Ologo II	Nuer
11. Tetteh Kole Ologo (Regent)	Tetteh Kole Ologo (Regent)	Ologo
12. Akrobetto II 1918	Kewsi Donkor Akrobetto II	Akrobetto
13. Tetteh Ologo IV 1920-1925	Tetteh Ologo	Ologo
14. Nuer Tetteh 1925-1927; 1930	Nuer Tetteh Ologo V	Nuer
15.	Tettey Korley (regent) 1930	Ologo
16.	Nuer Ologo V 1930-55	Nuer
17.	Padi Keteku Akrobetto III 1955-1978	Akrobetto
18.	Narh Ologo VI 1978-	Akrobetto

Appendix B
RULERS OF MANYA/DOSE KROBO
FROM THE EARLY 1700S

Noa Azu/S. Odonkor	Konor E. Mate Kole	*Okumo*
1. Madja	Madja	Madja
2.	Late Odoi	
3.	Akwe Tetteh Yome	Akwe Tetteh Yome
4.	Netenor	Netenor
5.	Ba Asare I	
6.	Nanote Asare	Nanote
7.	Okremeno	
8.	Ziome	Ziome
9.	Ba Asare II	
10.	Sinai	Sinai
11. Akutei Gbankobo	Odamkoto	Gbankobo
12. Ba Dua	Tsakate	
13.	Aniapima	Aniapima
14.	Muala Okumsra d. 1835 (Tsakati Lala) **(konor)**	
15. Odonkor Azu	Odonkor Azu 1835-1867	
16. (Ahmola) Sakite	(Abiatse) Sakitey 1867-1892	
17. Emmanuel Mate Kole	E. Mate Kole (1892-1939)	
18. Azzu Mate Kole (1939-1990)	Azzu Mate Kole	

The early part of this list is telescoped with Madja belonging to the origin of the Krobo settlement and the "rulers" 2-13 belonging to the eighteenth and early nineteenth centuries.

Appendix C
KROBO SETTLEMENTS ALONG THE
AKUAPEM FOOTHILLS, c. 1860s

Manya Krobo		Yilo Krobo	
Subtribe	Village	Subtribe	Village
Djebiam	Odumase Abudi Atuah Agomenya	Nyewe	Abokobi Trom Planey Sra
Piengua	Lom Amadam Yoquano	Bunase	Adjipo Kotokoli Somanya
Dom	Muchosisie Konopeah Asinty Nyasso	Ogome	Sradom Cromonyah Askoli
Akweno	Otalinya Kenglish Yoquano	Bonya	Sradom Akonyah Saloshi Pemoe
Manya	Tando Nawasipo Achonya	Plau	Pemoe Prapom
Susui	Ofuanseh Whapeh Manapo	Okpe	Tochonyah Somanya Kpeno Adjipo

Basel missionaries, the first Europeans to note that the "Krobo towns away from the Mountain, belong to the adjacent, vast extended Otschi [Twi] language, thus giving evidence that the Krobos have moved in their first settlements." "Kroboneger," (1867), p. 23. Dickson has noted the complete list of towns which are the homes of the various clans and subtribes. The first of these were Noaso, Somanya, and Odumase around the turn of the nineteenth century. By the 1830s and

1840s, with the accelerated rise of palm oil for export and huza farms established as far as fifteen miles to the west at the Pawnpawm River, all Krobo subtribes probably had homes along the Akuapem foothills.

Appendix D
PRINCIPAL TRADING FACTORIES
VOLTA DISTRICT 1889

	Firm	Agent	Nationality
Manya Krobo			
Odumase	F. & A. Swanzy	W.H. Williams	British
Akuse/Amedica	Bremen Factory	Weber	German
	Basel Trading Co.	J. Zimmermann	Swiss
	W.H. Ocansy	W.H. Ocansy	Ada
	G.B. Williams	A.C. France	Ada
	M.T. Lomoh	M.T. Lomoh	Ada
	Thomas Adaddy	Thomas Adaddy	Akwamu
Kpong	F. & A. Swanzy	W.H. Williams	British
	Alex Miller Bros.	Melnnes	British
	Bremen Factory	Webber	German
	W.B. Ocansy	W.B. Ocansy	Ada
	Basel Trading Co.	J. Zimmermann	Swiss
	B.G. Williams	G.B. Williams	Ada
	Sabbady	Sabbady	Ewe
	Joseph Tette	Joseph Tette	Ada
	Agbeschi	Agbeschi	Ewe
Yilo Krobo			
Sra	F. & A. Swanzy	W.H. Williams	British
Somanya	Alex Miller Bros.	Melnnes	British
	Sabbady	Sabbady	Ewe
	Agbeschi	Agbeschi	Ewe
Troon	Alex Miller Bros	Melnnes	British
	G.B. Williams	G.B. Williams	Ada

The Basel Mission Factory and Swanzy factories were established in December 1879; Miller Bros. (Akuse) in February 1884; the Ocansey factories in December 1889. C.O. 879/19 Commander R. Murray Rumsey, R.N. "General Report on the River Volta District, June 1882;" *Papers Relating to H.M. Colonial Possesions, Command Paper 5249-5, LXXII, 1888*, 177-79.

Appendix E
EUROPEAN MISSIONARIES STATIONED IN KROBOLAND 1858-1913

Name	Year Posted	Name	Year Posted
Johannes Zimmermann	1858	Theodora Josenhans	1889
J. Laisse	1858	Eunnike Mader	1887
Carl Aldinger	1859	E. Zwar	1887
C. Zimmermann	1860	Louise Spah	1888
Jakob Heck	1860	Dr. Alfred Erkhardt	1891
Marie Heck	1860	Christian Kolle	1891
M. Ros	1863	Adam Mischtich	1892
Robert Klaus	1864	Clara Finkh	1892
Jacob Weib	1865	Hanna Bauer	1892
Katharina Weib	1868	Luise Zerweek	1893
Johannes Kopp	1869		
Rosine Kopp		Arnold Deuber	1894
A. Haberle	1870		
N. Weber	1870		
Carl Schonfeld	1872		
Mathias Klaiber		Hanna Brugger	1896
Rosine Klaiber	1874		
Nathaniel Deiterle	1876	Dr. F. Hey	1897
Rudolf Furrer	1877	Sophie Im. Hof	1898
Elizabeth Furrer	1877	Emma Nothwang	1899
Jakob Weiss	1877	Bertha Guginbuhl	1900
Lydia Muh	1879	W. Dietrich	1903
Lydia Bender		Emilia Krautter	1903
		Adolf Berner	1904
August Buttner	1883	W. Zittel	1906
Heinrich Hurlimann	1883	Andrew Holm	1908
Heinrich Hurtmann	1885	Fredrich Ruff	1910
Henrich Glattli	1885	F. Rentz	1913
Gotthilf Maeger	1886	Otilie Shuhmacher	1913
Gottlob F. Josenhans	1887		

Source: *Jahresberichte*, Basel Mission Archives; Schott, *Basel Mission*, Appendix I and II; and Odjidja, *Mustard*, p. 71.

Appendix F
AFRICAN ASSISTANTS TO THE BASEL MISSIONARIES
AMONG THE KROBO 1857-1912

Name	Year Posted	Name	Year Posted
Paul Fleischer	1857	Sam N. Agbozo	1892
Thomas I. Akwetei	1858	John Notei	1894
Carl C. Reindorf	1858	Gottfried Medegbor	1894
Christian Obobi	1858	Windried Odjidja*	1894
T. B. Kwatei	1858	Sam Djane	1894
A. Briandt	1858	Christian Fleischer	1895
Peter Nyako Azu*	1863	S. Marshall	1896
Noa A. Azu*	1863	Emmanuel Tetteh	1897
Akutei Azu*	1863	G. Kpabitey	1898
Jakobo Nikoi	1870	N. Kuma	1898
Eammanuel T. Aku	1870	F. Ashie	1898
Solomon Kudjiju*	1871	Andrea Mate Saki*	1899
Carl Quist	1871	T. Sowa*	1899
Fred Larsen	1874	Charles Djaba*	1900
A. Kodji*	1874	E. Oko	1901
W. Buckman	1874	P. Djoleto	1902
Joh Adam	1877	John Koi	1903
Petro Mensah	1878	Andrews Holm	1903
Peter Sonne	1881	Sal. Kodji	1906
Emmanuel Mate Kole*	1881	Henock Azu*	1906
Nathan Adshie	1881	Christian Holm	1906
Andreas Padi*	1883	Jon Nikoi	1907
Is. Odoi	1885	F. Addo	1908
Emmanuel Odonkor	1885	Ioel Sonne	1908
Emmanuel Wentum	1885	John Teye	1908
Noah Aguae Azu*	1887	Ich. Kodji*	1908
Ebenezer Kofi	1887	Henry Hammond	1908
Abraham N. Azu*	1887	W. Neman	1908
Joshua Bartimeo	1889	John A. Dadi	1909
Nathaniel Date	1891	Samuel S. Odonkor	1910
Emmanuel Akuetei	1891	Robert Amano	1912
Joseph Boi	1891	Alexander C. Apo*	1912
William Quartey	1892	James P. Kofi*	1912

Source: *Jahresberichte*, Basel Mission Archives; Schott, *Basel Mission*, Appendix I and II; and Odjidja, *Mustard*, p. 72.

Appendix G
KROBO BASEL MISSION STATIONS
1858-1915

In Manya Krobo	In Yilo Krobo
Odumase (Main Station)	Sra
Manyakpongnor	Huhunya
Akuse	Kurakan
Kpong	Obawale
Bisa	Opersika
Anyaboni	Asekesu
Sekesua	Oterkpolu
Sesiamang	Trom
Adwenso	Bamanase
Akohia	Okpesi
Asesewa	Obenyemi
Akole	Obodaso
Ada	Kpemo
Bana	

In the Ga District, which included the Krobo, Odumase was the center of Basel missionary activity, as is evident by the fact that the first Synod of the Ga District was held in Odumase in 1910. *95: Funfundneunzigster*, p. 55. Akole and Trom declined in importance in the 1880s; by 1897 Trom was "dead—there were no personnel there." *94: Vierundneunzigster*, p. 124. Similarly Okepsi was "vacant" by 1910 as the Krobo population shifted farther into the forest in to cultivate cocoa and oil palm plantations or shifted to larger mission stations. *95: Funfundneunzigster*, pp. 62-65.

NOTES

Chapter 1

1. The other Adangme (Adangbe)-speaking people are the Prampram (Glugbla), the Ningo, the Ada, the La, the Shai (Se) and the Osudoku. *Population Census of Ghana 1970*, Vol. 2 (Accra: Government Printing Company, June 1972), pp. 264-89.
2. Robin Horton, "Stateless Societies in the History of West Africa," in *History of West Africa*, Vol. 1, ed. J. F. A. Ajayi and M. Crowder (New York: Columbia University Press, 1972), pp. 78-119.
3. The only exceptions are A. K. Quarcoo, "Processes of Social Control Among the Shai (Adangme)" (M.A. thesis, University of Ghana, Legon, Institute of African Studies, 1965); Irene Quay (Odotei), "The Ga and their Neighbours 1600-1742" (Ph.D. thesis, University of Ghana, Legon, 1971).
4. For a discussion of the state of Ghanaian history as determined by various scholars see *Proceedings of the Seminar on Ghanaian Historiography and Historical Research, May 20-22, 1976* (Legon: Department of History, University of Ghana, 1977).
5. *Proceedings*, 83.
6. "Krobo" or more correctly "Kro Obo So Fo," shortened to "Krobofo" (Rock or Mountain Dwellers) is the name still given these mountain dwellers, by the dominant group in the region, the Akan.
7. See chapters 2 and 3.
8. "Klo-yo" is of Akan origin.
9. Kwamina Dickson, *A Historical Geography of Ghana* (Cambridge: Cambridge University Press, 1969), pp. 18-20. For a precise location of the Krobo see Map NB 31-9, Keta,

Ghana, Series G504 Army Map Service Edition 1-AMS (First printing 9-60).

10. Jakob Heck, "Feindesliebe eines Negers," *Der Evangeslisches Heidenboten* (1849): 11.

11. Johannes K. Auer, "Die Traehotschaft aus West-Afrika," *Der Evangeslisches Heidenboten* 8/2 (1855): 146.

12. The Osudoku on the mountain of the same name have yet to be studied. There is limited archaeological data. Furthermore, Mt. Yogaga does not appear to have been settled, at least not by the Adangme.

13. The author also found both paths difficult to climb on several occasions in 1973-1974 and 1983-1984.

14. Auer, "Die Traehotschaft," 146.

15. The religious importance of these and other rocks and the *Dipo* ceremony will be discussed in chapters 2 and 3.

16. The origin of the Bose settlement will be discussed in chapters 2 and 3.

17. Social divisions among the Krobo will be discussed in chapter 2.

18. Auer, "Die Traehotschaft," p. 148.

19. Johannes Zimmermann, "Erfahrungen und Hoffnungen in Odumase," *Der Evangelisches Heidenboten* (1864): 89.

20. Hugo Huber, *The Krobo: Traditional Social and Religious Life of a West African People* (St. Augustin: The Antropos Institute, 1963), p. 35.

21. Kwame Daaku, *Trade and Politics on the Gold Coast 1600-1720: A Study of the African Reaction to European Trade* (London: Clarendon Press, 1970), pp. 1-20; Philip Curtin, *The Atlantic Slave Trade: A Census* (Madison: Wisconsin University Press, 1969), pp. 95-203; John Fynn, *Asante and Its Neighbours, 1700 to 1807* (London: Longman, 1971); Ivor Wilks, "The Rise of the Akwamu Empire, 1650-1710," *Transactions of the Historical Society of Ghana*, 3/2 (1957): 99-136.

22. The names of these rocks are: *Tsayi, Hogbate, Anikaka, Dsadsawu, Aku, Itroloku, Lanmako, Alamite, Okpe-ko, Nyew-eko, Lamisako,* and *Akweko.* Noa A. Azu, "Adangme (Adangbe) History," *The Gold Coast Review* 2 (1926): 246.

23. Johannes Auer, "Ein Ausflug von Akropong nach Odumase," *Der Evangelisches Heidenboten* (1859): 39.

24. Discussed in some detail in chapter 4.

25. Various aspects of the *huza* are discussed in chapters 2, 3, and 5.
26. Huber, *The Krobo*, p. 42.
27. Noa A. Azu, "Adangbe (Adangme) History," *Gold Coast Review* 2 (1926): 239-70; 3 (1927): 89-116; 4 (1928): 3-30.
28. Thomas Odonkor, *The Rise of the Krobo* (Legon: Institute of African Studies, 1966).
29. Tema: Ghana Publishing Corporation, 1971.
30. Margaret J. Field spent more than twenty years during the 1930s and again beginning in 1955 working among the Ga and Adangme. She initially came to the Gold Coast as a sociologist then returned to Britain and earned a medical degree and later a degree in psychology. According to Konor Azzu Mate Kole, she was the first European woman to climb the Krobo Mountain.
31. Hugo Huber provided the author with a copy of this unpublished manuscript.
32. D. A. Sutherland, "The Manya Krobo State" (Unpub. MS, 1931); GNA ADM 11/1124 F. G. Crowther, "Memorandum on Great Ningo"; S. W. Saxton, "Historical Survey of the Shai People," *The Gold Coast Review* 1/1 (1925): 126-45; Roger E. Page, "The Osu and Kindred Peoples," *The Gold Coast Review* 1 (1925): 67-70.
33. R. J. H. Pogucki, *Gold Coast Land Tenure*, Vol. 2, *Report on Land Tenure in Adangme Customary Law* (Accra: Government Printing Office, 1955).
34. Published by the Basel Mission.
35. M. E. Kropp, *Comparative African Wordlist: Ga, Adangbe, and Ewe (Lome)* (Legon: Institute of African Studies, 1972).
36. O. H. Hymes, "Glottochronology," *Current Anthropology* 1/1 (January 1960): 113-18; Robert G. Armstrong, "Glottochronology and African Linguistics," *Journal of African History* 3/2 (1962); C. Ehret, *Southern Nilotic History* (Evanston: Northwestern University Press, 1970).
37. Paul Ozanne, "Adwuku: Fortified Hill-Top Village," *Ghana Notes and Queries* 7 (January 1965): 6-8; "Ladoku: An Early Town Near Prampram," *Ghana Notes and Queries* 7 (January 1965): 6-7.
38. Rigsarkivet, København *Relationer om Forholdene i Guinea, 1733-1748*. Breve og Okumeter fra Guinea 1732-1745.

39. The author is grateful for the assistance of Professor Irene Qaye Odotei in translating some Danish archival material.

40. In 1976 the United Africa Company archives were opened to scholars. The records of the Alex Miller Brothers and Frank and Andrew Swanzy are deposited there.

Chapter 2

1. Migration histories were especially popular in the early 1960s, when many subsaharan nations gained their independence. B. A. Ogot's *History of the Southern Luo* (Cambridge: Cambridge University Press, 1961) became for over a decade the model used by many historians, especially of East Africa. Kennell Jackson has expressed criticism of this almost "formulaic approach" in his "Akamba Traditions" (paper presented at the Pacific Coast Branch meeting of the American Historical Association, August 11, 1979, Hawaii). West African historians have generally paid less attention to migration.

2. A. Adu Boahen, "Ghana Before the Coming of Europeans," *Ghana Social Science Journal* 4/2 (November 1977): 93-95; Francis Agbodeka, *Ghana in the Twentieth Century* (Accra: Ghana University Press, 1972), pp. 1-3. Also see J. M. Stewart, "Akan History, Some Linguistic Evidence," *Ghana Notes and Queries* 9 (1966): 54-58; A. Adu Boahen, "The Origins of the Akan," *Ghana Notes and Queries* 9 (1966): 3-10.

3. Noa A. Azu, "Adangbe (Adangme) History," *Gold Coast Review* 2 (1926): 242. M. E. Kropp Dakubu has attempted to identify the actual places visited and stopped between *Sameh* and Togalogo on the Accra plain. M. E. Kropp Dakubu, "Linguistic Pre-History and Historical Reconstruction: The Ga-Adangme Migrations," *Transactions of the Historical Society of Ghana* 13/1 (1972): 87-111.

4. Azu, "Adangbe" (1926), p. 242. Carl C. Reindorf, *The History of the Gold Coast and Ashantee* (Dublin: Browne and Nolan, 1966), p. 47; Donald A. Sutherland, "A History of the Manya Krobo State" (Unpublished manuscript, 1934), p. 10; W. J. Argyle, *The Fon of Dahomey: A History and Ethnography of the Old Kingdom* (Oxford: Clarendon Press, 1966), pp. 1-13;

I. A. Akinjogbin, *Dahomey and Its Neighbours 1708-1818* (Cambridge: Cambridge University Press, 1967), pp. 8-38.

5. Azu, "Adangbe" (1926), p. 242.
6. Odonkor, Thomas H. *The Rise of the Krobos*. Translated by Rev. S. S. Odonkor. Edited by E. O. Apronti. Legon: Institute of African Studies, University of Ghana, 1971, p. 17.
7. Paul Ozanne, "Ghana" in *The African Iron Age*, ed. P. Shinne, (London: Oxford University Press, 1971), p. 33. Merrick Posnansky, "Archaeological and Linguistic Reconstruction in Ghana," in *The Archaeological and Linguistic Reconstruction of African History*, ed. Christopher Ehret and Merrick Posnansky (Berkeley: University of California Press, 1987), pp. 256-66.
8. Paul Ozanne, "Ladoku: An Early Town," *Ghana Notes and Queries* 7 (January 1965): 6-7. Dr. James Anquandah's excavations in the summer of 1983 in the Shai hills provide the first radio-carbon dates, which place the sites some 200 years earlier than Ozanne's dates. Personal communication with Anquandah, June 1984.
9. Ozanne, "Ladoku," 8: 4-5.
10. The specific effects on the Krobo of these essentially Akan wars (including the Akyem, the Akuapem, the Akwamu, the Jakiti, the Apirede, and the Kotrepe) will be discussed in chapters 3 and 4. See also Wilks, "The Rise."
11. The assistance of Professor Christopher Ehret in preparing this chart is gratefully acknowledged. For a similar linguistic chart and discussion of migration see Kropp Dakubu, "Linguistic Pre-History," p. 111 and M. E. Kropp Dakubu, "The Peopling of Southern Ghana: A Linguistic Viewpoint," in *The Archaeological and Linguistic Reconstruction of African History*, ed. Christopher Ehret and Merrick Posnansky (Berkeley: University of California Press, 1982), pp. 245-55. The formula for employing a comparative wordlist is provided in D. H. Hymes, "Recent Trends in Glottochronology," *Current Anthropology* 1/1 (January 1960): 9-12.
12. Margaret J. Field, "The Krobo Constitution in Relation to the Nyewe-Ogome Dispute and the Significance of Priestly Stools" (Unpublished manuscript, May 1942). Odonkor, *The*

Rise, p. 2; Sutherland, "History," p. 10, Huber, *The Krobo*, p. 15.

13. Azu, "Adangbe" (1926); p. 2. Odonkor, *The Rise*, p. 2; Huber, *The Krobo*, p. 15.

14. Cited in Huber, *The Krobo*, p. 18. Other "Klama" songs and proverbs also recall past Adangme deeds, including Ladoku: "In the olden days it was at Ladoku where they traded with palm oil; they trade with palm oil at Nigo; they traded with palm oil at Tema. In the olden days at Ladoku." Additional historical analysis of the "Klama" is needed. Enoch Azu, *Adangbe Historical and Proverbial Songs* (Accra: Government Printing Office, 1929).

15. Akyem Abuakwa-Akwamu wars: 1659, 1682, 1699, 1700, 1719, 1722, 1723, 1730; Akyem Abuakwa-Asante wars: 1702, 1707, 1717, 1742, 1749, 1764, 1765, 1772, 1811, 1814, 1816, 1824, and 1826. Robert Addo-Fening, "Akyem-Abuakwa, c. 1874-1943: A Study of the Imposition of Missionary Activity and Colonial Rule on a Traditional State" (Ph.D. diss., University of Ghana, Legon, 1980), p. 324. Also see chapters 3 and 4.

16. See chapter 3 and Huber, *The Krobo*, pp. 242-43.

17. Huber, *The Krobo*, Appendix I, pp. 297-99; Sutherland, "History," pp. 30-32, 35, 41, 50-51.

18. Huber, *The Krobo*, pp. 25-26.

19. Except for the selection of paramount chiefs (konors); Nyewe is the Yilo's royal clan, and Djebiam-Nam that of the Manya.

20. Modified in recent times to *wetcho-Matse*.

21. Some of the kinship groups were originally Akan, hence matrilineal.

22. Huber, *The Krobo*, pp. 29-31.

23. Huber, *The Krobo*, p. 242.

24. The introduction of *Nana Kloweki* fostered the creation of an elaborate supportive priesthood, the *djemeli*.

25. Field, "Krobo Constitution"; Interviews with Konors Akrobetto and Mate Kole, January 15 and February 4, respectively, 1974.

26. Field, "Krobo Constitution"; Huber, *The Krobo*, pp. 17, 242; Sutherland, "History," pp. 11-13.

27. Interview with Reverend B. D. Tegaga, Pastor of the Presbyterian Church, Odumase-Krobo, December 10, 1973; and The Very Reverend E. M. C. Odjidja, Moderator of the Presbyterian Church retired, December 15, 1974.
28. Tegaga, Interview December 12, 1973; Huber, *The Krobo*, pp. 242-43 and Appendix I; Sutherland, "History," pp. 34-35.
29. Azu, "Adangbe History" (1926), pp. 244-45; Huber, *The Krobo*, pp. 244, 298.
30. Odonkor, *The Rise*, pp. 52-58; Sutherland, "History," pp. 58-60; Azu, "Adangbe," (1926), pp. 246-48; Gold Coast Colony Laws, Vol. III, Chapter 112, Sec. 4: "Native Customs Ordinance"; Huber, *The Krobo*, pp. 165-92, 243-45.
31. Huber, *The Krobo*, p. 243.
32. Quarcoo, "Process of Social Control." Donald A. Sutherland "Report on Enquiry into the Alleged Destoolment of Larbi Agbo II."
33. Nene Azzu Mate Kole (Konor), "The Historical Background of Krobo Customs," *Transactions of the Historical Society of the Gold Coast* (1955), p. 134.
34. "Okumo" appears to have been borrowed from the Akan word "Okumfo - priest." Huber, *The Krobo*, pp. 242-43.
35. Huber, *The Krobo*, p. 242.
36. Huber, *The Krobo*, p. 189.
37. The "okumo" is reputedly to have carried a "killing-staff" with which he directed the executioner. "Okumo is coming on the way, with his killing-staff, Run quick! Okumo is coming." Huber, *The Krobo*, p. 242.
38. Circumcision was one of the most distinguishing factors between the Adangbe (including the Krobo) and their neighbors and enemies the Akan.
39. Odonkor, *The Rise*, pp. 4-5; Azu, "Adangbe" (1926), p. 247; Sutherland, "History," pp. 11-12.
40. Field states incorrectly that the Akan among the Dom are Denkyira refugees; in fact they are Akyem. Field, "Krobo Constitution"; Azu, "Adangbe" (1926), p. 249; Odonkor, *The Rise*, pp. 4-5, and 47.
41. Huber, *The Krobo*, p. 242.
42. Field, "Krobo Constitution." Noa Azu contended that the Akan element was from Akyem. Initially, the original Piengua kasi settled among the Akweno and the Susui below the

mountain on the plains, hence, much of their oral tradition was overshadowed by these two subtribes. Azu, "Adangbe" (1926), p. 249.

43. Warfare among the Krobo is headed by the priests of their respective war deities—"Nadu" for the Manya and "Kotoklo" for the Yilo. Sutherland, "History," pp. 91-93; Huber, *The Krobo*, pp. 268-73; Odonkor, *The Rise*, pp. 52-53.

44. Odonkor, *The Rise*, p. 11. According to Akyem tradition, people called Kamana were indigenous to the area around present-day Kibi, before the arrival of the Akyem. These "Kamana" were scattered from their twelve towns around the beginning of the eighteenth century. *Ghana Gazette (Extraordinary)* "Stool Lands Boundaries (Manya Krobo) Order 1953," November 27, 1959, 1585.

45. Field, "Krobo Constitution"; Sutherland, "History," p. 45; Ghana National Archives (GNA), ADM 11/1115/2. Interview with Konor Azzu Mate Kole, December 5, 1973.

46. All sources refer to this rapid influx of "Akan" immigrants as "Denkyira Krobo" or "Krobo Denkyira." In some sources "Denkyira" is apparently used to mean all Akan, including Akyem, Akwamu, Akuapem, and Denkyira. For example, Thomas Odonkor states that some of the neighboring "Akan" refugees came from the Kingdom of Denkyira when it fell. Odonkor makes it clear that there were many groups of Akan who became part of the Krobo settlements. Odonkor, *The Rise*, pp. 4-5; Azu, "Adangbe" (1926), p. 247; Noa A. Azu, "Adangbe (Adangme) History," *Gold Coast Review*, 3 (1927): 112; Huber, *The Krobo*, pp. 19, 292; Sutherland, "History," pp. 145-47; Appendix D. GNA, ADM 11/1/1117 Yilo Krobo; GNA ADM 11/1/1118 Ogome (Yilo Krobo) Native Affairs. The fact that these refugees, mostly farmers and miners, "left behind their fertile forest region and came to the dry Krobo plains," Thomas Odonkor correctly asserts, reflected the harsh political realities of the day, namely the increased instability caused by chaotic wars between various Akan groups.

47. The physical proximity of the Akyem to the Krobo and oral traditions would account for this fact.

48. Azu, "Adangbe" (1926) p. 225; Field, "Krobo Constitution";
Odonkor, *The Rise*, pp. 2-7; Huber, *The Krobo*, pp. 25, 35;
Sutherland, "History," pp. 12-13, Appendix D.
49. Huber, *The Krobo*, p. 243.
50. Azu, "Adangbe" (1927), p. 116; Odonkor, *The Rise*, pp. 5,
6-7, 54; Sutherland, "History," pp. 10-11.
51. Azu, "Adangbe" (1927), p. 116.

Chapter 3

1. L. Texeira in Egon Klemp (ed.), *Africa on Maps Dating from
the Twelfth to the Eighteenth Century* (New York: McGraw
Hill, 1970); P. de Marees, *Beschryvinghe ende Historische
Verhael van het Gout Koninckrijck van Guinea 1602*
(Gravenhage: M. Nijhoff, 1912).
2. "Relationer om Forholdene i Guinea, 1733-48." "Breve og
Gokumeter fra Guinea 1732-45." *Guineiske journaler*,
Kobenhavn.
3. Ludvig F. Rømer, *Tilforladelig Efterretning om Kysten
Guinea* (Kobenhavn: L. H. Lillies, 1750), p. 249; "Breve
Indkomme Diverse Guineiske, 1755-59," *Rigsarkivet*,
Kobenhavn; Elmina Journal, Entry for 13 April 1749, Letter
from Brunner, Accra, 13 April 1749, Furley Collection, Balme
Library, University of Ghana, Legon; Kay Larsen, *Guvernører:
Residenter, Kommandanter og Chefter* (Kobenhavn: A.
Jensen, 1940), pp. 24-25.
4. This map was originally published in 1729 (April); the 1760
edition is in Freda Wolfson, *Pageant of Ghana* (London:
Oxford University Press, 1960), p. 8.
5. Rømer, *Tilforladelig*, p. 249.
6. "Breve Indkomme Diverse Guineiske, 1755-59," *Rigsarkivet*,
Kobenhavn; Elmina Journal; Larsen, *Guvernører*, pp. 24-25.
7. There were apparently two "Dadokus." According to Paul
Ozanne, the kingdom of Ladoku was located near Prampram
in the Shai Hills (5°45'30" N, 0°05'00" E). The second
Dadoku, or La-Doku, was located near the Krobo Mountain
and, according to Noa Azu, was founded by the Las, "the last
Adangbe tribe who crossed the Volta." Drawe, its capital,
was not part of the coastal network. Azu, "Adangbe

(Adangme) History," 2 (1926): 265; Ozanne, "Ladoku," pp. 6-7.

8. Wilks, "The Rise," p. 109. Carl Reindorf noted that the Ladoku kingdom consisted of twenty-two villages about the Shi Mountain: Legbeshe, Manya, Lenodshe, Kpofu, Asmodshe, Solone, Bonase, Mapong, Dodo, Ladoku, Zoma, Abotiaa, Klepe, Nogala, Mogbien, Mla, Drawe, Laga, Kayikpo, Gblaka, Hiowe, and Kinawe. Klepkpe was the capital. Ghana National Archives (GNA) ADM 11/1115 S.N.A. 73. See also: R. E. Kea, "Akwamu-Anlo Relations c. 1750-1813," *Ghana Notes and Queries* 11 (1969): 29-63; Seth Acolatse, "Government and Politics in the Akwamu State, 1730-1930" (B.A. honors diss., University of Ghana, Legon, June 1979); A. O. Akoto, "History of Akwamu" (B.A. honors diss., University of Ghana, Legon, May 1974).

9. Fynn, *Asante*, p. 67. An example of the harshness of Akwamu rule was recorded by W. Bosman of the "Lampi [Adangme] people. [They] have a king of their own, with the title of King of Landingcour; though in reality he and his subjects (if they may be so called) depend entirely on the King of Aquamboe [Akwamu], according to whose will and pleasure he is obliged to regulate himself; for upon the least disquest, which he or his people give to those Aquamboe, they are so severly punished that the remembrance of it remains for several years." W. Bosman, *A New and Accurate Description of the Coast of Guinea* (London: St. Pauls' Church-Yard, 1705), p. 327.

10. These Akwamu refugees settled near present day Ho. Rømer, *Tilforladelig*, p. 251.

11. Ghana National Archives (GNA) ADM 11/1/404 Awuna Native Affairs, SNA No. 64/1912; N. K. Gaikpa, "History of Ada: A Quest for Security" (B.A. honors diss., University of Ghana, Legon, 1982), pp. 15-16.

12. According to Kea, this alliance lasted more than 150 years. Kea, "Akwamu-Anlo," p. 31; Wilks, "Akwamu," p. 110.

13. Marion Johnson, "Migrants' Progress," Part I, *Bulletin of the Ghana Geographical Association* 9/2 (July 1964): 1-27; Marion Johnson, "Migrants' Progress" Part II, *Bulletin of the Ghana Geographical Association* 10/1 (May 1965): 13-29.

Also see chapters 5 and 7 for a discussion of Krobo territorial expansion.

14. Addo-Fening, "Akyem-Abuakwa," chapters 2 and 3.
15. For a discussion of the economic implications of the war see chapter 4.
16. According to Kwame Arhin, many of the eighteenth century Asante wars were directed at establishing control over states formerly under the Denkyira who had been defeated by the Asante in 1701. Kwame Arhin, "The Structure of Greater Ashanti (1700-1824)," *Journal of African History* 6/8 (1967): 65-85.
17. Wilks, *Asante*, chapter 1; Fynn, *Asante*, chapter 1.
18. Arhin, "Greater Asante," pp. 76-78.
19. Arhin, "Greater Asante," p. 78.
20. Wilks, *Asante*, chapter 1.
21. Between 1659 and 1826 there were at least twenty major conflicts or wars between the Asante and Akyem Abuakwa. Addo-Fening, "Akyem-Abuakwa," p. 324.
22. Kea, "Akwamu-Anlo," p. 33; Fynn, "Asante," p. 80; Kwamena-Poh, *Government and Politics in the Akuapem State 1730-1850* (London: Longman, 1973), p. 81.
23. Kea, "Akwamu-Anlo," p. 38; Fynn, "Asante," p. 80.
24. A. Afrifa, "History of the Akyem" (unpublished manuscript, London University, School of Oriental and African Studies, n.d.).
25. Public Record Office (PRO) T70/31, David Mill, Cape Coast Castle, 30 August 1770; Azu, "Adangbe (Adangme) History," *Gold Coast Review* 3 (1927): 91.
26. PRO T70/31 W.I.C. 118, Pieter Woortman and Lefdael, El Mina, 30 August 1770; Azu, "Adangbe" (1927), p. 91.
27. Azu, "Adangbe" (1927), pp. 91-95.
28. Upon hearing of the defeat of Bana, a dismayed Asantehene Osei Kwadwo reputedly asked, "'Are the Krobos more numerous than my numberless army? No, was the reply. I shall now send any army of greater strength to dig the mountain down and I will see where they dwell.'" While the Krobo's account of the brief conflict cannot be confirmed, the legend's salient feature is that the Asante were unable to defeat the Krobo or to incoporate them into their Greater Asante empire, an unprecedented accomplishment. Only a

few decades earlier, the Krobo had been an unimportant small-scale polity; now they merited the attention, indeed the anger, of the Asantehene himself. Enoch Azu, *Adangbe Historical and Proverbial Songs*, p. 88.

29. Azu, "Adangbe" (1927), p. 94; *Native Reports in Tishi* (Akropong, 1913), pp. 38-40.
30. PRO T70/949 Accra Day Book, 10 December 1772.
31. Azu, "Adangbe" (1927), p. 94; "The Asante did not succeed in winning the mountain and they had to make peace with the Krobo without making heavy stipulations." Johannes Zimmermann, "Aus der Mission unter den Krobo-Neger," *Der Evangelisches Heidenboten* (1864): 137.
32. Thomas Edward Bowdich, *Mission from Cape Coast Castel to Ashantee* (London: J. Murray, 1819), p. 241; Reindorf, *History*, p. 153; Brodie Cruickshank, *Eighteen Years on the Gold Coast of Africa* (London: Frank Cass, 1953), pp. 92-93; PRO, T70/35 White to Committee, Cape Coast, 25 March and 23 May 1811; Reindorf, *History*, pp. 153-55.
33. William W. Claridge, *A History of the Gold Coast and Ashanti* (London: Frank Cass, 1964), p. 264.
34. Opoku's forces on one of these attacks did reach the Ogome on the western side of Klo-yo (Yilo Krobo), before they were repulsed by a combined counterattack by the Yilo and the Manya Krobo. Azu, "Adangbe" (1927), p. 95; Claridge, *A History*, p. 265.
35. In early 1811 the Asante and the Ga had formed an alliance in which the Asante would protect the Ga's interest along the coast against foreign intrusion; in return the Asante gained greater direct influence along the southeastern coast of Ghana. Irene Quaye, "The Ga and Their Neighbours, 1600-1742" (Ph.D. thesis, University of Ghana, Legon, 1972), p. 45; Azu, "Adangbe" (1927), p. 95.
36. Kwamena-Poh, "The Emergence of the Akuapem State 1730-1850," *Ghana Notes and Queries* 11 (November 1970): 26-36; Kwamena-Poh, *Government*, p. 87; David Brokensha, ed., *Akwapim Handbook* (Accra: Ghana Publishing Corp., 1972), p. 46; Reindorf, *History*, p. 154.
37. Reindorf, *History*, p. 156. Odonkor, *The Rise*, p. 17; Alfred Burdon Ellis, *A History of the Gold Coast of West Africa*, 2nd ed. (Totowa: Rowman and Littlefield, 1971), p. 222.

38. Among the Krobo the 1826 Asante war is called the Gua war. Henry Ricketts, *Narrative of the Ashantee War* (London: Simpkin and Marshall, 1831); John J. Crooks, *Records Relating to the Gold Coast Settlement from 1750 to 1874* (London: Frank Cass, 1973); Brohensha, *Akwapim*, p. 45.
39. Reindorf, *History*, p. 196; Odonkor, *The Rise*, p. 9.
40. Odonkor, *The Rise*, p. 9.
41. Odonkor, *The Rise*, pp. 9-10; Azu, "Adangbe" (1927), pp. 97-98.
42. *Guineisk Journaler* (Kobenhavn), 1825, Nos. 462, 512; George Nørregard, *Danish Settlements in West Africa 1658-1850* (Boston: Boston University Press, 1966), pp. 194-95.
43. Kwamena-Poh, *Government*, p. 98.
44. The Danish plantation was called "the Republic of the Krobbo." The Krobo people had no apparent knowledge of the agreement. A copy of this treaty is in Kwamena-Poh, *Government*, pp. 160-61. Also see Paul E. Isert, *Reise nach Guinea und den Caribaischen Inseln in Columbian in briefen an sein freude beschrieben* (Copenhagen: J. F. Morthorst, 1788); Paul E. Isert, *Voyanges en Guinee et dans les Iles Caraibes en Amerique* (Paris: Maradan, 1793); H. Jeppesen, "Danske plantageanlaeg paa Buldkysten 1788-1850" (Reprinted from the publication of the Danish Geographical Association) (Copenhagen, 1966); Ole Justesen "Aspects of Eighteenth Century Ghanian History as Revealed by Danish Sources," *Ghana Notes and Queries* 12 (June 1972): 9-12.
45. Andreas Riis, "Akropong auf der Goldkuste," *Der Evangelisches Heidenboten* (1836): 34; GNA EC 6/3 "Digest of Articles on Ghana," in *Basel Mission Periodicals*, 1828-51, compiled and edited by Paul Jenkins.
46. Mørch had arrived on the Gold Coast only on 12 August 1834, and was appointed acting governor 26 December 1834; he knew virtually nothing about the history of Akuapem-Krobo relations. Larsen, *Guvernører*, p. 94; Azu, "Adangbe" (1927), pp. 92-96.
47. Riis, "Akropong," p. 34.
48. Riis, "Akropong," p. 34; Nørregard, *Danish*, p. 208.

49. Andreas Riis, "Goldkuste in West-Akrika," *Der Evangelisches Heidenboten* (1835): 61-62.
50. The leader of the Shai was later killed by his people for having waged war against their Adangme neighbors, the Krobo. *Guineiske Journaler*, Morch to Copenhagen, 12 February 1836; Nørregard, *Danish*, p. 208.
51. There are other versions of the war. One is that the Krobo came down from the mountain to collect water from the nearby Okwe stream and were attacked by the Akuapem without Mørch's permission. The Akuapem were defeated. George E. Metcalfe, *Maclean of the Gold Coast* (London: Oxford University Press, 1962), p. 200. Kwamena-Poh's version of the war is decidedly pro-Akuapem; he contends that the Governor refused additional ammunition to the Akuapem after the battle had begun, also that "Addo Dankwa and his men decided to leave the field of battle, for they realised that Sum [Mørch] was secretly sending arms to the Krobo." Kwamina-Poh, *Government*, p. 148. Azu, "Adangbe" (1927), pp. 91-92; Odonkor, *The Rise*, p. 11. According to Nørregard, Krobo casualties were 42 dead and 60 to 70 wounded. Clearly this was a major war. Governor Mørch and merchant Richter were knighted for their actions against the Krobo (Order of Dannebrog); the two sergeants received the Cross of Dannebrog. Nørregard, *Danish*, pp. 208-209.
52. Azu, "Adangbe" (1927), pp. 96-101; Odonkor, *The Rise*, p. 60.
53. Danish merchant John Richter contracted to collect his fine. Riis, "Akropong," p. 35. Nørregard, *Danish*, p. 209.
54. Metcalfe, *Maclean*, pp. 196-200; Sutherland, "History."
55. Azu, "Adangbe" (1927), p. 101.
56. Elaborating further on the political rise of Odonkor Azu as a result of his exploits in the Dum War, Noa Azu recorded that Odonkor Azu's "Uncle Muela Okumsom of Drom [Dom] also gave his stool to him [Odonkor Azu] in addition to his own of the Djebiam tribe. This is the reason why Odonkor Azu's stool is spoken of as two stools." Azu, "Adangbe" (1927), p. 103.

Chapter 4

1. An earlier version of this chapter was presented at a Faculty Seminar at the University of Ghana, Legon in 1984. I wish to express my appreciation to the constructive comments and suggestions offered by Professor A. Boahan, John Fynn, Kwame Arhin, Albert Van Danzig, M. E. Kropp Dakubu, James Anquandah, Irene Odetoi (Auay), and Mr. Garett Austin.

2. There is considerable material on the legendary founders of the Asante Kingdom. Reindorf, *History*, pp. 48-49; R. S. Rattray, *Ashanti Law and Constitution* (Oxford: Oxford University Press, 1929), pp. 270-84; R. S. Rattray, *Ashanti* (London: Oxford University Press, 1923), pp. 287-94; A. A. Y. "Ashanti Royal Regalia: Their History and Function" (Doctoral thesis, Oxford University, 1966); J. Agyeman-Duah, "Ashanti-Mampong; a traditional history to the reign of Nana Safo Katanka," *Transactions of the Historical Society of Ghana* 4: 21-25; Ivor Wilks, *Asante in the Nineteenth Century* (Cambridge: Cambridge University, 1975), p. 112.

3. The ethnic/language distribution in Ghana, according to the 1983 Census, is as follows by percentage: Akan (44.1), Mole-Dagbani (15.9), Ewe (13.0), Ga-Adangme (8.3), Guan (3.7) and Gurma (3.5). M. E. Kropp Dakubu, "The Peopling of Southern Ghana: A Linguistic Viewpoint," in *The Archaeological and Linguistic Reconstruction of African History* ed. Christopher Ehret and Merrick Posnansky (Berkeley: University of California, 1982), pp. 245-55; Dakubu, "Linguistic Pre-History."

4. Unlike among the Akan, the *Asafo* does not refer to a military group or "company." Huber, *The Krobo*, p. 28.

5. Huber stated in personal communication to the author that the konor was a title for "an entirely new batch of strangers [who were] put in charge of the new war-stool, the priestly tribe having no intention [at the time of relinquishing political authority]." Also see Field, "Krobo Constitution."

6. Richard J. H. Pogucki, *Gold Coast Land Tenure Volume 2: Report on Land Tenure in Adangme Customary Law* (Accra: Government Printing Office, 1955), pp. 3-5.

7. Huber, *The Krobo*, p. 25.

8. Fynn, *Asante*; Wilks, *Asante*, chapter 1; Addo-Fening, "Akyem Abuakwa," pp. 30-34.
9. Field, "Krobo Constitution."
10. With the influx of refugees, the Krobo and other Adangme devised a systematic way of culturally integrating neighboring peoples into their society. Refugees had to agree to the following (1) male circumcision, (2) the *Dipo* ceremony, (3) taking of Adangme names, and (4) speaking of Adangme languages on the mountain. Azu, "Adangbe (1926)," p. 250; Huber, *The Krobo*, pp. 165-92.
11. All traditions insist that the earliest immigrants were Denkyira, with other Akan groups including the Akyem and the Akwamu arriving later. Thus the term "Denkyira" refers to Akan immigrants in general. On this subject Odonkor wrote "most of the Akans (the Denkyiras)." Odonkor, *The Rise*, pp. 4, 6, and 47. Sutherland, "Manya Krobo," p. 11. Noa Azu and Henry S. Newlands, Deputy Commissioner Eastern Province, suggest that these refugees were from Akyem. Azu, "Adangbe" (1926), pp. 247-48; Azu, "Adangbe" (1928), p. 27; (GNA) ADM 11/1650 H. S. Newlands Report, August 1922, p. 3. However, Yilo Krobo tradition claims a remote connection with the ancient Denkyira State. Interview with Konor Padi Keteku Akrobetto, 22 January 1984. Pogucki also mentions assimilated Akans from Kwawu, and Kamana tribes. Pogucki, *Gold Coast*, p. 3.
12. Azu, "Adangbe" (1926), pp. 248-49; Field, "Krobo Constitution."
13. Field, "Krobo Constitution."; Sutherland, "Manya Krobo," p. 11.
14. Azu, "Adangbe" (1926), pp. 247-48; Odonkor, *The Rise*, p. 3; GNA ADM 11/1116 King Akrobetto, Case No. 4836/1899; GNA ADM 11/830 Bunase Adjikpo, Case No. 15/1923; GNA ADM 11/877 Okper Nam (Yilo Krobo), Case No. 22/1924; GNA ADM 11/1117 Krobo (Yilo), 1899-1930, Case No. 28/1921; GNA ADM 11/877 Okpes (Yilo Krobo), Case No. 22/1924.
15. Azu, "Adangbe" (1928), pp. 19-21; GNA ADM 11/1116 The Ogome Tribe of Western Krobo, Case No. 439/1908; GNA ADM 11/1116 Western Stool Dispute Case No. 581/14/08, 18 November 1917; GNA ADM 11/1116 Western Krobo Native

Affairs, Case No. 547/1906; Sutherland, "History," Appendix D.

16. GNA ADM 11/1116 Western Stool Dispute; Field, "Krobo Constitution"; GNA ADM 11/1116 King Akrobetto; GNA ADM 11/1117 Krobo (Yilo); GNA CSO S.D. Adjiracker to Sec. Native Affairs, 10 December 1931; Odonkor, *The Rise*, p. 47; Donald A. Sutherland, *State Emblems of the Gold Coast* (Accra: Government Printing Office, 1954), p. 69.
17. Odonkor, *The Rise*, p. 47; Interview with Konor Akrobetto, Oct. 20, 1973.
18. For a discussion of the Akan borrowings surrounding the enstooling of chiefs see Zuta Odonkor, "The Origin, Settlement and Traditional Government of the Yilo-Krobo with an Account of the Institution of Chieftaincy Among Them" (B.A. History honor's thesis, University of Ghana, 1976), pp. 14-35; Huber, *The Krobo*, pp. 229-32, 292.
19. Four of the six Bose/Yilo Krobo subtribes were of Akan ancestry.
20. Huber suggests that Bonya's shift to Bose may have been the result of marriage between the Bonya and a section of the Bose community. Personal correspondance, 30 March 1981. Noa Azu and Field both refer to Bose as "Bose of Bonya." Noa Azu, "Adangbe" (1926), p. 248; Field, "Krobo Constitution;" Sutherland , "History," Appendix D.
21. Huber, *The Krobo*, pp. 242-43.
22. GNA ADM 11/1650 H.S. Newlands Report, 3-28; *Ghana Gazette Extraordinary*, "Stool Lands Boundaries, Manya Krobo Order 1953," No. 105, (27 November 1959); Johnson, "Migrants' Progress," Part I.
23. Huber, *The Krobo*, p. 292.
24. Pogucki, *Gold Coast*, p. 5.
25. Margaret Field, "The Agricultural System of the Manya Krobo of the Gold Coast," *Africa* 14/2 (1943): 54-65; Polly Hill, "Three Types of Southern Ghanaian Cocoa Farmers," in *African Agrarian Systems*, ed. Daniel Biebuck (London: 1970), pp. 203-23; Polly Hill, *Migrant Cocoa-Farmers of Southern Ghana* (Cambridge: Cambridge University Press, 1963), pp. 72-85; George Benneh, "The Huza Strip Farm System of the Krobo of Ghana," *Geographica Polonica* 19

(1970): 185-206; Pogucki, *Gold Coast*, p. 20; Azu, "Adangbe" (1927), p. 107; Sutherland, "History," pp. 16-17.
26. Field, "Agricultural," p. 54.
27. Field, "Agricultural," pp. 57-59.
28. Field, "Agricultural," p. 56-58; Benneh, "The Huza," pp. 187-90; Huber, *The Krobo*, p. 293.
29. Field, "Agricultural," pp. 58-59; Benneh, "The Huza," pp. 190-91; Johnson, "Migrants'," pp. 12-13, 17-19.
30. Mate Azzu Kole, "The Historical Background of Krobo Customs," *Transactions of the Gold Coast and Togoland Historical Society* 1 (1955): 133-40.
31. Krobo was an integral part of the Asante's overland and river transportation system. Wilks, *Asante*, p. 11.
32. Since the defeat of the Akwamu in 1730 there had been an increasing numbers of Krobo who ventured farther and farther away from the protective range of the mountain. Although the exact date for the change in name is unclear, given the movement of the Krobo, both Dose and Yilo, into the region north of the mountain, the term "Manya" probably was well established on the eve of the introduction of legitimate trade.
33. GNA ADM 11/477 Chief Odonkor of Kpong, Case No. 49/1913. The most famous of these villages chiefs was Thomas Harrison Odonkor, author of *The Rise of the Krobos*.
34. Huber, *The Krobo*, pp. 46-49.
35. Azu, "Adangbe" (1927), pp. 89-97; Odonkor, *The Rise*, pp. 7-11; Field, "Krobo Constitution," p. 9. Qarcoo is of the opinion that the Shai did not have paramount chiefs during the colonial period; Saxton disagrees. Qarcoo, "Processes," p. 27. Saxton, "Historical Survey," pp. 132-33.
36. Odonkor, *The Rise*, pp. 7-9, 11; Sutherland, "History," pp. 45-46 and Appendix D.
37. Only Koyo and Odonkor reached adulthood. As for the origin of Odonkor's name, which means slave, by giving this last son such a name it was believed by the Krobo and other people, including the Asante, that such a derogatory name would protect the enfant or child from evil/death. Personal discussions with Adu Boahen and Kropp Dakubu, Legon, Ghana, October 13, 1984.

38. The Krobo were part of the left column along with other Adangme and the Akuapem. Henry Ricketts, *Narrative of the Ashantee War: with a view of the Present State of the Colony of Sierra Leone* (London: Simpkin and Marshall, 1831); Odonkor, *The Rise*, p. 9; Azu, "Adangbe" (1927), p. 97; Page, "Historical Survey," pp. 134-35.

39. Noa Azu has recorded traditions which suggest that the *Adontehene* stool passed to four of Boafo's half-brothers in succession—Ozeno, Akrote, Jang, and Tete Ano. Azu, "Adangbe" (1927), pp. 89-99.

40. Odonkor, *The Rise*, p. 8; Azu, "Adangbe" (1928), pp. 21-22; Field, "Krobo Constitution."

41. Kole, "Historical Background," p. 134.

42. Field, "Krobo Constitution." Odonkor Azu's ascendancy, according to David Henige, marked a shift from a collateral to a linear line of succession. David Henige, "Seniority and Succession in the Krobo Stools," *International Journal of Historical Studies* (1977), p. 204. He is critical of Konor E. Mate Kole's attempt to bring the Yilo under his authority. Mate Kole's actions were motivated by at least two considerations. First, the belief that historically the Bose/Yilo settlements had been under the authority of the okumo. Konor Mate Kole considered himself the successor of the okumo. Also, Mate Kole's action was an attempt to gain political preeminence over the Yilo with the assistance of the British. Sutherland, "Manya Krobo," p. 45; Odonkor, *The Rise*, p. 60; Azu, "Adangbe" (1927), p. 91; Field, "Krobo Constitution," p. 9.

43. Odonkor, *The Rise*, p. 11.

44. Field, "Krobo Constitution."

45. Generaltoldkammer og Kommerce-Kollegiets arkiv (Gtk.) *Guineiske journaler* (G.j.) 1835 No. 154; Azu, "Adangbe" (1927), pp. 110-12.

46. Yilo Konor Ologo Patu also attended the meeting. Azu, "Adangbe" (1927), p. 111.

47. Colonial Office (CO), 96/44 Governor Bird to Lytton, 9 September 1858; Colin Newbury, *British Policy Towards West Africa: Select Documents, 1786-1874* (Oxford: Clarendon Press, 1965), pp. 617-19.

48. Johannes Zimmermann, "Lebensende des Krobo-Konigs," *Der Evangelishces Heidenboten* (1868), p. 18; Otto Schott, *The Basel Mission on the Gold Coast, Western Africa on the First January 1879: Retrospect of Fifty Years of Mission Work*, (Basel, 1879), Vol. 12, No. 43; E. M. L. Odjidja, *Mustard Seed: The Growth of the Church in Kroboland* (Accra: Waterville Publishing House, 1973), pp. xiii-74; S.K. Odamtten, *The Missionary Factor in Ghana's Development 1820-1880* (Accra: Waterville Publishing House, 1978), pp. 102-4, 133.

49. All the permanent villages of the twelve Krobo subtribes were established along the Akuapem foothills during Sakite's reign. Dickson, *Historical Geography*, pp. 353-54; Field, "Agricultural," p. 54; Huber, *The Krobo*, p. 19.

50. Only Konor Sakite of all the chiefs in the Eastern consistantly supported the British efforts to defeat the Asante. His support was publicly recognized by colonial officials and Captain John Glover, who was in charge of the Volta campaign. Noa Azu, "The Late King Sakitey and the Ashanti War," *Gold Coast Review* 84 (1929); C.O. 879/4 Captain J. Glover, R.N. to the Earl of Kimberley, 30 July, 1873; Elizabeth (Lady) Glover and Richard (Sir) Temple (ed.), *The Life of Sir John Hawley Glover* (London: 1897), p. 153. Sakite received a specially made silver medallon for his military exploits. Heskett J. Bell, "The Fetish Mountain of Krobo," *Macmillan's Magazine* [London] 68 (July, 1893): 210-19.

51. The Volta District included both Krobo states, the Shai, the Akuapem, Akyem Abuakwa, Akwamu, and a number of smaller chiefdoms.

52. Odonkor, *The Rise*, p. 34.

53. Between 1874 and 1901, the British enacted a number of laws which were designed to bring the colony and the protectorate under more direct control of the colonial officials. Of these laws, the Jurisdiction Ordinance of 1878, which was not applied until 1883, defined the authority of paramount chiefs as head chiefs under the express authority of the British. Sakite and Akrobetto were so identified as the head-chiefs of their respective chiefdoms. David Kimble, *A Political History of Ghana* (Oxford: Oxford University Press, 1963), pp. 303-6.

54. Adam Mischlich, "Wichtige Tag fur das Kroboland," *Der Evangelishces Heidenboten* (1892): 81; Ghana National Archives, Accra, (GNA), ADM 31/1/7, James Williams to Colonial Secretary, 16 March 1892; GNA, ADM 1/9/4, 275 Governor B. Griffith to J. Williams, 1 August 1892; Mangus J. Sampson, *Gold Coast Men of Affairs (Past and Present)* (London: Dawsons of Pall Mall, 1969), pp. 174-77.

55. Emmanuel Mate Kole's rival was Akute of the Dom subtribe, despite his legitimate claim to the Konor, Griffith overruled Williams, the District Office. GNA ADM 31/1/17 Williams to Colonial Secretary, 18 March 1892; Heinge, "Seniority," p. 216.

56. Konor Mate Kole was the first African to serve on the Legislative Council which was established in 1911; he was knighted for his long and meritorious service to the Crown.

57. GNA ADM 11/11115/S.N.A. Governor Griffith to Secretary of State, 24 August 1892. The Krobo's neighbors, the Shai and the Osudoku, were also forced to abandon their mountain settlements and permanently settle on the plains. "The Stool Lands Boundaries Settlement (Osudoku and Nigo)," *Gold Coast Gazette Extraordinary* 95 (December 1955): 1864.

58. Mischlich, "Wichtige," p. 82.

59. Mischlich, "Wichtige," p. 83.

60. Mischlich, "Wichtige," p. 83; Sampson, *Gold Coast*, pp. 174-76.

61. Mischlich, "Wichtige," p. 88; Sampson, *Gold Coast*, p. 175; Sutherland, "History," p. 36; *8: Achtundsiebensigster Jahresbericht der Evangelischen Missionsgesllschaft zu Basel; auf 1 Juli 1893* (Basel: Missionsverwaltung, 1893), pp. 17-18.

62. Mischlich, "Wichtige," p. 88.

63. Mischlich, "Wichtige," p. 89; Sampson, *Gold Coast*, p. 176.

64. Mischlich, "Wichtige," pp. 89-90.

65. *94: Vierundneunsigster Jahresbericht der Evangelischen Missionsgesellschaft zu Basel; auf 1 Juli 1909* (Basel: Missionsverwaltung, 1909), p. 46.

66. Azu, "Adangbe" (1928), p. 11.

67. Henige, "Seniority," p. 204.

Chapter 5

1. The most complete discussion of this topic to date is Anthony G. Hopkins, *An Economic History of West Africa* (London: Longman, 1973). For a discussion of the impact of international trade in slaves and/or vegetable oils on a larger society in West Africa see Kwame Y. Daaku, *Trade and Politics on the Gold Coast, 1600 to 1720* (Oxford: Clarendon Press, 1970), pp. 21-47, 144-81; Kwame Y. Daaku, "Trade and Trading Patterns of the Akan in the Seventeenth and Eighteenth Centuries," in *The Development of Indigenous Trade and Markets in West Africa*, ed. Claude Mellassaux (Oxford: Oxford University Press, 1971), pp. 168-81; A. J. H. Latham, *Old Calabar 1600-1891* (Oxford: Oxford University Press, 1973), pp. 55-150; Robin Law, "Royal Monopoly and Private Enterprise in the Atlantic Trade: The Case of Dahomey," *Journal of African History* 28/4 (1977): 555-77; Karl Polanyi, *Dahomey and the Slave Trade* (Seattle: University of Washington Press, 1966); Catherine Coquery-Vidrovitch, "De la traite des esclaves a l'exportation de l'huile de palme et des palmistes au Dahomey," in Meillassoux, *Development*, pp. 107-23; Edward Reynolds, *Trade and Economic Change on the Gold Coast, 1807-1874* (London: Longman, 1974); Martin Lynn, "Change and Continuity in the British Palm Oil Trade with West Africa, 1830-55," *Journal of African History* 22/3 (1981): 331-48.
2. 1891 Gold Coast Census.
3. Briefly, the huza is a uniquely West African system of land tenure in which individuals formed companies to purchase large tracts of land. Field, "Agricultural," p. 54; Hill, "Three Types," pp. 203-23; Hill, *Migrant Cocoa-Farmers*, pp. 72-74; Freda Wolfson, "A Price Agreement on the Gold Coast—the Krobo Oil Boycott, 1858-66," *The Economic History Review* 6/1 (1953): 68-77; Johnson, "Migrants' Progress," Part 1, Johnson, "Migrants' Progress," Part 2; Inez Sutton, "Labour in Commercial Agriculture in Ghana in the late Nineteenth and Early Twentieth Centuries," *Journal of African History* 24 (1983): 461-83; George Benneh, "The Huza Strip Faming System," *Geographia Polonica* 7/19 (1970): 185-206; Ghana National Archives (GNA) ADM 11/1650 *H. S. Newlands*

Report, 1922, pp. 2-16; Poguchi, *Gold Coast*, pp. 6-28; Kole, "Historical Background," p. 135.

4. Field, "Agricultural," pp. 57-65.
5. George Nørregard, *Danish Settlements in West Africa, 1658-1850* (Boston: Boston University Press, 1966), pp. 84-93.
6. Albert van Dantzig, *Forts and Castles of Ghana* (Accra, 1980), pp. 53-64. Forts built in the 1780s were primarily for defense. A. W. Lawrence, *Trade Castles and Forts of West Africa* (Stanford: Stanford University Press, 1964); Nørregard, *Danish*, pp. 92-93. *Atlas of the Gold Coast* (Accra: Government Printing Office, 1949), p. 20.
7. Hopkins, *Economic History*, p. 137; Kimble, *Political History*, pp. 7-8.
8. *Guineiske journaler* (1891), No. 311; Paul E. Isert, *Reise nach Guinea und den Caribaischen Inseln*, pp. 338-40; Paul E. Isert, *Dokumeter angaaende de a P. E. Isert*, Thaarups Archiv.; C. Adams, "Activities of Danish Botanists in Guinea 1783-1850," *Transactions of the Historical Society of Ghana* 3/1 (1957): 30-46; Nørregard, *Danish*, pp. 174-75.
9. Similar commercial agricultural schemes were attempted at Big Ada, Asentema [Akuapem], and Krachi in the north. These were cultivated by slaves; cotton, tobacco, groundnuts, and maize were the main crops. C.O. 267/93 Rowan Report, Appendix 30; GNA EC 1/33 Digest of Basel Missionary Archives of Ghana; George MacDonald, *The Gold Coast, Past and Present* (London: Longmans, Green, 1898), pp. 319-28; Dickson, *Historical Geography*, pp. 120-28.
10. Kwamina B. Dickson, "Trade Patterns in Ghana at the Beginning of the Eighteenth Century," *Geographical Review* 56 (July 3, 1966): 417-31. The Asante's route V connected the Krobo with the interior and the coast. Wilks, *Asante*, pp. 1-18.
11. *Evangelische Missions-Magazin* (1853), Part 2, p. 63; *Evangelische Missions-Magazin* (1856), Part 2, p. 68; Johnson, "Migrants," pp. 21-24.
12. "Legitimate trade" was a term used by Europeans to include any non-slave item in the aftermath of Britain's ending of the slave trade in 1807.
13. After the defeat of the Akwamu by the Akyem Abuakwa and others, the Krobo moved into the plains region north of the

Krobo Mountain, forcing out the smaller and militarily weaker Kotrepe, Jakiti, Apirede, and Begoro. "Das Kroboland," *Der Evangelische Heidenboten*, (1867): 8; Addo-Fening, "Akyem Abuakwa," chapters 2 and 4. Kole, "Historical Background," p. 134.

14. Mate Kole and the government records suggest the huza began at least by the beginning of the nineteenth century; Field and Hill suggest a later date, the middle of the century; missionary accounts make no reference to the origin of the huza; the author's evidence suggests an even earlier date, possibly late eighteenth century.

The sale of land is termed *zigma yibopom* or *zigba bayipom*. The language which usually accompanies the outright sale, not leasehold, of land in Adangme is: *"Zigba no ike ha mo kwraa ono keya nenene, ibe no hewam ko nu"* ("This land I have given to you entirely, it is yours forever I have no claim on it." Sutherland, "Manya Krobo," p. 83. Noa Azu has recorded a similar expression for the sale of land. "I have parted away with this parcel of land bounded so and so; my ancestors shall have no right to reclaim it forever"; Azu, "Adangbe," (1927), 108. Most accounts agree with Field, that the huza "system has since revolutionized Krobo social life and Krobo politics." Field, "Agricultural," p. 54.

15. Field, "Agricultural," pp. 54-65; Hill, "Three Types," pp. 203-23; Hill, *Migrant*, pp. 72-74; Benneh, "Huza," 185-205; S. La Anyane, *Aweso: A Manya Krobo Huza Husa* (Accra, 1956); Walter Manshard, "Afrikanische Waldhufen-und Waldstreifenfluren," in *Die Erde*, Heft 4 (Berlin), 1961.

16. *H.S. Newlands Report*, 2-4; *Gold Coast Gazette, Extraordinary*, "The Stool Lands Boundaries Settlement—(Osudoku) Order" 95 (1 December 1955): 1870; *Gold Coast Gazette Extraordinary*, "In the Matter of the Stool Lands Boundaries Settlement (Akwamu)" 6 (17 January 1956): 93-94; *Ghana Gazette Extraordinary*, "Stool Lands Boundaries (Manya Krobo) Order," 105 (27 November 1959): 1583; Johnson, "Migrants," Part I, p. 14.

17. Johnson, "Migrants," Part I, pp. 36-37.

18. Kwamina B. Dickson, "The Development of Road Transport in Southern Ghana and Ashanti Since 1850," *Transactions*

201

of the Historical Society of Ghana, 5/1 (1961): 331-42; H. J. Bevin, "Some Notes on Gold Coast Exports 1886-1913," *Economic Bulletin of Ghana* 4(1960), 13-20; Peter R. Gould, *The Development of the Transportation Pattern in Ghana* (Evanston: Northwestern University Press, 1960).

19. Volta River District Record Book 12; *Newlands*, p. 3; *Gold Coast Gazette, Extraordinary* (1 December 1955), 1870; *Gold Coast Gazette Extraordinary*, (17 January 1956): 93-94; *Ghana Gazette Extraordinary* (27 November 1959): 1583-92; Johnson, "Migrant," p. 11; Pogucki, *Gold Coast*, p. 7.

20. Kole, "Historical Background," pp. 139-40.

21. It is logical that after the area on the plains surrounding the Krobo Mountain had been settled, the forested area would have marked the beginning of the next phase. Missionaries who arrived in Odumase and Sra in the 1850s record that the palm oil groves planted there were planted by the parents of konors Odonkor Azu and Ologo Patu, or about 1800. Odonkor Azu is reported to have told Aldinger in 1867, "the now so wonderful green and fertile plain at the feet of the Akuapem mountains, had been a large desert about the end of the last century." Johannes Zimmermann, "Der Kroboneger," *Der Evangelische Heidenboten* (1867): 36; *Newlands*, p. 3.

22. Accompanying the huza farms came family villages such as Noaso, Somanya and Odumase all along the base of the Akuapem foothills in close proximity to their huza farms and the Krobo Mountain. Volta River District Record Book 12; *Newlands*, p. 3; Dickson, *Historical Geography*, p. 353.

23. Reverend M. Rös, "Aus der Mission unter den Krobo-Negern," *Der Evangelische Heidenboten*, (1864): 138-39.

24. Zimmermann, "Kroboneger," p. 22.

25. Carl Aldinger, "Das Kroboland," *Der Evangelische Heidboten* (1867): 6.

26. *Newlands*, p. 4; *Gold Coast Gazette, Extraordinary* (1 December 1955): 1870; *Gold Coast Gazette Extraordinary* (17 January 1956): 95; *Ghana Gazette Extraordinary* (27 November 1959): 1584.

27. "I cannot give the exact number of the villages, he noted, . . . it might have been more than one hundred." These were the largest villages also. Johannes Kopp, "Von der

Missionsarbeit auf der Station Odumase," *Der Evangelische Heidenboten* (1875): 45.

28. Africanus B. Horton, *West African Countries and Peoples* (London: W. J. Johnson, 1868), p. 141; Johnson, "Migrants," Part I, p. 37.

29. Johnson, "Migrants," Part I, p. 27.

30. The *gugwe* was the unit of length, that is the length which a tall man can compass when he stretches his arms sideways; the *kpa* or *rope* was also a measure of length equivalent to between fourteen and sixteen yards, sometimes five or twelve. Field, "Agricultural," p. 55. In the second half of the twentieth century the measure system was modified slightly. Benneh, "Huza," p. 188.

31. The "Akuapem [huza] model" of the huza differed from the Krobo in that land was often purchased in a non-contiguous manner. This method also was used by the Shai and other Adangme. Hill, *Migrant*, pp. 72-74; Benneh, *Huza*, pp. 188-92.

32. Hill, *Migrant*, pp. 72-74; Field, "Agricultural," p. 55; Benneh, "Huza," pp. 188-92.

33. The earliest recorded decription of Krobo markets is as follows: "The markets are important in Krobo for trade and as centers of traffic. They are a peculiar characteristic of the country and of their existence to the scattered residences. They are held on the open field at certain days of the week. The traders come together from all over. They put a few posts in the ground under a shade tree, put others crossway, take some palm branches as a rook and the booth is ready." Jakob Auer, "Ein Ausflug von Akropong nach Odumase," *Der Evangelische Heidenboten* (1859): 38.

34. It is not until 1854 that palm oil is included as an export from the Akyem Abuakwa. Addo-Fening, "Akyem Abuakwa," pp. 62-70. In the 1860s Horton observed that gold mining continued to be the main occupation of the Akyem Abuakwa; "agriculture forms but a small part of their labour." Horton, *West African*, p. 138. Between 1860 and 1876 over 120 square miles of Begoro stool land alone were sold to the Krobo. GNA ADM 11/1122 Hull to Colonial Secretary, 25 July, 1895; GNA ADM 11/1440 Enquiry into Disputed Land Question Between Jakites and Begoro 4 July 1876; Addo-

Fening, "Akyem Abuakwa," p. 322; Johnson, "Migrants," pp. 15-16; Anthony Agyei Addo, "The History of Begoro" (B.A. honors thesis, history, University of Ghana, Legon, April 1975), pp. 9-10.

35. Andreas Riis, *Magazin fur die neuste Geschichte der Evangelischen Missions- und Bibelgesellschaften*, 3: 556.

36. Johnson, "Migrant," pp. 6, 19, 21; Hill, *Migrant Cocoa-Farmers*, pp. 73-74. Marion Johnson, "The Migration," in *Akwapim Handbook*, ed. David Brokensha (Accra: Ghana Publishing Company, 1972), p. 58.

37. The Akuapem had a direct route to the Accra markets, however, unlike the Krobo they were also involved in other commercial ventures, including slave trading, moreover internal conflict continued to plague any united economic policy toward palm oil commercial production.

38. The population of southern Ghana increased with the decline of the exportation of slaves, and the rise of commercial activity along the southeastern coast with Europeans. The poor soils and frequent flooding along the southeastern coast and along the banks of the lower Volta River made it difficult to cultivate food crops on a large scale for commercial purposes. Krobo land at the base of the Akuapem mountains was the nearest and most logical choice for growing food crops for the region.

39. The Proclamation of the Protectorate 1874 extended Britain's power and was defined to extend to (1) preservation of public peace, protection of individuals, life and property; (2) civil and commercial jurisdiction, including the establishment of Superior Courts of Justic and the regulation of Native Courts; (3) extinction of human sacrifices; (4) abolition of slave dealing; (5) increased opposition to domestic slavery and pawning; and (6) establishment of police force, administration of health, education and raising revenue. Fearing renewed attacks from the Asante, the costal states generally welcomed the protection and colonial status of the British. Francis Agbodeka, *African Politics and British Policy in the Gold Coast 1868-1900*, (London: Longman, 1971), pp. 34-61; Kimble, *Political History*, pp. 301-29.

40. David Henige has suggested that the Yilo were politically dominant during the first half of the nineteenth century. He

considered the Yilo konor as having being well established whereas Odonkor Azu had only recently become konor. Henige is only partially correct as I have attempted to explain elsewhere. David Henige, "Seniority and the Succession in the Krobo Stools," *Journal of African Historical Studies* (1977): 203-27; Louis E. Wilson, "Evolution of Paramount Chiefs Among the Adangme: The Krobo (Ghana)," *Geneve-Afrique* 24/2 (1986): 74-100.

41. According to contemporary nineteenth-century Basel missionaries, "The chiefs share power with a council of eldermen, [and] in some circumstances, they govern without the council; they [the chiefs] unite the administrative and judicial power. . . . Sometimes the eldermen are gathered as representatives of the peoples." Zimmermann, "Krobonegers," p. 26.

42. Zimmermann, "Kroboneger," p. 23; Aldinger, "Kroboland," (1867), p. 10. That the Yilo purchased land from various Akan peoples including the Akuapem, the Begoro, the Aprede and the Tafo is evident from their territorial expansion, although that expansion was almost half that of the Manya. Except from one reference in the *Ghana Gazette Extraordinary* (1959) previous cited on page 1590 the Yilo are not specifically identified with any particular aspects of Krobo expansion, whereas the Manya Krobo and their konors are continually referred to in the *Newlands Report*, in the *Gazettes*, Basel Missionary records, and scholarly works.

43. The first arbitration between the Krobo was with the Akuapem in August 1872, involving land purchased from the Akuapem between 1833 and 1872. Odonkor, *The Rise*, p. 25; *Newlands*, p. 4; *Gold Coast Gazette, Extraordinary* (1 December 1955): 1863-73; *Gold Coast Gazette Extraordinary* (17 January 1956): 93-103; *Ghana Gazette Extraordinary* (27 November 1959): 1583-92.

44. *Gold Coast Gazette* (1956): 94 and 95; *Newlands*, pp. 6-34; *Ghana Gazette* (1959): 1585.

45. It is significant that all accounts of this landmark case agree, that no challenge was made of the decision until after Sakite's death. "The Krobo claim," Newlands reported, "stands or falls by the contention that jurisdiction under

native customary law is tribal." For land to be considered tribal the following conditions had to be met "(a) that the land is immediatley contigous [sic] to the division of which the purchaser is a member; (b) that the purchase is made by or on behalf of a community; (c) that the head chief of the division to which the community belongs is notfied of the purchase." The Krobo maintained that all these conditions had been fulfilled. *Newlands*, p. 6; *Gold Coast Gazette* (1956): 95-96; *Ghana Gazette* (1959): 1585-86.

46. *Ghana Gazette* (1959): 1985.
47. Field, "Agricultural," p. 54; Johnson, "Migrants," pp. 3 and 8-11.
48. Newlands gives a rather Eurocentric explanation for when the sale of land began. "[The] sale of land is believed to have commenced after the nominal abolition of the slave trade in 1807 and ceremony used to effect the sale (*'guah'* in Twi) is merely an adaptation of the one formerly employed when a slave was sold (*'trama'* in Twi)". Cited in *Gold Coast Gazette* (1956): 99.
49. Paul Steiner, "50 Jahre Missionaarbeit in Krobo," *Der Evangelische Heidenboten* (1909): 90.
50. The ownership of multiple huzas led mid-nineteenth century Basel missionaries to note "that is why everybody has three houses, one in the home area [i.e., along the Akuapem foothills such as Odumase], the other one in the larger villages, [such as Bisa], and the third one here on the newly acquired plantations." Zimmermann, "Kroboneger," p. 26. Field, "Agricultural," p. 59.
51. Field, "Agricultural," p. 61.
52. Aburi Botanical Station, on the Akuapem ridge, was the experimental farming station established by the British government in the mid-1870s; cotton, coffee, rubber, and cocoa were some of the crops experimented with for the purpose of added financial independence of the Gold Coast Colony. GNA ADM 1/492 No. 345 9 November 1891 acting governor Hodgson to Secretary of State, "Aburi Botanical Station: Development of Coffee Cultivation Among the People: Trade in Coffee: Cotton Cultivation;" GNA 1/495 6 April 1895 Governor Brandford Griffith to Secretary of State, "Cultivation of Coffee, Cocoa and Bananas at Aburi Botanical

Station: Its Educative Effect on the People; Their Increasing Interest in Farming; State of the Road to Aburi;" GNA ADM 1/496 26 February 1897, Governor W. E. Maxwell to Secretary of State, "A More Promising Report of Aburi Garden." When cocoa did become a cash crop by the early 1900s, the Krobo continued to expand. 95: *Funfneunzigster Jahresbericht der Evagelischen Missionsgesellsechaft zu Basel auf den 1 Juli 1910* (Basel: Missionsverwaltung, 1910), pp. 57-58.

53. *Gold Coast Gasette* (1956): 99. Later, Hill made a similar observation, "The cultivation of one crop [palm oil] therefore led directly to the development of another [cocoa]." Hill, *Migrant Cocoa-Farmers*, p. 74. Also, colonial officials encouraged and were generally pleased with how quickly the Krobo, and the Akuapem attempted to cultivate coffee as a commercial crop. "The cultivation of Coffee by the Krobos was becoming universal." GNA ADM 1/492.

54. Zimmermann, "Kroboneger," p. 37.

55. Zimmermann, "Kroboneger," p. 37.

56. GNA ADM 5/2/1 "Report on the Census of the Gold Coast Colony, 1891," *Gold Coast Census, 1891* (see below).

57. 1984 Cenus of Ghana.

58. Jewelry was a major item of trade also. Zimmermann, "Kroboneger", p. 23. The first European description of a Krobo market was by Auer, "Ein Ausflug von Akropong nach Odumase," *Der Evangelische Heidenboten* (1859): 39.

59. Huber, *The Krobo*, p. 57.

60. Imported textiles replaced bark cloth in Kroboland around 1800. "The Krobo shares with the other negroes the pleasure of European garments." Zimmermann, "Kroboneger," p. 23; Huber, *The Krobo*, p. 58.

61. In 1867, Kukutsunya was still considered "the most important market in Western Krobo." Zimmermann, "Kroboneger," p. 38; Huber, *The Krobo*, p. 58f.

62. In addition to a wide range of African and American foods, traders in these markets also sold European cloth, guns, sabers, knives, locks, filed tools, iron, lead, mats and baskets, sacks, and the the like. Zimmermann, "Kroboneger," p. 38; *Magazin für die neuste Geschichte der Evangelischen Missions- und Bibelgesellschaften* (1853), II, 63; *Magazin*

für die neuste Geschichte der Evangelischen Missions-und Bibel-gesellschaften (1856) II, 68-69; Huber, *The Krobo*, pp. 58-59; Johnson, "Migrants," pp. 21-22.

63. Huber, *The Krobo*, p. 58; Hill, *Migrant Coca-Farmers*, p. 74.

64. Zimmermann, "Kroboneger," p. 37. GNA ADM 1/473 No. 337 Administrator Alfred Moloney to Secretary of State, "Condition and Prospects of Trade on the River."

65. For a contemporary description of traffic along the Volta at Kpong see Aldinger, "Kroboland," (1867), pp. 12-13; GNA ADM 1/494 No. 171 Governor Brandford Griffith to Secretary of State, "Navigation of the Volta and Ankobra River," 12 June 1893; Dickson, "The Development of Road Transport," pp. 331-42; George Dodson, "The River Volta, Gold Coast, West Africa," *Journal of Manchester Geographical Society* 8 (1892): 19-25; James A. Croft, "Exploration of the River Volta, West Africa," *Proceedings of the Royal Geographical Society* (1873-74): 183-93; J. H. Bevin, "Some Notes on Gold Coast Exports, 1886-1913," *Economic Bulletin of Ghana* 4 (1960): 13-20; J. H. Bevin, "The Gold Coast Economy About 1800," *Transactions of the Gold Coast and Togoland Historical Society* 2, part 2 (1956): 14-23; Gould, *Development*.

66. Johannes Zimmermann, *A Grammatical Sketch of the Akra or Ga Language, with some specimens of it from the mouth of the natives and a vocabulary of the same, with an appendix on the Adanme dialect* (Stuttgart: Basel Missionary Society, 1858); *Gold Coast Gazette* (1956): 94-95; *Gold Coast Gazette* (1955): 1867.

67. Zimmermann, *Grammatical sketch*; Johnson, "Migrants," p. 8; Croft, "Explorations," pp. 183-85.

68. Zimmermann, *Grammatical sketch*.

69. In addition to the destruction of Kpong, Akuse, and Auschare de Lima also destroyed the Basel trading mission at Dawroamadam in 1863; Dawroamadam was sacked again in 1873 and thereafter ceased to be a center of commercial trade. *Die Baseler Handelsgesellschaft 1859-1959* (Paul Jenkins Abstract); Africanus B. Horton, *Letters on the Political Condition of the Gold Coast* (London: Johnson, 1870), pp. 91-104; Divine Amenumey, "Geraldo de Lima: A

Reappraisal," *Transactions of the Historical Society of Ghana* 9 (1968): 65-69; Reynolds, *Trade*, pp. 141-42.

70. Auer, "Ein Ausflug," p. 51; Inez Sutton, "The Volta Salt Trade: The Survival of an Indigenous Industry," *Journal of African History* 22/1 (1981): 52-53; Zimmermann, *Vocabulary*; Johnson, "Migrants," p. 22; Aldinger "Kroboland," (1867), p. 9.

71. Odonkor, *The Rise*, pp. vii, 35; E. M. L. Odjidja (Very Reverend) *Mustard Seed: The Growth of the Church in Kroboland* (Accra: Waterville, 1973), p. 82. In the 1920s, the rise of road traffic by motor vehicles and the increased rise in the production of cocoa far away from the Volta led to the demise of the Volta as a major means of transportation. GNA ADM 1/493 No. 113 20 April 1893 Governor Brandford Griffith to Secretary of State, "State of Roads: Relation Between Transport and Trade"; Dickson, *Historical Geography*, p. 296.

72. "Akuse," *Der Evengelische Heidenboten*, 1878, 12; GNA ADM 1/473 No. 337, 24 July 1882 Administrator Moloney to Secretary of State "Condition and Prospects of Trade on the River."

73. The European merchant community in Akuse was well established by the 1880s and included the Basel missionaries' first missionary-merchant, Karl Weigle. See chapter 9. "Akuse," 13; GNA ADM 1/473 No. 337, 91. Zimmermann, "Kroboneger," p. 38; Croft, "Explorations," pp. 185-86.

74. "In such a case, for example, the favorite wife of Odonkor Azu, the King of East Krobo, took the seat of her absent husband in the chapel of Odumase at the Sunday service." Zimmermann, "Kroboneger," (1868), p. 26. The cultivation of palm grove trees tended to be dominated by men, although it was not their exclusive right; the harvesting of corn (Welsh maize) was the right of women. Zimmermann, "Kroboneger," p. 37.

75. Zimmermann, "Kroboneger," p. 24.

76. In the case of wives with only female children, "the eldest daughter," if unmarried, "inherits [land] on behalf of her sister, but her interest in the land abrogates upon marriage." Sutherland, "Manya," 79; Benneh, "Huza," 192.

77. Huber, *The Krobo*, pp. 42-44, 59, 61; Field indicated that by the beginning of the twentieth century, the market skills of a young women were a valuable asset for securing a husband, as was his ability as a successful huza farmer. Field, "Agricultural," p. 60. Huber, *The Krobo*, pp. 59-60.

78. Given the small number of women who converted to Christianity in the nineteenth century, Christianity had little effect on the female Krobo population.

79. For the Krobo, market women in that society date from at least the last quarter of the nineteenth century.

80. Millet was the traditional crop of the Krobo and Adangme until the introduction of maize and other foods from the Americas. It is also used in all religious ceremonies. Huber, *The Krobo*, p. 58.

81. Hopkins, *Economic*, p. 133; Field, "Agricultural," p. 58; Huber, *The Krobo*, p. 48; Reynolds, pp. 146-47.

82. Inez Sutton suggests that the Krobo used some slave labor on their plantations. Sutton, "Labour," pp. 465-70. Much later, in the early 1890s, Accra colonial officials were of the opinion that the "Krobo plantations . . . were made entirely by slave labour, long before the Gold Coast Colony was formed." GNA ADM 1/494 No. 171, 12 June 1893, Governor Brandford Griffith to Secretary of State, "Oil Plam Cultivation: The Rubber Trade."

83. Zimmermann, "Kroboneger," pp. 38-39.

84. Zimmermann, "Kroboneger," p. 24.

85. Chiefdoms visited by Firminger included Akuapem, Krobo, Akwamu, Krepi, Inkonya, and the Kratchi Confederation. GNA ADM 1/88 Firminger to Sec. of State, 4 April 1889, "Report on the Slave Trade at Salaga and on Slave-Trading in the Protectorate."

86. Zimmermann, "Kroboneger," p. 39; Huber, *The Krobo*, pp. 165-90.

87. Zimmermann, "Kroboneger," p. 40; Huber, *The Krobo*, pp. 192-216, 219-25; *96: Siebenundneunzigster Jahresbericht der Evangelischen Missionsgesellschaft zu Basel auf 1 Juli 1912* (Basel: Missionsverwaltung, 1911), p. 76.

88. Zimmermann, "Kroboneger," pp. 40-42; Azu, "Adangbe," (1928): 23; Huber, *The Krobo*, pp. 266-73.

89. GNA ADM 11/1115 S.N.A. 24 August 1892 Governor Brandford Griffith to Secretary of State, Dispatch No. 229; "Wichtige Tage für das Kroboland," *Der Evangelische Heidenboten* (1892): 81.

90. Estimated population of Adangme 100,000, Krobo 30,000 and Ga 24,000. "Kroboneger," (1867), p. 22.

91. Reverend Johann G. Christaller, *Dictionary of the Asante and Fante Language*, 2nd ed. (Basel: Evangelical Missionary Society, 1933); Manya Krobo 28,119; Yilo Krobo 17,363. *Gold Coast Census, Report, 1891*; "Appendix K," pp. 32-34.

92. *Gold Coast Census 1891*, pp. 37-39.

93. *Gold Coast Census 1891*; Christaller, *Dictionary*, p. 601; *Gold Coast Gazette* (1955): 1866; Johnson "Migrants," 2: 14.

Chapter 6

1. Wolfson, "Price Agreement," pp. 68-77. This important article presents the agreement itself; there is little attempt to understand the Rebellion or the Boycott in the context of Krobo history or in the context of Britain's attempt to gain control of the palm oil trade in Kroboland.

2. In the eastern region, the people rejected the tax because they paid over one-third of the collected revenue (£2,697 10s. 6d.), 60 percent of which was in gold, but they represented only about one-fifth of the colony's population. Although collected revenue increased slightly in 1853 to 7,567 pounds sterling, it was hardly enough to fulfill Governor Stephen J. Hill's (1851-1854) grand promises of schools, roads, medical facilities and stipends for chiefs. In 1854, opposition to the tax was fierce, organized, and widespread, especially among the Akyem, the Akuapem, the Ga, and the Krobo. The exact amount collected from the Krobo is not available; they were grouped along with the "Accra" [Ga] and the "Aquapim," who collectively paid £2,697 10s. 6d. in cowries and "Akim gold." In 1857, Governor Sir Benjamin C. Pine (1857-1858) estimated that only about one-fifth of the amount collected from the eastern district had been properly allocated. C.O. 96/41 Gov. B. Pine to Labourchere, 30 April 1857, Dispatch 35. C.O. 96/30 Gov. S. Hill to Newcastle, 31 May 1854; Reindorf,

History, p. 324. *Parliamentary Papers*, 1855, xxxvii (383), 83. Marion Johnson, "The Cowrie Currencies of West Africa, Part II," *The Journal of African History* 11/3: 337-38; Kimble, *Political*, pp. 4-9, 168-69; Claridge, *A History*, pp. 479-95; William E. F. Ward, *A History of Ghana* (London: George, Allen and Unwin, 1958), pp. 196-97; George E. Metcalf, *Great Britain and Ghana: Documents of Ghana History 1807-1957* (Legon, 1964), pp. 230-34; Edward Reynolds, *Trade*, pp. 124-25; Newbury, *British Policy*, pp. 616-17.

3. The Manya Krobo were not involved in the Asibe War. For a description of the method of warfare and military organization used in the 1860s as observed by missionaries see Zimmermann, "Kroboneger," pp. 25-26.

4. Azu, "Adangbe," (1927), p. 112; Odonkor, *The Rise*, p. 15; Reindorf, *History*, pp. 324-25.

5. C.O. 96/44 Bird to Lytton, 9 September 1858; Odonkor, *The Rise*, pp. 15-16; Azu, "Adangbe" (1927), pp. 111-12; Sutherland, "Manya Krobo," p. 13, Newbury, *British Policy*, 616; C.O. 96/44.

6. There is no evidence that Konor Ologo Patu was engaged in slave trading. Both Krobo chiefdoms engaged in human sacrifices to the gods of war: *Kotoklo* (Yilo) and *Nadu* (Manya). C.O. 96/44; Huber, *The Krobo*, pp. 266-73; Zimmermann, "Kroboneger" (1867), pp. 40-41.

7. Colonial officials also incorrectly assumed that Odonkor Azu was paramount chief of all the Krobo, a position generally shared by the Basel Missionaries. C.O. 96/44.

8. C.O. 96/44; Alfred B. Ellis, *A History of the Gold Coast of West Africa* (London: Chapman and Hall, 1893), pp. 222-23.

9. C.O. 96/44.

10. The other members of the Council were Richard Ross, Chief Justice, and Robert Dalrymple, Acting Colonial Secretary. C.O. 96/44.

11. C.O. 96/44. The GCAC, formerly the Gold Coast Police Force, was created in 1856. It was plagued with discipline problems, primarily because it was composed of ex-slaves. C.O. 96/44; William H. Gillespie, *A History of the Gold Coast Police, 1844-1939* (Accra: Government Printing Office, 1955), pp. 5-6; Newbury, *British Policy*, pp. 617-19. Composition of African forces: Akwamu and Krepi, 1,500

jointly; Akuapem, 3,000; and several hundred Accra and Christiansborg volunteers. C.O. 96/44; John J. Crooks, *Records Relating to the Gold Coast Settlements from 1750-1874* (London: Frank Cass, 1973), pp. 341, 351-52.

12. All were members of the small group of educated "natives" of Accra and important and wealthy merchants. Kimble, *Political History*, p. 239. The Accras received eight barrels of powder (300 lbs.) and 200 lead bars; the Akuapem received eleven barrels of powder (1,000 lbs.), eight kegs of ball cartridges, and 200 lead bars. C.O. 96/44 Bird to Lytton, 9 October 1858.

13. C.O. 96/44 Bird to Lytton, 15 October 1858.

14. Johannes Zimmermann, "The Crobo Expedition from the 6th September to the 4th November 1858, (Extract from Missionary Report, translated by Rev. [E. M. J.] Odjidja 1935.)" This manuscript was provided by E. M. J. Odjidja, Moderator (retired) of the Presbyterian Church in 1974.

15. Several hundred warriors deserted. African auxiliaries who held their position included the Shai, a few Accras, the Prampram, the Akwamu, and the Akuapem. C.O. 96/44 Bird to Lytton, 15 October 1858; Claridge, *A History*, pp. 499-500. Casualties (European and/or volunteers): killed—Thomas Cringle, Henry Cobbe, and John Wheeler; wounded—C. Twish, C. Hunter, C. Bruce, R. Peel, C. Palm, W. Scott, and J. Doolan. The number and names of Africans killed was not recorded. C.O. 96/44 Bird to Lytton, 10 November 1858. C.O. 96/44 Cochrane to Bird, 9 October 1858.

16. Azu, "Adangbe" (1927), p. 113. The procedure for destooling [deposing] a konor is discussed in Huber, *The Krobo*, p. 231.

17. Within the context of violation of the oath Odonkor Azu had taken when he became konor, there was a strong case against him. Consider the second part of the oath taken by the konor: "I swear this oath; should anything come upon the town and you call upon me, and should I then refuse to take the lead, woe is me." Huber, *The Krobo*, p. 231.

18. Azu, "Adangbe" (1927), p. 113.

19. Azu, "Adangbe" (1927), pp. 113-14.

20. Azu, "Adangbe" (1927), p. 113.

21. The other members of the court were Acting Colonial Secretary Bulmer Hedtley, T. B. Freeman, Captains Cochrane,

Brownell, and H. Danell, and T. C. Hansen, Esq., an African merchant. C.O. 96/44 Bird to Lytton, 10 November 1858, Dispatch 67. C.O. 96/44 Bird to Lytton, 10 November 1858.

22. C.O. 96/44 Bird to Lytton, 10 November 1858.
23. C.O. 96/44.
24. Both konors spent only about six months in prison before they were freed by Sakite, Odonkor Azu's son. Johannes Zimmermann, "Lebensende des Krobo-konigs," *Der Evangeliche Heidenboten*, 1868. There was apparently no attempt to carry out the destooling of Konor Ologo Patu, which was part of the assigned punishment. C.O. 96/44 Bird to Lytton, 10 November 1858, Dispatch 68. Wolfson, "Price Agreement," pp. 68-77.
25. The boycott has become part of the Krobo heroic traditions: they fought bravely against the powerful British and their allies; the Krobo Mountain was never militarily taken; and although their konors were imprisoned, they were freed by the heroic deeds of Krobo warriors led by Odonkor Azu's son, Sakite. Wolfson, "Price Agreement," pp. 68-69.
26. Robert Hutchison's reported net worth in 1855 was 60,000 pounds sterling, a considerable sum for anyone. C.O. 96/34 H. Hutchison to Secretary of State, 10 September 1855, Dispatch 85.
27. Frank and Andrew Swanzy and Messrs. Forster and Smith were the largest trading companies in palm oil at the time; both were based in Liverpool. Later Hutchison sold 300 pounds sterling of his surety to W. Edwards, a principal agent of Forster and Smith, and 750 pounds sterling to William Addo, an independent African merchant. C.O. 96/50 Bird to Colonial Secretary, 15 December 1858; C.O. 96/53 Andrews to the Duke of Newcastle, 16 July 1861; Wolfson, "Price Agreement," p. 73.
28. Odonkor Azu estimated that the Krobo produced 10,000 pots of oil per year, hence, the Krobo could pay the indemnity in two years. Carl Aldinger, "Quartalsbericht," Baud Afrika, XII, 1 April to 30 June 1860; C.O. 96/50 Bird to Colonial Secretary; Wolfson, "Price Agreement," p. 73.
29. C.O. 95/50 Bird to Colonial Secretary.
30. C.O. 96/53 Andrews to the Duke of Newcastle, 16 July 1861.

31. C.O. 96/53 Andrews to the Duke of Newcastle, 9 August 1861, Dispatch 77. Carl Aldinger was extremely critical of Britain's collection methods and especially Hutchinson, whom he called a speculator. Carl Aldinger, "Quartalsbericht," *Baud Afrika*, 1 April to 30 June 1860.
32. C.O. 96/51 Andrews to the Duke of Newcastle, 12 January 1861, Dispatch 189.
33. C.O. 96/51 Andrews to the Duke of Newcastle, 12 January 1861, Dispatch 190.
34. C.O. 96/51 Andrews to the Duke of Newcastle, 12 January 1861, Dispatch 190B; C.O. 96/51 Andrews to the Duke of Newcastle, 12 January 1861, Dispatch 193.
35. GNA ADM 11/1115 Zimmermann to Major C. de Ruvignes, Odumase, 20 November 1861; C.O. 96/51 Andrews to the Duke of Newcastle, 12 January 1861, Dispatch 160.
36. GNA ADM 11/1115 C. de Ruvignes to W. A. Rop, Colonial Secretary, 21 November 1861; C.O. 96/51.
37. C.O. 96/53 Andrews to the Duke of Newcastle, 22 July 1861; "West-Afrika Berichte," *Der Evangelische Heidenboten* (1861): 14; C.O. 96/59 Edwards to Colonial Office, 17 June 1862; C.O. 96/59 Hutchison to Colonial Office, 10 June 1862; C.O. 96/60 Pine to the Duke of Newcastle, 13 February 1863, No. 2441. According to the same statistics, the eastern region led in exports, despite the boycott. C.O. 442/10-42 Blue Books, pp. 1850-76.
38. Missionaries reported that the actual payment by the Krobo amounted to more than "100 per cent in interest." *Baud Afrika*, "Jahresbericht vom Jahr 1860," 30 January 1861.
39. The author has seen some of these storage places.
40. Colonial administration was also in a state of chaos because de Ruvignes, Civil Commandant of the eastern region, was accused of "grave misconduct"; Charles and James Bannerman were accused of extortion and embezzlement. The litigation of these cases brought the Christiansborg administration to a standstill. C.O. 96/62 Andrews to the Duke of Newcastle, 1 September 1863. Johannes Zimmermann, "Erfuhrungen und Hoffnungen in Odumase," *Der Evangelische Heidenboten* (1864): 89.
41. William Addo received no settlement from the government, for reasons the colonial records or Wolfson do not make

clear. C.O. 96/70 Conrad to Cardwell, 3 February 1866; Wolfson, "Price Agreement." p. 45. Carl Aldinger, "Quartalsbericht," *Baud Afrika*, 1 April to 30 June 1860. There were ten mission reports between December 1858 and early 1860; the Krobo fine is not mentioned until April 1860.

42. Aldinger, "Quartalsbericht", 1 April to 30 June, 1860.

43. Aldinger, "Quartalsbericht", 1 April to 30 June, 1860.

44. Aldinger, "Quartalsbericht," 1 April to 30 June, 1860.

45. Hutchinson, according to Johnannes Zimmermann, had originally implemented this scheme for collection. Aldinger, "Quartalsbericht," 1 April to 20 June 1860; C.O. 96/53 Colonial Secretary Ross to de Ruvignes, 24 July 1861.

46. The actual extent of territorial expansion during the boycott years is not known. We do know, however, that expansion did continue. M. Ros, "Aus der Mission under den Krobo-Negern," *Der Evangelische Heidenboten* (1864): 137. See also chapter 5.

47. Aldinger, "Quartalsbericht," 1 April to 30 June 1860.

48. Henige suggests that in the 1840s and 1850s, Ologo Patu was wealthier, and exercised more political authority, than Odonkor Azu. Henige, "Seniority," pp. 215-20. Basel Missionary accounts appear to disagree with Heinge's assessment. Aldinger, "Quartalsbericht," 1 April to 30 June 1860; Johannes Zimmermann "Jahresbericht vom Jahr 1860," *Baud Afrika*, 30 January 1861; "Kroboneger" (1867), p. 22.

49. Oil prices peaked in 1854-1861; oil merchants and Gold Coast administrators in 1858 must have been aware of the rise of palm oil prices. Hopkins, *Economic History*, p. 132; Martin Lynn, "Change and Continuity in the British Palm Oil Trade with West Africa, 1830-55," *Journal of African History* 22/3 (1981): 331-48.

50. C.O. 96/44 Bird to Lytton, 9 September 1858.

51. Kimble, *Political History*, p. 6.

Chapter 7

1. The author has seen this portrait of Konor Sakite in the main hall of the konor of Manya Krobo residence.

2. The exact method by which Sakite was selected differed from the present day procedure; he was only the second

konor selected. The current succession procedure was essentially established during the reign of Sakite's successor, Emmanuel Mate Kole (1892-1939), and has been recorded by Sutherland. "The selection of the *Paramount Chief* of Manya Krobo follows the male line of descent and it is not necessarily the eldest son who succeeds. The nomination of the stool candidate is performed by the head of the deceased Paramount Chief's house (through the male line) and Gyasse-Asaoatse, who consult with the Odumase Council and the two Nam Asofiatsemei of Susui and Abordornya in Camera." Sutherland, "Manya Krobo," p. 36; Azu, "Adangbe" (1927), pp. 2-4. Odonkor Azu died on 29 September 1867; he was eulogized by his friend of ten years Rev. Johannes Zimmermann, who was at his bedside. Johannes Zimmermann, "Lebensende des Krobo-Konigs," *Der Evangelische Heidenboten* (1868): 18.

3. Zimmermann, ignoring or rejecting these political realities, says that all three refused because they were "too young" in the Christian faith. Zimmermann, "Lebensende," p. 18.

4. Kole, "Historical Background," p. 133; Huber, *The Krobo*, p. 19; David Henige, "Seniority and the Succession in the Krobo Stools," *International Journal of African Historical Studies* (1977): 203-27; Odonkor, *The Rise*, pp. 11-13.

5. Azu, "Adangbe" (1927), p. 89. Azu, "Adangbe" (1927), pp. 89-100. Interview with Konor Azzu Mate Kole, 22 November 1973, Odumase-Krobo.

6. Divine Amenumey, "Geraldo de Lima: A Reappraisal," *Transactions of the Historical Society of Ghana* 9 (1968): 65-66; Divine E. Amenumey, "The Ewe People and the Coming of European Rule, 1850-1914" (M.A. thesis, University of London, 1964), p. 86; Edward Reynold, *Trade and Economic Change on the Gold Coast 1807- 1874* (London: Longman, 1974), pp. 141-42; C.O. 96/97 Julio Ungar to F. W. Richards, 14 May 1865. In addition to the destruction of Akuse, Kpong, and Auschare, de Lima also destroyed the Basel Trading Mission about a mile inland at Dawroamadam in 1863. *Die Baseler Handelsgesellschaft 1859-1959* (Paul Jenkins' Abstract). Africanus B. Horton, *Letters on the Political Condition on the Gold Coast*

(London: Johnson, 1870), pp. 91-104; Resolutions of the Select Committee, 26 June 1865, C. 412.

7. Odonkor, *The Rise*, pp. 25-26.

8. Odonkor, *The Rise*, p. 34.

9. The presence of Akan symbols in the Manya Krobo state emblem is evident in the stool and the ceremony swords; this state emblem probably appeared during the reign of Emmanuel Mate Kole in the late nineteenth century. Sutherland, *State Emblems*, p. 47.

10. Zimmermann, "Kroboneger," p. 22.

11. Odonkor, *The Rise*, p. 34.

12. Agnes A. Aidoo, "Political Crisis and Social Change in the Asante Kingdom, 1867-1901" (Ph.D. diss., University of California, Los Angeles, 1975), chapter 1.

13. Wilks, *The Asante*, pp. 497-512; Sir Henry Brackenbury, *The Ashanti War: A Narrative* (London: Frank Cass, 1968); William E. F. Ward, "British and Asanti, 1874-1896," *Transactions of the Historical Society of Ghana* 15/2 (1974): 131-64; Thomas J. Lewin, *Asante Before the British* (Lawrence: The Regents Press of Kansas, 1978), chapter 1; W. D. McIntyre, "British Policy in West Africa: The Ashanti Expedition of 1873-74," *Historical Journal* 5 (1962): 19-46; Francis Agbodeka, *African Politics and British Policy in the Gold Coast, 1868-1900* (London: Longman, 1971), pp. 122-67.

14. *Cape Coast Standard*, 2 October 1873.

15. Glover had an established reputation as an able administrator while in Lagos Colony. His rank was Commander, but he was affectionately called "Captain." W. D. McIntyre, "Commander Glover and the Colony of Lagos, 1861-73," *Journal of African History* 4/1 (1963): 57-80; C.O. 879/4 Captain J. Glover, R.N. to the Earl of Kimberley, 30 July 1873; Elizabeth (Lady) Glover and Richard (Sir) Temple, eds. *Life of Sir John Hawley Glover* (London: Smith, Elder, 1897); Glover Papers, Royal Commonwealth Society (London).

16. Great Britain, *Irish University Press Series of Parliamentary Papers: Further Correspondence on the Ashanti Invasion, Colonies Africa* 59 (Shannon: Irish University Press, 1967), p. 66.

17. *Further Correspondence* 59: 66.

18. *Further Correspondence* 59: 53-54, 66; Glover, *Life*, pp. 153-54, 178; C.O. 96/101 Earl of Kimberly to Captain Glover, 18 August 1873; Glover, *Life*, pp. 153-54, 178.

19. On 28 September 1873, Glover held a meeting with the paramount chiefs of Akyem Abuakwa and Akyem Kotoko, and "the other Kings and Chiefs of the Eastern District." C.O. 96/101 Glover to H. W. Harley, 28 September 1873; Azu, "Adangbe" (1928), pp. 4-5; Odonkor, *The Rise*, p. 28. Many European and African merchants, who were residents of Ada and Keta, strongly opposed any attacks by Glover on the Anlo (Awuna), fearing it would disrupt trade. *Further Correspondence* 59: 73-74, 82-83, 383, 426, 523-24, 569-70.

20. Each "king" received large quantities of gin, rum, and tobacco, as well as axes and cutlasses and between 200 and 300 silver coins. Additional costs incurred included rations for the men, estimated at 3s. 1/2 d. per diem. *Further Correspondence* 59: 569-70.

21. Other chiefs at the Accra meeting: "Amoakko Attah, Eastern Akim [Akyem Abuakwa], with his principal chiefs and captains; Tackie Taviah, King of Accra and the Eastern Districts; Ansah, King of Awuapim, with his principal chiefs and captains, consisting of chiefs of the Akropong, Aparade, Addomarug, Aburi, Tootoo, Lartey, Mampong, Marnefee, and Oboosoomassey; the King of Crepee and his chiefs and captains; the Caboceers of James Town, Christiansborg, Labaddy, Teshie, Ninquah, Semmah, Poney, Pram Pram, Ningo, and Addah, all in the district of Accra." (Original spelling) C.O. 96/101 Wolseley to the Earl of Kimberley, 18 October 1873, Incl. 3, No. 182. Brackenbury, *Ashanti War*, p. 388.

22. The other troops were to come from the following tribes: Accra and Ada, 12,000; Akuapem, 7,000; Akyem Abuakwa, 4,000; Krepi, 14,000. Brackenbury, *Ashanti War*, p. 388.

23. Glover also recruited Hausa troops from the southern part of the Gold Coast, primarily around Accra. Glover again angered Wolseley because he actively recruited enslaved Hausa; the fact that he paid their former masters did not end the controversy. *Further Correspondence* 59: 53, 64-65, 165, 217, 323, 334, 342, 498-99, 537; Glover, *Life*, p. 173.

24. C.O. 96/102 Wolseley to the Earl of Kimberley, 13 November 1873. Noa Azu, "The Late King Sakitey and the Ashanti War," *Gold Coast Review* (1929): 105-117. For an opposing view see William W. Claridge, *A History*, p. 84; Brackenbury's account is similar to Claridge's. Brackenbury, *Ashanti War*, p. 390; A. B. Ellis, *A History of the Gold Coast* (London: Chapman and Hall, 1893), pp. 322-23.

25. C.O. 96/102 Wolseley to the Earl of Kimberley, 13 November 1873.

26. Sakite's loyalty to the British was first questioned by some of the Accra chiefs in February 1873. *Further Correspondence* 58: 664-65.

27. Sakite first pledged his support for the British against the Asante in March 1873. *Further Correspondence* 58: 406. Glover recognized the reluctance of some eastern chiefdoms to participate in the Asante campaign when, after the Akropong meeting, he reported: "It may not be out of place to remark upon the indifference manifested by the Kings Tackie and Solomon of Accra, and the favourable contrast displayed by the Kings, Chiefs and people of Akropong, Croboe, and Creepee." C.O. 96/102 Harley to the Earl of Kimberley, 30 September 1873; Glover, *Life*, pp. 156 and 158. Chief Tutu Yao of Pkei, Chief Boso Nyako of Anum, Chief Doe of Shai, and Konor Sasraku of the Yilo Krobo questioned Sakite's loyalty. Odonkor, *The Rise*, pp. 28-29.

28. C.O. 96/102 Wolseley to the Earl of Kimberley, 12 November 1873, Inc. 1, No. 18.

29. Odonkor, *The Rise*, p. 49.

30. Little is remembered of Chief Lamie; he was *Wetse Matse* of Ogome (Yilo Krobo) and a cosigner of the 1872 Krobo-Akuapem treaty. *British Parliamentary Papers*, 58: 161-62.

31. C.O. 96/102 Wolseley to the Earl of Kimberley, 16 December 1873, Incl. 2 and Incl. 3; C.O. 96/102 Wolseley to the Earl of Kimberley, 18 December 1873, Inc. 2; Brackenbury, *Ashanti War*, p. 391; *Further Correspondence* 59: 556 and 602.

32. The exact number of Krobo who participated in the war is unknown. Noa Azu states there were 500 troops under Tei Dakro and Mate Adkipa Kokrobo. Azu "Adangbe" (1928), p. 8; Odonkor, *The Rise*, p. 29; C.O. 96/102 Wolseley to the Earl of Kimberley, 26 December 1873, Incl. 1.

33. The reserves included an estimated 5,000 Akyem Abuakwa and 3,000 Akuapem. C.O. 96/102 Wolseley to the Earl of Kimberley, 26 December 1873.
34. C.O. 96/102 Wolseley to the Earl of Kimberley, 1 January 1874, Incl. 2; *Further Correspondence* 59: 615, 617-18. Glover overspent his budget of 27,000 pounds sterling and Wolseley accused him of attempting to bribe the chiefs with gifts. *Further Correspondence* 59: 55-56, 62, 127-28, 347, 352-56; Claridge, *The History*, pp. 84-87.
35. C.O. 96/102 Wolseley to the Earl of Kimberley, 1 January 1874; *Further Correspondence* 59: 617-18.
36. C.O. 96/102 Wolseley to the Earl of Kimberley, 1 January 1874; *Further Correspondence* 59: 55-56, 127-28, 352-56.
37. Lieutenant Cameron had to return to Blappah because of illness, and was replaced by Dr. Bale. *Further Correspondence* 59: 352. Commissioner Goldsworthy was left in charge of the Volta region.
38. The Krobo who remained at Blappah and elsewhere along the Volta were probably Yilo. In addition to the Krobo, there were some 11,870 other troops. Glover, *Life*, p. 187; *Further Correspondence* 59: 353.
39. Odonkor incorrectly called these snider rifles "303 M.E.'s", which did not appear in West Africa until about 1900. Sartorious noted that every man wanted to carry a gun, making it difficult to find porters. A porter was paid 10d. per day and a fighting man 1s. C.O. Sartorius to Glover 22 November 1873. Konor Azzu Mate Kole suggests that the Krobo received these snider rifles because there was a surplus, which seems doubtful. Interview with Konor Azzu Mate Kole, 26 November 1973, Odumase-Krobo.
40. C.O. 96/102 Wolseley to the Secretary of State for War, 15 January 1874.
41. Sakite appointed his uncle Noa Azu acting konor in his absence. Azu, "Adangbe" (1928), p. 12.
42. The exact number of Krobo involved in the expedition is unclear; the records state only that they were a "considerable number under Chief Sakkity." C.O. 96/102 Glover to Wolseley, 2 January 1874; C.O. 96/102 Glover to Wolseley, 9 January 1874; C.O. 96/102 Wolseley to the

Secretary of State for War, 15 January 1874; Ellis, *A History*, pp. 342, 346-47.

43. C.O. 96/102 Wolseley to the Secretary of State for War, 13 February 1874. Glover's forces numbered about 4,448 at this time. C.O. 96/102 Wolseley to the Earl of Kimberley, 15 February 1874; Glover, *Life*, p. 217.

44. J. J. Crooks, *Records Relating to the Gold Coast Settlement from 1750-1874* (London: Frank Cass, 1973), pp. 530-36.

45. Glover was initially awarded 2,000 pounds sterling. John Whitford stated that Glover's "march from the Volta to take Coomassie in the rear with a fickle, undisciplined, and constantly dwindling army of unmanageable natives was in a strategic point of view, a no less meritorious achievement than Sir Garnett Wolseley's victorious campaign." Few other writers appear to share this view. John Whitford, *Trading Life in Western and Central Africa* (London, 1877), pp. 63-64.

46. Great Britain, *C. 962 Asante Invasion: Report by Captain Glover, R.N., on the Conduct of the Deputy Commissioners, Officers, and Men, April 1874*; Glover, *Life*, p. 54; *Further Correspondence* 59: 53-54.

47. Sakite, Konor Azzu Mate Kole claims, had actually been nominated for the KCMG, and when London officials rejected this nomination, he was given part of the KCMG's regalia.

48. Major-General P. B. Gillett, C.B., C.V.O., O.B.E., Secretary to the Central Chancery of the Orders of Knighthood, insists that no African was nominated for or received the KCMG during the war or at any time. Furthermore, "it should not have been possible for an African Chief to wear the KCMG Insignia without the permission of the Order." Letter to the author dated 28 February 1978. The regalia was observed on Sakite by Hesket J. Bell. H. J. Bell, "The Fetish-Mountain of Krobo," *Macmillan's Magazine* 68 (July 1893): 210-19.

49. Picture of medallion in Odonkor, *The Rise*. The author saw the sword, medallion, and chain in 1974 and again in 1984.

50. C.O. 879/7 Governor Stephen Strahan to the Earl of Carnarvon, 27 June 1874; Odonkor, *The Rise*, p. 34.

51. Others present: "Tackie of Accra, Edward Solomon, King Dosu of Adda, Cocumay from Aholu, war captain of Anlo,

222

Tameklo, chief of Hootsay, Joseph Akrobotu, Chief Seruboy, Trigee, Captain of Anyoko, Tubolu interpreter, Afadee interpreter, Posoo, Captain of Jellah Coffe." (original spelling) C.O. 879/7 C. C. Lees to Carnarvon, 23 June 1874.

52. Jakob Kopp, "Von der Missionsarbeit auf der Station Odumase," *Der Evangelische Heidenboten* (1875): 53.

53. Sutherland, "History," p. 37.

Chapter 8

1. Noel Smith, *The Presbyterian Church of Ghana, 1835-1960*, (Accra, Ghana Universities Press: 1966), p. 135.

2. Ralph M. Wiltgen, *Gold Coast Mission History 1471-1880*, (Chicago, 1956), pp. 14-17, 20-24, 42-47; Hans W. Debrunner, *History of Christianity in Ghana* (Accra: Waterville Publishing House, 1967), pp. 13-30; Hans W. Debrunner, "Notable Danish Chaplains on the Gold Coast," *Transactions of the Gold Coast and Togoland Historical Society, Part 1*, 4 (1956): 73-86; Charles Pelham Groves, *The Planting of Christianity in Africa, Vol I* (London, Lutterworth: 1948), pp. 299-307; Francis L. Bartels, *The Roots of Ghana Methodism* (Cambridge: Cambridge University Press, 1965); S. K. Odamtten, *The Missionary Factor in Ghana's Development (1820-1880)* (Accra: Waterville Publishing House, 1978), pp. 11-29.

3. Frances L. Bartels, "Philip Quaque 1741-1816," *Transactions of the Gold Coast and Togoland Historical Society* 1/5 (1955): 170.

4. "Amo became chaplain at Elmina, despised by the whites and rejected by the Africans." He translated the Apostles' Creed into Fante. Smith, *Presbyterian*, p. 24; Groves, *Planting* 1: 152; Odamtten, *Missionary*, pp. 14-15; Henry O. A. McWilliam, *The Development of Education in Ghana*, (Longman, 1970), pp. 9-10.

5. McWilliam, *Development*, p. 10.

6. Hans Debrunner, "Friedrich Pederson Svane, 1710-1789," *Der Evangelisches Missions-Magazin* (February 1957); Smith, *Presbyterian*, pp. 24-25.

7. W. Schlatter, *Geschichte der Basler Mission, 1815-1915* 1 (Basel: Verlag der Basler Missionsbuchhandlung, 1916), p.

223

12; Paul Steiner, *Hundert Jahre Missionsarbeit, 1815-1915* (Basel: Verlag der Basler Missionsbuchhandlung, 1915), pp. 4-17; Paul Eppler, *Geschichte der Basler Mission, 1815-1900* (Basel: Verlag der Basler Missionsbuchhandlung, 1900), pp. 1-37; Hans Debrunner, "Anfange evangelischer Missionsarbeit auf der Goldkuste bis 1828," *Der EvangelischesMissions-Magazin* (January-March, 1954); Otto Schott, *The Basel Mission on the Gold Coast, Western Africa, on the 1st January 1879: A Retrospect of Fifty Years of Mission Work* (Basel: Basel Mission Society, 1879), pp. 1-22; Groves, *Planting* 1: 302-6 and 2: 224-26. Reverend Thomas Birch Freeman was probably the most notable early member of the Wesleyan Missionary Society.

8. The Wesleyan Missionary Society arrived at Cape Coast in 1835; the Roman Catholic Church in 1881. The Wesleyan schools and religious instruction were in English; Twi was not used in instruction until 1850 when Christiansborg came under the authority of Britain. A. W. Parker, an African minister, produced the first Twi (Fante) translation of two Christian gospels in 1877.

9. From the earliest years there had been some emphasis on practical skills, such as carpentry and tailoring; in the late nineteenth century there was even greater emphasis on "manual education." "The basis of this reform came from the famous Booker T. Washington of Tuskegee in America with his program for Negro schools; it is healthy for the Negroes to be educated not only in their minds, but also to know the practical work. They should have a healthy attitude towards work." *96: Sechsundneunzigster Jahresbericht der Evangelischen Missionsgellschaft zu Basel, auf 1 Juli 1911* (Basel: Missionsverwaltung, 1911): 67. By 1913 manual skills courses included carpentry, the locksmith trade, book binding and weaving; there was a mininum of 7 1/2 to 10 hours per week for manual instructions. In 1910 Basel mission schools received 68,100 Franks in subsidy from the colonial government; thereafter the colonial needs dominated missionary and secondary schools. English became the language of instruction that same year. *96: Sechsundneunzigster Jahresbericht,* 67; *98: Achtundneunzigster Jahresbericht der Evangelischen*

Missionsgesellschaft zu Basel auf 1 Juli 1913 (Basel: Missionsverwaltung, 1913), pp. 87-88.

10. Smith, *Presbyterian*, pp. 26-29; McWilliam, *Development*, pp. 23-25.

11. By comparison, Johannes Gottlieb Christaller produced a dictionary of Twi in 1881. Zimmermann and Christaller were also instrumental in preserving many Ga, Adangbe, and Twi traditions by recording them in their writings. A Ewe grammar was produced in 1858, and a dictionary in 1905. Eppler, *Geschichte*, p. 209; W. Ringwald, *Stafette in Africa* (Stuttgart: Evangelische Missionsverlag, 1957), pp. 31-35; Odjidja, *Mustard Seed*, p. 73; Smith, *Presbyterian*, pp. 54-56; Groves, *Planting* 2: 229.

12. Cited in McWilliam, *Development*, p. 20.

13. McWilliam, *Development*, p. 20.

14. Reindorf, *History*, p. 222.

15. Smith, *Presbyterian*, p. 49; E. A. Boateng, *A Geography of Ghana* (Cambridge, 1959), p. 161.

16. "Uber Westafrika," *Der Evangeliche Heidenboten* (1828): 70-72; "Uber danische Goldküste," *Der Evangelische Heidenboten* (1829): 53-55; Schlatter, *Geschichte* 3: 23-24; Odamtten, *Missionary*, pp. 32-33; Groves, *Planting* 1: 299-301; McWilliam, *Development*, pp. 18-19.

17. Johannes Henke, "Uber Goldküste," *Der Evangelische Heidenboten* (1831): 19-20; Andreas Riis, "Danische Goldküste, Jager und Riis," *Der Evangelische Heidenboten* (1832): 93-95; "Danische Goldküste," *Der Evangelische Heidenboten* (1834): 63-76; W. Oelschner, *Landung in Osu* (Stuttgart: Evangelische Missionsverlag, 1959), pp. 25-30; Smith, *Presbyterian*, pp. 28-30; Odamtten, *Missionary*, pp. 32-33; Schlatter, *Geschichte* 3: 21.

18. Andreas Riis, "Goldküste in West-Afrika," *Der Evangelische Heidenboten* (1835): 62-67; Schlatter, *Geschichte* 3: 28-30. This was in the Dum War; see chapter 4.

19. "Reise der Brüder Riis und Mürdter bei Akropong," *Der Evangelische Heidenboten* (1839): 53-55.

20. Andreas Riis, "Die Mission auf der Goldküste," *Der Evangelische Heidenboten* (1843): 17-24; Andreas Riis, "Der Wiederersatz," *Der Evangelische Heidenboten* (1843): 81-84;

"Aus einem Brief von Riis," *Der Evangelische Heidenboten* (1844): 92-95; Schott, *The Basel Mission*, pp. 6-10, 18.

21. Before the 1880s there were essentially two types of schools, *Erziehungsanstalten* (boarding school) and the *Gemeindeschulen* (day primary school). The first boarding schools for each sex were at Christiansborg, Akropong, Aburi, Odumase, and Abokobi. Eppler, *Geschichte*, p. 205.

22. "Miss. Schrenks Reise nach Kape Koast," *Der Evangelische Heidenboten* (1871): 77-81; Smith, *Presbyterian*, p. 45.

23. Basel missionary reports do not support this claim.

24. Jakob Auer, "Ein Ausflug von Akropong nach Odumase," *Der Evangelische Heidenboten* (1859): 39.

25. Auer, "Ein Ausflug," p. 49.

26. Auer, "Ein Ausflug," p. 39; Odjidja, *Mustard Seed*, pp. 37-50; Odonkor, *The Rise*, pp. 18-19.

27. See Azu, "Adangbe (Adangme) History," (1926): 239-70; 3 (1927): 89-116; 4 (1928): 3-30; Noa Azu, "The Late King Sakitey and the Ashanti War," *Gold Coast Review* 1 (1929): 105-17; *Adangbe Historical and Proverbial Songs* (Accra, 1929).

28. Odjidja, *Mustard Seed*, pp. 37-64, 73-74.

29. Jakob Kopp, "Von der Missionsarbeit auf der Station Odumase," *Der Evanglische Heidenboten*, 1875, 53.

30. Auer, "Ein Ausflug," p. 40.

31. *85: Funfundachtzigster Jahresbericht der Evangelischen Missionsgesellschaft zu Basel auf 1 Juli 1900* (Basel: Missionsverwaltung, 1900), pp. 26-28. Also working against missionary conversion was "European culture," that is, the ability for Krobo to make money. *98: Achtundneunzigster Jahresbericht der Evangelischen Missionsgesellschaft zu Basel auf 1 Juli 1913* (Basel: Missionsverwaltung, 1913); Odjidja, *Mustard Seed*, pp. 68-70.

32. Odjidja, *Mustard Seed*, pp. 61-62.

33. "Nachrichten von der Goldküste, etc.," *Der Evangelische Heidenboten* (1876): 22.

34. *84: Vierundachtzigster Jahresbericht der Evangelischen Missionsgesellschaft zu Basel auf 1 Juli 1899* (Basel: Missionsverwaltung, 1899), p. 62.

35. *79: Neunundsiebenzigster Jahresbericht der Evangelischen Missionsgesellschaft zu Basel auf 1 Juli 1894* (Basel: Missionsverwaltung, 1894), pp. 9-10.

36. Missionaries had difficulty throughout the region gaining converts, not just among the Krobo. In the 1890s the colonial government began to establish their own public schools in which conversion was not required or stressed for admission.

37. *94: Vierundneunzigster Jahresbericht der Evangelischen Missionsgesellschaft zu Basel auf 1 Juli 1909* (Basel: Missionsverwaltung, 1909), p. 53.

38. *80: Achtzigster Jahresbericht der Evangelischen Missionsgesellschaft zu Basel auf 1 Juli 1895* (Basel: Missionsverwaltung, 1895), p. 17.

39. The annual report also suggests that there are more men than women who have begun to reject traditiional religious practices. *81: Einundachtzigster Jahresbericht der Evangelischen Missionsgesellschaft zu Basel auf 1 Juli 1896* (Basel: Missionsverwaltung, 1896), p. 19.

40. Only Okpesi, the newest Krobo substation in the "Krobo plantations," increased its membership. *82: Zweiundachtzigster Jahresbericht der Evangelischen Missionsgesellschaft zu Basel auf 1 Juli 1897* (Basel: Missionsverwaltung, 1897), p. 19.

41. Missionaries claimed that there existed more than 16,000 Christians, more than in India; Begoro had the greatest increase in 1898 with 376; Odumase and its substations registered the lowest increase. *83: Dreiundachtzigster Jahresbericht der Evangelischen Missionsgesellschaft zu Basel auf 1 Juli 1898* (Basel: Missionsverwaltung, 1898), p. 22.

42. *83: Dreiundachtzigster*, p. 49. "Odente," a powerful new deity, had emerged by 1900 in Kroboland. *85: Funfundachtzigster*, p. 62.

43. *83: Dreiundachtzigster*, p. 49.

44. Somanya was the second least desirable Krobo town from the missionaries' perspective; it was referred to as "Sodom and Gomora." *83: Dreiundachtzigster*, p. 22; *95: Funfundneunzigster Jahresbericht der Evangelischen*

Missionsgesellshaft zu Basel auf 1 Juli 1910 (Basel: Missionsverwaltung, 1910), p. 67.

45. The missionaries were also displeased with Konor Mate Kole, because he had a "music band, which makes a hell of noise and is the source of much anger to us, it also spoils our work for it became the center of attraction and a meeting point for the dregs of the society . . . the expelled and runaway school children, and other dark characters." *83: Dreiundachtzigster*, pp. 48-49; *80: Achtzigster*, p. 17; *84: Vierundachtzigster*, pp. 63-64; *95: Funfundneunzigster*, pp. 65-66.

46. *83: Dreiundachtzigster*, p. 49.

47. *84: Vierundachtzigster*, pp. 23-24. In the 1890s Islam also provided competition, especially Moslem Hausa. In 1913 "American Zionists" with their "peculiar methods" established a mission in Odumase. *98: Achtundneunzigster*, p. 103.

48. *84: Vierundachtzigster*, p. 64; *85: Funfundachtzigster*, pp. 26-28.

49. *97: Siebenundneunzigster Jahresbericht der Evangelischen Missionsgesellschaft zu Basel auf 1 Juli 1912* (Basel: Missionsverwaltung, 1912), p. 69.

50. Odjidja, *Mustard*, p. 31.

51. *84: Vierundachtzigster*, p. 23; *85: Funfundachtzigster*, pp. 61-65; *94: Vierundneunzigster*, p. 124.

52. *85: Funfundachtzigster*, p. 65; *84: Vierundachtzigster*, p. 23.

53. *79: Neunundsiebenzigster*, p. 11.

54. *84: Vierundachtzigster*, pp. 64-65.

55. *85: Funfundachtzigster*, p. 64.

56. *83: Dreiundachtzigster*, p. 49.

57. *Der Evangelische Heidenboten* (1867).

58. *85: Funfundachtzigster*, p. 63.

59. As late as 1912 polygamy among Christians and non-Christians in Kroboland continued virtually unaffected by missionary opposition. *97: Siebenundneunzigster*, p. 49.

60. Jakob Kopp, "Von der Missionsarbeit auf der Station Odumase," *Der Evangelischen Heidenboten* (1875), p. 44.

61. Jakob Kopp, "Die Heidnische Frauenwelt in Kroboland," *Missionsmagazin* (1893), p. 403; *83: Dreiundachtzigster*, p. 49. Some Christian Krobo women, however, apparently

did not object to a polygamous marriage. *95: Funfundneunzigster*, pp. 62-63.

62. *96: Sechsundneunzigster Jahresbericht der Evangelischen Missionsgesellschaft zu Basel auf 1 Juli 1911* (Basel: Missionsverwaltung, 1911), p. 63.
63. *84: Vierundachtzigster*, pp. 63-65. The konor's first wife, who was baptized in 1900, exerted no influence on her husband. *85: Funfundachtzigster*, p. 63.
64. *96: Sechsundneunzigster*, p. 63.
65. *97: Siebenundneunzigster*, p. 50.
66. In addition to Konor Mate Kole, one of his brothers was dismissed from the church in 1894, and one of his sisters, Johanna, was dismissed from the church in 1912. *97: Siebenundneunzigster*, p. 50.
67. *84: Vierundachtzigster*, p. 64.
68. *76: Sechsundzsiebenzigster*, p. 14.
69. *76: Sechsundsiebenzigster*, pp. 15, 17, 23.
70. *77: Siebenundsiebenzigster*, p. 17.
71. *79: Neunundsiebenzigster*, p. 16.
72. *95: Funfundneunzigster*, p. 59.
73. Krobo Christians tended to be urban and involved in the cash economy. *94: Vierundneunzigster*, p. 47; *95: Funfundneunzigster*, pp. 61-63.
74. Zimmermann, "Kroboneger." Little had changed in 1910; the Krobo plantations continued to hamper the formation of a closely controlled Christian community. *95: Funfundneunzigster*, p. 58.
75. *79: Neunundsiebenzigster*, p. 9.
76. Zimmermann, "Kroboneger" (1867), p. 34.
77. *94: Vierundneunzigster*, pp. 53-54, 124-27.
78. Odumase was the exception. *98: Achtundneunzigster*, p. 96.
79. *77: Siebenundsiebenzigster*, p. 42. Dr. Christian Heinz, who arrived in the Gold Coast with Riis, was a medical doctor, he died in 1832. Thereafter the Basel missionaries only had chests of medicine until Dr. E. Mahly arrived in 1882, followed by Dr. Fisch in 1883, both were stationed at Christiansborg. Dr. Carl A. Eckhardt and Klara Finckh, a nursing sister, were the first medical team to arrive in Kroboland. They had arrived in Christiansborg in 1887 and moved to Odumase in 1891; both died in 1893.

Zimmermann, "Kroboneger," p. 38; Paul Steiner, "50 Jahre Missionsarbeit in Krobo," *Der Evangelische Heidenboten*, p. 92.

80. 77: *Siebenundsiebenzigster*, pp. 42, 44.

81. The treatment of a very ill member of Konor Mate Kole's family demonstrates the competitiveness between the traditional healers and missionary doctors. Konor Mate Kole, although he disagreed with missionaries on many issues including Dipo and polygamy, however, strongly supported missionary doctors and their techniques, and followed their medical advice. 77: *Siebenundsiebenzigster*, pp. 46-48; 97: *Siebenundneunzigster*, pp. 60-61.

82. 77: *Siebenundsiebenzigster*, pp. 45-46.

83. 77: *Siebenundsiebenzigster*, pp. 46, 49.

84. 96: *Sechsundneunzigster*, pp. 66-68; 98: *Achtundneunzigster*, p. 88; Schott, *Basel Mission*, pp. 30-34.

85. 96: *Sechsundneunzigster*, p. 67.

86. C.O. 96/17 C.H. Bartels to M. Forster, 28 September 1849.

87. For example, students established a stratification based on their level in school "the first class are called slaves, the second class are called princes; third class are called lawyers, and the fourth class are kings." 97: *Siebenundneunzigster*, p. 48.

88. 97: *Siebenundneunzigster*, pp. 48-49.

89. 96: *Sechsundneunzigster*, p. 76. As a result, therefore, the people in lower Volta, and Ada, and Odumase, were least responsive to missionary efforts, as were all the major urban centers along the Eastern Region, such as Christiansborg. 76: *Sechsundsiebenzigster*, pp. 13-14. 97: *Siebenundneunzigster*, pp. 46-47.

90. 95: *Funfundneunzigster*, pp. 61-63; 98: *Achtundneunzigster*, pp. 92-93.

91. 94: *Vierundneunzigster*, p. 48.

92. 95: *Funfundneunzigster*, p. 61.

93. 97: *Siebenundneunzigster*, pp. 69-70; 98: *Achtundneunzigster*, pp. 84-88, 108.

94. The earlier attempts by colonial officials, in 1844 and 1852, to implement an education policy in the Gold Coast failed. John J. Crooks, *Records Relating to the Gold Coast Settlements*, p. 308. By 1902 a school received a grant of 2s. per

student per year for each pass in arithmetic, reading and writing and 6d. to 2s. per student based on average attendance. McWilliams, *Development*, p. 33. Missionary officials reluctantly accepted this development. "Without the help and control from the government we would not have achieved such high standards at our schools." *96: Sechsundneunzigster*, p. 67; *98: Achtundneunzigster*, pp. 87-88.

95. Beginning in 1909, schools, government and missionary, received a subsidy based on attendance and efficient teaching; the latter criteria replaced the previous subsidy based on payment by results, which awarded subsidies based on the number of students who passed each 'standard' [grade level]. *98: Achtundneunzigster*, pp. 88-89; *96: Sechsundneunzigster*, pp. 77-78; McWilliam, *Development*, pp. 32-43.

96. *98: Achtundneunzigster*, p. 108.

97. In 1910 as Kroboland celebrated its Fiftieth Anniversary in September, there were reported to be 1385 Christians, 14 schools with 845 pupils, 25 native assistants and 3 ordained missionaries. *95: Funfundneunzigster*, pp. 56-60. By 1911 Christian holidays were observed by the general Krobo population; however, non-Christians celebrated these Christian holidays in the traditional Krobo manner. *96: Sechsundneunzigster*, p. 64; *97: Siebenundneunzigster*, p. 49; Zimmermann, "Krobonegers", p. 25; Alfred Erhardt, "Krobo einst und jetst," *Der Evangelische Heidenboten*, (1918) p. 50.

98. *Jahresberichte der Basler Mission* (1914), pp. 90-95. See also *76: Sechsundsiebenzigster*, p. 14.

BIBLIOGRAPHY

Books, Articles, and Dissertations

Accam, T. N. N. *Dangme and Klama Proverbs*. Edited by M. E. Kropp Dakubu. Legon: Institute of African Studies, 1972.

Acolatse, Seth. "Government and Politics in the Akwamu State, 1730-1930." B.A. Honors diss. University of Ghana Legon, June 1979.

Adams, Captain John. *Sketches Taken During Ten Voyages to Africa Between 1768 and 1800*. London: Hurst, Robinson, 1821.

Adams, C. D. "Activities of Danish Botanists in Guinea, 1783-1850." *Transactions of the Historical Society of Ghana* 3, pt. 1 (1957): 30-46.

Addo, Anthony Agyei. "The History of Begoro." B.A. History Honors thesis, University of Ghana Legon, April 1975.

Addo-Fening, Robert. "Akyem-Abuakwa, c. 1874-1943: A Study of the Imposition of Missionary Activity and Colonial Rule on a Traditional State." Ph.D. thesis, University of Ghana, Legon, 1980.

African Historical Demography: Proceedings of a Seminar held in the Centre of African Studies, University of Edinburgh, 29th and 30th April 1977. Edinburgh: Centre for African Studies, 1977.

Agbodeka, Francis. *African Politics and British Policy in the Gold Coast 1868-1900: A Study in the Forms and Force of Protest*. London: Longman, 1971.

_____. *Ghana in the Twentieth Century*. Accra: Ghana University Press, 1972.

Agyeman-Duah, J. "Ashanti-Mampong; A Tradition History to the Reign of Nana Safo Katanka." *Transactions of the Historical Society of Ghana* 4: 21-25.

Aidoo, Agnes A. "Political Crisis and Social Change in the Asante Kingdom, 1867-1901." Ph.D. diss., University of California, Los Angeles, 1975.

Akinjogbin, I. A. *Dahomey and Its Neighbours 1708-1818*. Cambridge: Cambridge University Press, 1967.

Akoto, A. O. "History of Akwamu." B.A. Honors diss., University of Ghana Legon, May 1974.

Allen, Marcy. *The Gold Coast*. London: Hodden and Stoughton, 1874.

Amenumey, Divine. "The Ewe People and the Coming of European Rule, 1850-1914." M.A. thesis, University of London, 1964.

_____. "Geralido de Lima: A Reappraisal." *Transactions of the Historical Society of Ghana* 9 (1968): 60-72.

Ameyaw, K. "Traditions of Kwaben (Akeym-Abuakwa)." Institute of African Studies (Legon), Acc. No. KAG/70 (June 1965).

_____. "Kwawu—An Early Akan State." *Ghana Notes and Queries* 9 (November 1966): 8-10.

_____. "Traditions of Akim Oda (Kotoku)." Institute of African Studies (Legon), Acc. No. KAG/7 (January 1966).

Anjorin, A. O. "European Attempts to Develop Cotton Cultivation in West Africa, 1850-1910." *Odu* 3 (1966): 3-15.

Ansah, J. K. *The Centenary History of the Larteh Presbyterian Church, 1853-1953*. Larteh: Larteh Presbyterian Church, 1955.

Arhin, Kwame. "The Structure of Greater Ashanti (1700-1824)." *The Journal of African History* 6/8 (1967): 65-85.

Argyle, W. J. *The Fon of Dahomey: A History and Ethnography of the Old Kingdom*. Oxford: Clarendon Press, 1966.

Armstrong, Robert. "Glottochronology and African Linguisti5cs." *Journal of African History* 3/2 (1962): 283-90.

Azu, Noa A. "Adangbe (Adangme) History." *Gold Coast Review* 2 (1926): 239-70; 3 (1927): 89-116; 4 (1928): 3-30.

_____. "The Late King Sakitey and the Ashanti War." *Gold Coast Review* 1 (1929): 105-17.

Azu, Enoch. *Adangbe Historical and Proverbial Songs*. Accra: Government Printing Office, 1929.

Barbot, John. *A Description of the Coasts of North and South Guinea*. London, 1732.

Bagyire, Otutu, IV. "The Guans: A Preliminary Note." *Ghana Notes and Queries* 7 (January 1965).

Bartels, Francis L. "Philip Quaque 1741-1816." *Transactions of the Gold Coast and Togoland Historical Society* 1/5 (1955): 166-75.

_____. *The Roots of Ghana Methodism*. Cambridge: Cambridge University Press, 1965.

Beecham, John. *Ashantee and the Gold Coast*. London: J. Mason, 1841.

Bell, Hesket J. "The Fetish-Mountain of Krobo." *Macmillian's Magazine* 68 (July 1893): 210-19.

_____. "History, Trade, Resources, and Present Conditions of the Gold Coast Settlement." *Journal of Commerce*. Liverpool, 1893.

_____. *Outline of the Geography of the Gold Coast Colony and Protectorate*. London: Sampson, Low & Co., 1894.

Bellon, I. *Die Gewaltsame Vertreibung der Basler Missionare von der Goldküste*. Stuttgart, 1918.

Benneh, George. "The Huza Strip Farm System of the Krobo of Ghana." *Geographica Polonica* 19 (1970): 185-206.

Bertho, J. "La Parente des Yoruba aux Peuplades de Dahomey et de Togo." *Africa* 21 (April 1949): 121-32.

Bevin, H. J. "The Gold Coast Economy About 1800." *Transactions of the Gold Coast and Togoland Historical Society* 2, pt. 2 (1956): 14-23.

_____. "Some Notes on Gold Coast Exports, 1886-1913." *Economic Bulletin of Ghana* 4 (1960): 13-20.

_____. *Economic History of the Gold Coast, 1874-1914, Select Documents*. Legon: Department of History, University of Ghana, 1960.

Birmingham, Walter, N. and Omaboe, E. N., eds. *A Study of Contemporary Ghana: Some Aspects of Social Structure Vols. I and II*. London: George Allen and Unwin, 1967.

Blake, John W. *European Beginnings in West Africa, 1454-1578*. London: Longmans, Green & Co., 1937.

Boahen, A. Adu, "Ghana Before the Coming of Europeans" *Ghana Social Science Journal* 4/2 (November 1977): 93-95.

_____. "The Akan of Ghana." *Ghana Notes and Queries* 9 (1966): 3-10.

Boateng, E. A. *A Geography of Ghana*. Cambridge: Cambridge University Press, 1966.

Bosman, William. *A New and Accurate Description of the Coast of Guinea: Divided into the Gold, the Slave, and the Ivory Coasts.* London: J. Knapton, 1705.

Bowdich, Thomas E. *Mission From Cape Coast Castel to Ashantee.* London: J. Murray, 1819.

Boyle, Frederick. *Through Fanteeland To Coomassie: A Diary of the Ashantee Expedition.* London: Chapman and Hall, 1874.

Brackenbury, Henry (Sir). *The Ashanti War: A Narrative.* 2d ed. 2 vols. London: Frank Cass, 1968.

Brokensha, David. *Social Change at Larteh, Ghana.* Oxford: Clarendon Press, 1966.

_____, ed. *Akwapim Handbook.* Accra: Ghana Publishing Corp., 1972.

Brooks, George E. *Yankee Traders, Old Coasters and African Middlemen.* Boston: Boston University Press, 1970.

Büchner, H. "Die allemeine und kirschliche Lage auf der Goldküste." *Evangelisches Missions-Magazin, Basel,* January 1944.

Buhl, Carl. *Die Basler Mission auf der Goldküste.* Basel: Basel Mission Society, 1882.

Burton, Sir Richard Francis and Verney Lovett Cameron. *To The Gold Coast For Gold.* 2 vols. London: Chatto & Windus, 1883.

Butler, W. F. Major. *AKIM-FOO: The History of a Failure.* London: Sampson Low, Marston, Low, & Searle, 1875.

Cardinall, A. W. *The Gold Coast 1931.* Accra: Government Printing Office, 1931.

Christaller, Johannes G. *A Grammar of the Asante and Fante Language.* Basel: Basel Mission Society, 1875.

_____. *Dictionary of the Asante and Fante Language.* Basel: Basel Mission Society, 1881.

_____. "Recent Explorations in the Basin of the Volta (Gold Coast) by Missionaries of the Basle Missionary Society." *Proceedings of the Royal Geographical Society* (New Series), 8 (1886): 246-56.

Claridge, William, W. *A History of the Gold Coast and Ashanti.* 2d ed. 2 vols. London: Frank Cass, 1964.

Coquery-Vidrovitch, Catherine. "De La Traite des Esclaves a l'exportation de l'huile de palme et des palmistes au Dahomey." In *The Development of Indigenous Trade and*

Markets in West Africa, edited by C. Mellassoux, 107-23. Oxford: Oxford University Press, 1971.

Cornevin, Robert. *Histoire du Dahomey*. Paris: Berger-Levrault, 1959.

_____. *Histoire du Togo*. Paris: Berger-Levrault, 1962.

_____. *La Colonisation Intérieure du Togo par les Kabre-Losso*. Paris: Berger-Levrault, 1972.

_____. *Le Peuple Akposso*. Paris: Berger-Levrault, 1970.

Croft, James A. "Exploration of the River Volta, West Africa." *Proceedings of the Royal Geographical Society* (1873-74): 183-93.

Crooks, John J. *Records Relating to the Gold Coast Settlements From 1750-1874*. London: Frank Cass, 1973.

Crowther, F. G. "The Epwe Speaking People." *The Gold Coast Review* 3/1 (1927): 11-43.

Crowther, Francis, "Notes on a District of the Gold Coast," *Quarterly Journal* 1/3 (1906): 167-78, Liverpool University Institute of Commercial Research in the Tropics; London: Williams Norgate.

Cruickshank, Broderick. *Eighteen Years on the Gold Coast of Africa*. 2 vols. London: Frank Cass, 1953.

Curtin, Philip D. *The Atlantic Slave Trade: A Census*. Madison: University of Wiscons Press, 1969.

Daaku, Kwame Yeboa. *Trade and Politics on the Gold Coast 1600-1720: A Study of the African Reaction to European Trade*. Oxford: Clarendon Press, 1970.

Dahse, P. "Die Goldküste," *Deutsche geographische Blätter* 2: 81-111.

Dalgleish, W. Scott. "Ashanti and the Gold Coast." *Scottish Geographical Magazine* 12 (1896): 10-21.

Dakubu, M. E. Kropp, "Linguistic Pre-History and Historical Reconstruction: The Ga-Adanme Migrations." *Transactions of the Historical Society of Ghana* 13/1 (1972): 87-111.

_____. *One Voice: The Linguistic Culture of An Accra Lineage*. Netherlands: African Studiis Centre, 1981.

_____. "The Peopling of Southern Ghana: A Linguistic Viewpoint." In *The Archaeological and Linguistic Reconstruction of African History*, edited by Christopher Ehret and Merrick Posnansky, 245-55. Berkeley: University of California Press, 1982.

Dalzel, Archibald. *The History of Dahmey: an Inland Kingdom of Africa*. London: printed for author, 1793.

Davies, Oliver. *West Africa Before the Europeans: Archaeology and Prehistory*. London: Methuen, 1971.

Dantzig, Albert van. *Forts and Castles of Ghana*. Accra: Sedco Publishers, 1980.

Debrunner, Hans. "Notiable Danish Chaplains on the Gold Coast, 1830-1844." *Transactions of the Gold Coast and Togoland Historical Society* 1/4 (1956): 73-86.

_____. *History of Christianity in Ghana*. Accra: Waterville Publishing House, 1967.

_____. "Wie Sollen wir dem Hexeglauben auf der Goldküste in Predigt und Seelsorge begegnen?" *Evangelisches Missions-Magazin, Basel*, January 1955.

_____. "Freidrich Pederson Svane, 1710-1789." *Evangelisches Missions-Magazin, Basel*, February 1957.

_____. "Anfänge evangelischer Missionsarbeit auf der Goldküste bis 1828." *Evangelisches Missions-Magazin, Basel*, January and March 1954.

De Graft-Johnson, J. C. "The Population of Ghana 1846-1967." *Transactions of the Historical Society of Ghana* 10: 1-12.

Dickson, Kwamina B. "Evolution of Seaports in Ghana: 1800-1928." *Annals of the Association of American Geographers* 55/1 (1965): 98-111.

_____. "The Development of Road Transportation in Southern Ghana and Ashanti Since 1850." *Transactions of the Historical Society of Ghana* 5/1 (1961): 331-42.

_____. *A Historical Geography of Ghana*. Cambridge: Cambridge University Press, 1969.

_____. "Trade Patterns in Ghana at the Beginning of the Eighteenth Century." *Geographical Review* 56 (3 July 1966): 417-31.

Dike, K. Onwuka. *Trade and Politics in the Niger Delta 1830-1885: An Introduction to the Political and Economic History of Nigeria*. Oxford: Clarendon Press, 1966.

Djang, S. S. "Full Description on Akantamansu Battle," *The Sunglight Magazine of History and Progress* Aburi 3/1 (1976): 65-80.

Dodson, George. "The River Volta, Gold Coast, West Africa" *Journal of Manchester Geographical Society* 8 (1892): 19-25.

Dumett, R. A. "British Official Attitudes to Economic Development on the Gold Coast, 1874-1905." Ph.D. thesis University of London, 1966.

Duncan, John. *Travels in Western Africa in 1845 and 1846*. 2 vols. London: R. Bentley, 1847.

Ehret, Christopher. *Southern Nilotic History*. Evanston: Northwestern University Press, 1970.

Ellis, Alfred Burdon. *The Land of Fetish*. London: Chapman and Hall, 1883.

_____. *West African Sketches*. London: Chapman and Hall, 1883.

_____. *The Tshi-Speaking Peoples of the Gold Coast of West Africa, Their Language, Religion, Manners, Customs, Laws, Etc*. London: Chapman and Hall, 1890.

_____. *The Ewe-Speaking Peoples of the Slave Coast of West Africa, Their Religion, Manners, Customs, Laws, Language, Etc*. London: Chapman and Hall, 1890.

_____. *A History of the Gold Coast of West Africa*. London: Chapman and Hall, 1893.

Eppler, Paul. *Geschichte der Basler Mission, 1815-1899*. Basel: Basel Mission Society, 1900.

Fage, John D. "Administration of George Maclean on the Gold Coast 1830-1844." *Transactions of the Gold Coast and Togoland Historical Society* 1/4 (1944): 102-22.

Field, Margaret, J. *Social Organization of the Ga People*. London: Oxford University Press, 1940.

_____. "The Agricultural System of the Manya-Krobo of the Gold Coast." *Africa* 14/2 (1943): 54-65.

_____. *Akim-Kotoku, an Oman of the Gold Coast*. London: Crown Agents, 1948.

_____. *Search for Security*. London: Crown Agents, 1960.

Fischer, F. *Kuturelle Wandlungen an der Goldküste im 19. Jahrhundert. (Sonderdruck aus Mitteilungen der Ostschweiz Geograph-Commerce Gesellschaft.)* St. Gallen: Ostschweizerische geographisch-commercielle gesellschaft, 1911.

Fynn, John K. "The Reign and Times of Kusi Obodum, 1750-1764." *Transactions of the Historical Society of Ghana* 8 (1965): 24-32.

_____. "The Rise of Ashanti." *Ghana Notes and Queries* 9 (November 1966): 24-30.

Gaikpa, N. K. "History of Ada: A Quest for Security." B.A. Honors diss., University of Ghana Legon, 1982.

Gannon, Margaret, "The Basle Mission Trading Company and British Colonial Policy in the Gold Coast, 1918-1928." *Journal of African History* 24/4 (1983): 498-519.

Gillespie, William H. *The Gold Coast Police 1844-1938*. Accra: Government Printing Office, 1955.

Gleave, Michael B. "Hill Settlements and their Abandonment in Western Yorubaland." *Africa* 33 (1936): 343-52.

Glover, Elizabeth (Lady) and Temple, Richard (Sir). *Life of Sir John Hawley Glover*. London: Smith, Elder & Co., 1897.

Glover, John. "Notes on the Country Between the Volta and the Niger." *Proceedings of the Royal Geographical Society* (1874): 286-300.

Goody, John. "Ethnological Notes on the Distribution of the Guany Languages." *Journal of African Languages* 2/3 (1963): 322-44.

Gordon, Charles A. *Life on the Gold Coast*. London: Bailliere, Tindall, 1874.

Gould, P. R. *The Development of the Transportation Pattern in Ghana*. Evanston: Northwestern University Press, 1960.

Governor Carstensen's Diary 1842-1850. (Translated by the Institute of African Studies, n.d.)

Groves, Charles P. *The Planting of Christianity in Africa*. 4 vols. London: Lutterworth Press, 1948.

Hargreaves, John. *West African Partitioned*. Vol. 1, *The Loaded Pause, 1885-1889*. Madison: University of Wisconsin Press, 1974.

Harrop, Sylvia. "The Economy of the West African Coast in the Sixteenth Century." *Economic Bulletin of Ghana* 8/3 (1964): 15-33; 8/4 (1964): 19-36.

Hay, John C.D. *Ashanti and the Gold Coast; and What we Know of It*. London: Edward Stranford, 1874.

Henige, David. "Seniority and the Succession in the Krobo Stools." *Journal of Historical Studies* (1977): 203-27.

Henking, H. *Durch Nacht zum Licht: 125 Jahre Basler Missionsarbeit auf der Goldküste*. Basel: Basel Mission Society, 1953.

239

Henty. G. A. *The March to Coomassie*. London: Tinsley Brothers, 1874.

Hill, Polly. "The History of the Migration of Ghana Cocoa Farmers." *Transactions of the Historical Society of Ghana* 4/1 (1959): 12-32.

_____. "Some Characteristics of Indigenous West African Economic Enterprise." *Economic Bulletin of Ghana* 6 (1962): 3-14.

_____. *The Native Tribunal of Okorase-Akwapim: Selected Land Cases 1918-1919*. Legon, 1964. (Mimeographed).

_____. *Migrant Cocoa-Farmers of Southern Ghana; A Study in Rural Capitalism*. Cambridge: Cambridge University Press, 1970.

_____. "Three Types of Southern Ghanaian Cocoa Farmers." In *African Agrarian Systems*, ed. Daniel Biebuyck. Oxford: Oxford University Press, 1970, 203-23.

Hilton, Thomas E. *Ghana Population Atlas*. Edinburgh: T. Nelson, 1960.

Hopkins, Anthony G. "Economic Imperialism in West Afarica: Lagos, 1880-92." *Economic History Review* 21 (1968): 580-606.

_____. *An Economic History of West Africa*. London: Longman, 1973.

Horton, James Africanus B. *West African Countries and People*. London: W. J. Johnson, 1868.

_____. *Letters on the Political Condition of the Gold Coast Since the Exchange of Territory Between the English and Dutch Governments, Together with a Short Account of the Ashantee War, 1862-64, and the Awoonah War, 1866*. London: W. J. Johnson, 1870.

Horton, Robin, "Stateless Societies in the History of West Africa." In *History of West Africa*, vol. 1, ed. J. F. A. Ajayi, and M. Crowder. New York: Columbia University Press, 1972, 78-119.

Huber, Hugo. "Krobo Marriage Customs." *Anthropos* 46, 5/6 (September-December 1951): 996-97.

_____. "Initiation to Womanhood Among the Se (Ghana)." *The Nigerian Field* 23/3 (1958): 99-119.

_____. "Ceremonie pour les filles uberes d'origine Adangme a Anecho (Togo)." *Bulletin do l'F.A.N.*, ser. B., 20/3-4 (1958): 415-31.

_____. "Adangme Purification and Pacification rituals." *Anthropos* 53, 1/2 (1958): 161-91.

_____. "Ritual Oaths as Instruments of Coercion and Self-Defence Among the Adangme of Ghana." *Africa* 29/1 (January 1959): 41-49.

_____. *The Krobo: Traditional Social and Religious Life of a West African People*. St. Augustin: The Antropos Institute, 1863.

Hymer, Stephen H. "Economic Forms in Pre-Colonial Ghana." *Journal of Economic History* 31 (1970): 33-50.

Hymes, D. H. "Recent Trends in Glottochronology." *Current Anthropology* 1/1 (January 1960): 9-12.

Isert, Paul E. *Reise nach Guinea und den Caribaischen Inseln in Columbian in Briefen an sein Freunde Beschrieben.* Kobenhaven: J. F. Morthorst, 1788.

_____. *Voyages en Guinee et dans les Iles Caraibes en Amerique*, Par Paul Erdman Isert. Paris: Maradan, 1793.

Jackson, Kennell. "Akamba Traditions." Paper presented at the Pacific Coast Branch meeting of the American Historical Association, August 11, 1979, Hawaii.

Jehle, A. *Kostlicher denn das vergagliche Gold: 100 Jahre Basler Missionsarbeit auf der Goldküste.* Basel: Basel Mission Society, 1828.

Jeppesen. H. "Danske plantageanlaeg paa Buldkysten 1788-1850." Reprinted from the publication of the Danish Geographical Association. Kobenhaven, 1966.

Johnson, Marion. "Migrants' Progress," Part I, *Bulletin of the Ghana Geographical Association* 9/2 (July 1964): 1-27.

_____. "Migrants' Progress," Part II, *Bulletin of the Ghana Geographical Association* 10/1 (May 1965): 13-29.

_____. "Ashanti East of the Volta." *Transactions of the Historical Society of Ghana* 7 (1966): 33-59.

_____. "M. Bonnat on the Volta." *Ghana Notes and Queries* 10 (1968): 4-17.

_____. "The Cowrie Currencies of West Africa, Part II." *The Journal of African History* 11/3 (1970): 330-50.

Jones, G. I. *The Trading States of the Oil Rivers*. Oxford: Oxford University Press, 1963.

Justesen, Ole. "Aspects of Eighteenth Century Ghanaian History as Revealed by Danish Sources." *Ghana Notes and Queries* 12 (June 1972): 9-12.

Kea. R. A. "Akwamu-Anlo Relations, c. 1750-1813." *Ghana Notes and Queries* 11 (1969): 29-63.

_____. "Four Asante Officials in the Southeast Gold Coast (1808)." *Ghana Notes and Queries* 11 (1970): 42-47.

_____. "Osei Kwame's Interdiction on Danish Trade, 1788-1789" *Ghana Notes and Queries* 11 (1970): 36-41.

Kellerhals, E. "Staat und Kirche auf der Goldküste." *Evangelisches Missions-Magazine, Basel*: January 1944.

Kemp, Dennis. *Nine Years at the Gold Coast*. London: Macmillan, 1898.

Kimble, David. *A Political History of Ghana*. Oxford: Clarendon, 1963.

Klemp, Egon, ed. *Africa on Maps dating from the Twelfth to the Eighteenth Century*. New York: McGraw-Hill, 1970.

Kole, Mate Azzu. "The Historical Background of Krobo Customs." *Transactions of the Gold Coast and Togoland Historical Society* 1 (1955): 133-40.

Kropp, M. E. *Comparative African Wordlists No. 2: Ga, Adangme and Ewe (Lome)*. Legon: Institute of African Studies, 1966.

Kwamena-Poh, M. A. "The Emergence of Akuapem State 1730-1850." *Ghana Notes and Queries* 11 (November 1970): 26-36.

_____. *Government and Politics in the Akuapem State 1730-1850*. London: Longman, 1973.

_____. *Government and Politics in the Akuapem State*. London: Longman, 1973.

Kyerematen, A. A. Y. *Panoply of Ghana*. London: Longmans, 1964.

La-Anyane, Seth. *Aweso: A Manya Krobo Huza*. Accra: Division of Agriculture, 1956.

_____. *Ghana Agriculture*. London: Oxford University Press, 1963.

Larsen, Kay. *Guvernører: Residenter, Kommandanter Og Chefer*. Kobenhaven: A. Jensen, 1940.

_____. *De Danskei Guinea*. Kobenhavn, Nordiske Forfatteres Forlag, 1945.

Latham, A. J. H. "Old Calabar, 1600-1891: the Economic Impact of the West Upon a Traditional Society." Ph.D. thesis, University of Birmingham, 1970.
_____. *Old Calabar, 1600-1891: The Economic Impact of the West Upon a Traditional Society*. Oxford: Oxford University Press, 1974.
Lawrence, A. W. *Trade Castles and Forts of West Africa*. Stanford: Stanford University Press, 1964.
Lynn, Martin, "Change and Contunity in the British Palm Oil Trade with West Africa." *Journal of African History* 22/3 (1981): 331-48.
MacDonald, George. *The Gold Coast, Past and Present*. London: Longmans, Green & Co., 1898.
Mahly, E. "Studien von der Goldküste." *Globus*, LXVIII (1895): 149-51, 169-72.
Manning, Patrick. "Slaves, Palm Oil and Political Power on the West African Coast." *African Historical Studies* 2 (1969): 279-88.
Manoukin, M. *Akan and Ga-Adanme Peoples of the Gold Coast*. London: Clarendon Press, 1950.
_____. *The Ew-Speaking People*. London: Clarendon Press, 1952.
Marees, Pieter de. *Beschryvighe ende Historische Verhael van het Gout Koninckrijck van Guinea anders der Gout-Custe de Mina genaemt liggende in het dael van Africa*. Gravenhage: M. Nijhoff, 1912.
Marree, J. A. de. *Reizen op en Beschrijving van de Goldkust van Guinea, voorzien met de noodige ophelderingen, journalen, kaart, platen en bewijzen*. 2 Vols. Gravenhage: Gebroeders van Cleef, 1817-1818.
Maurice, J. F. *The Ashantee War*. London: Henry S. King, 1874.
McIntyre, W. D. "British Policy in West Africa: The Ashanti Expedition of 1873-74." *Historical Journal* 5 (1962): 19-46.
_____. "Commander Glover and the Colony of Lagos, 1861-1873." *Journal of African History* 4/1 (1963): 57-80.
McPhee, Allan. *The Economic Revolution in British West Africa*. 2d ed. London: Frank Cass, 1971.
McWilliam, Henry O. A. *The Development of Education in Ghana*. London: Longman, 1959.

McSheffrey, Gerald. "Slavery, Indentured Servitude, Legitimate Trade and the Impact of Abolition in the Gold Coast, 1874-1901." *Journal of African History* 24/3 (1983): 344-75.

Meillassoux, Claude, ed. *The Development of Indigenous Trade and Markets in West Africa*. Oxford: Oxford University Press, 1971.

Metcalfe, George E. "After Maclean: Some Aspects of British Gold Coast Policy in the Mid-Nineteenth Century." *Transactions of the Gold Coast and Togoland Historical Society* 15 (1955).

_____. *Maclean of the Gold Coast*. London: Oxford University Press, 1962.

_____. *Great Britain and Ghana: Documents of Ghana History 1807-1957*. Legon: Thomas Nelson, 1964.

Nadel, S. F. *A Black Byzantium: The Kingdom of Nupe in Nigeria*. London: Oxford University Press, 1969.

Native Reports in Tishi. (Originally published as Papers in Tishi in the 1860s and based on oral traditions collected by David Asante, P. Keteku, and Isaac Ado; collected works later enlarged under title Twi Kasa mu Akuapem ne eho Aman Nsem anase Abasem: History of the Gold Coast or Native Reports in Tshi.) Akropong: no publisher, 1913.

Newbury, Colin W. *British Policy Towards West Africa: Selected Documents, 1786-1874*. London: Clarendon Press, 1965.

_____. *British Policy Towards West Africa 1875-1914*. London: Clarendon Press, 1971.

Nørregard, Georg P. ed. *Governor Edward Carstensens Indberentninger fra Guinea, 1842-1850*. Copenhagen: Selskabet for Udgivelse AF Kilder Til Dansk Historie, 1964.

_____. *Danish Settlements in West Africa 1658-1850*. Boston: Boston University Press, 1966.

Norris, Robert. *Memoirs of the Reign of Bossa Ahadee King of Dahomey*. 2d ed. London: Frank Cass, 1968.

Odamtten, S. K. *The Missionary Factor in Ghana's Development (1820-1880)*. Accra: Waterville Publishing House, 1978.

Odjidja, E. M. L. *Mustard Seed: The Growth of the Church in Kroboland*. Accra: Waterville Publishing House, 1973.

Odonkor, Thomas H. *The Rise of the Krobos*. Translated by Rev. S. S. Odonkor. Edited by E. O. Apronti. Legon: Institute of African Studies, University of Ghana, 1971.

Odonkor, Zuta. "The Origin, Settlement and Traditional Government of the Yilo-Krobo with an Account of the Institution of Chieftaincy Among Them." B.A. History Honors thesis, University of Ghana Legon, March 1976.

Oelschner, Walter. *Landung in Osu*. Stuttgart: Evangelische Missionsverlag, 1959.

Ozanne, Paul. "Adwuku: Fortified Hill-Top Village." *Ghana Notes and Queries* 4 (January 1965): 4-5.

_____. "Ladoku: An Early Town." *Ghana Notes and Queries* 7 (January 1965): 6-7.

_____. "Ghana" In *The African Iron Age*, ed. P. Shinne. London: Oxford University Press, 1971.

Page, Roger E. "The Osu and Kindred Peoples." *The Gold Coast Review* 1 (June/December 1925): 67-70.

Painter, C. "The Guang and West African Historical Reconstruction," *Ghana Notes and Queries* 9 (November 1966): 22-43.

Parringer, Edward G. "Yoruba-Speaking Peoples in Dahomey." *Africa* 17 (April 1947): 122-28.

_____. *The Story of Ketu*. Ibadan: Ibadan University Press, 1967.

Pedler, Frederick. *The Lion and the Unicorn in Africa: A History of the Origins of the United Africa Company, 1787-1931*. London: Heinemann, 1974.

Platt, D. C. M. "Economic Factors in British Policy During the 'New Imperialism.'" *Past and Present* 39 (April 1968): 120-38.

Pogucki, R. J. H. *Gold Coast Land Tenure*. Vol. 2, *Report on Land Tenure in Adangme Customary Law*. Accra: Government Printing Office, 1955.

Polyanyi, Karl. *Dahomey and the Slave Trade*. Seattle: University of Washington Press, 1966.

Population Census of Ghana 1970. Vol. 2. Accra: Government Printing Office, June 1972.

Posnansky, Merrick. "New Radiocarbon Dates from Ghana." *Sankofa* 2 (1976): 60-63.

_____. "The Archaeological Foundations of the History of Ghana," in *Proceedings of the Seminar on Ghanian Historiography and Historical Research*, ed. John Hunwick. Legon: University of Ghana, 1977, pp. 1-25.

_____. "Archaeological and Linguistic Reconstruction in Ghana" in *The Archaeological and Linguistic Reconstruction of*

African History ed. by Christopher Ehret and Merrick Posnansky. Berkeley: University of California Press, 1982, pp. 256-66.

Proceedings of the Seminar on Ghanaian Historiography and Historical Research, May 20-22, 1976. Legon: Department of History, University of Ghana, 1977.

Quarcoo, A. K. "Processes of Social Control Among the Shai (Adangme)," M.A. thesis, University of Ghana, Institute of African Studies, 1965.

Quay, Irene. "The Ga and Their Neighbours 1600-1742." Ph.D. thesis, University of Ghana, Legon, Institute of African Studies, 1971.

Raaflaub, F. "Ein wichtiges Dokument aus der Geschichte der Goldküste." *Evangelisches Missions-Magazin, Basel* (February 1958).

Rattray, R. S. *Ashanti Law and Constitution.* Oxford: Oxford University Press, 1929.

Reade, William W. *The Story of the Ashantee Campaign.* London: Smith, Elder, 1874.

Reade, Winwood. *The African Sketch-Book.* London: Smith, Elder & Co., 1873.

Reindorf, Carl C. *The History of the Gold Coast and Ashantee.* 2d ed. Dublin: Browne & Nolan Ltd., 1966.

Reynolds, Edward. *Trade and Economic Change on the Gold Coast, 1807-1874.* London: Longman, 1974.

Ricketts, Henry T. *Narrative of the Ashantee War: With A View of the Present State of the Colony of Sierra Leone.* London: Simpkin and Marshall, 1831.

Ringwald, Walter. *Stafette in Africa* (der Weg einer jungen Kirche in Ghana). Stuttgart: Evangelische Missionsverlag, 1957.

Roberts, Andrew, ed. *Tanzania Before 1900.* Nairobi: East African Publishing House, 1968.

Rømer, Ludvig. F. *Tilforladelig Eferrentining om Kystem Guinea.* Copenhagen: L. H. Lillies, 1750. Translated into English by Kirsten Bertelsen for the Institute of African Studies, Legon, 1965.

Rodney, Walter. "Gold And Slaves on the Gold Coast." *Transactions of the Historical Society of Ghana* 10 (1969): 13-28.

Rogers, Ebenezer. *Campaigning in Western Africa and the Ashantee Invasion.* London: Major E. Rogers, 1874.

Sampson, Magnus J. *Gold Coast men of Affairs: (Past and Present)*. London: Dawsons of Pall Mall, 1969.

Sarbah, J. Mensah. *Fanti National Constitution*. London: William Clowes and Sons, 1906.

Saxton, S. W. "Historical Survey of the Shai People." *The Gold Coast Review* 1 (1927): 126-45.

Schlatter, W. *Geschichte der Basler Mission, 1815-1915*. 4 Vols. Basel: Verlag der Basler Missionbuchhandlung, 1916.

Schott, Otto. *The Basel Mission on the Gold Coast, Western Africa, on the 1st January 1879. A Retrospect of Fifty Years of Mission Work*. Basel: Basel Mission Society, 1879.

Smith, Noel. "Andreas Riis." *The Christian Messenger* (May 1960-August 1961), Accra.

_____. *The Presbyterian Church of Ghana, 1835-1960*. Accra: Ghana University Press, 1966.

Sprigge, R. G. S. "Eweland's Adangbe: An Enquiry into Oral Tradition." *Transactions of the Historical Society of Ghana* (1969): 67-125.

Steiner, Paul. "Die Opfer der Akraneger auf der Goldküste" *Globus*, 65 (1894): 178-80.

_____. *Saat und Ernte der Baseler Mission auf der Goldküste*. Basel: Missionbuch, 1896.

_____. "Kulturversuche der Basler Mission auf der Goldküste" *Evangelisches Missions-Magazin, Basel* (April 1902).

_____. *Kulturabeit der Basler Mission in Westafrika*. Basel: Verlag der Basler Missionbuch landlung, 1904.

_____. *Die Basler Mission auf der Goldküste*. Basel: Verlag der Basel Missionsbuchhandlung, 1909.

_____. *Hundert Jahre Missionsarbeit, 1815-1915*. Basel: Verlag der Basler Missionbuchhandlung, 1915.

_____. *Im Heim des afrikanischen Bauern*, von P. Steiner. Stuttart: Evangelische Missionsverlag, 1922.

Stewart, J. M. "Akan History, Some Linguistic Evidence." *Ghana Notes and Queries* 9 (1966): 3-10.

Stilliard, N. H. "The Rise and Development of Legitimate Trade in Palm Oil with West Africa." M.A. thesis, University of Birmingham, 1938.

Sunderstrom, Lars. *The Exchange Economy of Pre-Colonial Tropical Africa*. New York: St. Martin's Press, 1975.

Sutherland, D. A. *State Emblems of the Gold Coast*. Accra: Government Printing Office, 1954.

Sutton, Inez. "The Volta Salt Trade: The Survival of an Indigenous Industry." *Journal of African History* 22/1 (1981): 48-67.

_____. "Labour in Commercial Agriculture in Ghana in the Nineteenth and Early Twentieth Centuries." *Journal of African History* 24 (1983): 461-83.

Swanzy, Andrew. "Civilization and Progress on the Gold Coast of Africa, as affected by European Contact with Native Inhabitants." *Journal of the Royal Society of Arts* 23 (1875): 415-26.

Swanzy, Henry. "A Trading Family in the Nineteenth Century Gold Coast." *Transactions of the Gold Coast and Togoland Historical Society* 2 (1956): 78-120.

Szerszewsk, R. *Structural Changes in the Economy of Ghana 1891-1911*. London: Oxford University Press, 1965.

Tenkorang, S. "The Importance of Firearms in the Struggle between Ashant and the Coastal States, 1708-1807." *Transactions of the Historical Society of Ghana* 9 (1968): 1-16.

Tordoff, William. "Griffith's Offer of British Protection to Ashanti 1891." *Transactions of the Historical Society of Ghana* 6 (1962): 31-49.

_____. "The Ashanti Confederacy." *Journal of African History* 2/3 (1962): 339-47.

Tranakides, G. "Observations on the History of Some Gold Coast Peoples." *Transactions of the Gold Coast and Togoland Historical Society* 1/2 (1952): 33-43.

Tufuoh, Isaac. "Relations Between Christian Missions, European Administrations, and Traders in the Gold Coast, 1828-1874." In *Christianity in Tropical Africa*, ed. C. G. Baeta. London: Oxford University Press, 1968.

Wanner, Gustav A. *Die Basler Handels-Geseltschaft A. G., 1859-1959*. Basel: Basler Handels-Gesellschaft, 1959.

_____. *Basel Und Die Goldküste, das Heutige Ghana*. Stadtbuck, 1960.

_____. *The First Cocoa Trees in Ghana, 1858-1868*. Basel: Basel Trading Co., 1962.

Ward, William E. F. *A History of Ghana*. 2d ed. London: George Allen and Unwin, Ltd., 1958.

_____. "Britain and Ashanti, 1874-1896." *Transactions of the Historical Society of Ghana* 15/2 (December 1974): 131-64.

West African-Sketches. Compiled from the Reports of Sir G. R. Collier, Sir Charles MacCarthy. Legon: Institute of African Studies, 1963.

Whiteford, John. *Trading Life in Western and Central Africa.* 2d ed. New York: Barnes and Noble, 1867.

Wilks, Ivor. "The Rise of the Akwamu Empire, 1650-1710." *Transactions of the Historical Society of Ghana* 3/2 (1957): 99-136.

_____. "Aspects of Bureaucratization in Ashanti in the Nineteenth Century." *The Journal of African History* 8/2 (1966): 215-32.

_____. *Asante in the Nineteenth Century: The Structure and Evolution of a Political Order.* Cambridge: Cambridge University Press, 1975.

Wills, J. Brian, ed. *Agriculture and Land Use in Ghana.* London: Oxford University Press, 1962.

Wiltgen, Ralph M. *Gold Coast Mission History, 1471-1880.* Techny, Illinois: Divine World Publications, 1956.

Wilson, Louis E. "Evolution of Paramount Chiefs Among the Adangme: The Krobo (Ghana)." *Geneve-Afrique* 24/2 (1986): 74-100.

Wolfson, Freda. "A Price Agreement on the Gold Coast—The Krobo Boycott, 1858-66." *Economic History Review* 6/1 (1953): 68-77.

_____. *Pageant of Ghana.* London: Oxford University Press, 1958.

Wood, Evelyn. *From Midshipman to Field Marshal.* London: Methuen & Co., 1874.

_____. *The Ashanti Expedition of 1873-74.* London: Royal United Service Institution Lecture, 1874.

Yeboa, A. A. "Ashanti Royal Regalia: Their History and Function." Ph.D. diss., Oxford University, 1966.

Zimmermann, Johannes. *A Grammatical Sketch of the Akra- or Ga-Language, with some specimens of it from the mouth of the natives and a vocabulary of the same with an appendix on the Adanme-dialect.* Stuttgart: Basel Mission Society, 1858.

Archives

Ghana

Ghanaian National Archives (GNA), Accra.

Crowther, F. G. "Memorandum on Great Ningo," ADM 11/1124.

"Yilo Krobo," ADM 11/1117.

"Ogome (Yilo Krobo) Native Affairs," ADM 11/1/1118.

Sutherland, Donald A. "Report on Enquiry into the Alleged Destoolment of Larbi Agbo II, Manche of Prampram with some Preliminary Notes on the History and Constitution of Prampram," ADM 11/1128 Prampram Native Affairs, Case No. 6675/1899.

"Henry S. Newlands Report, August 1922," ADM 11/1650.

"King Akrobetto," ADM 11/1116 Case No. 4836/1899.

"Oper Nam (Yilo Krobo)," ADM 11/877 Case No. 22/1924.

"Krobo (Yilo) 1899-1930," ADM 11/1117 Case No. 28/1921.

"Opes (Yilo Krobo)," ADM 11/877 Case No. 22/1924.

"The Ogome Tribe of Western Krobo," ADM Case No. 439/1908.

"Western Stool Dispute," ADM 11/1116 Case No. 581/14/08. 18 November 1917.

"Western Krobo Native Affairs," ADM 11/1116 Case No. 547/1906.

"Chief Odonkor of Kpong," ADM 11/477 Case No. 49/1913.

"Digest of Basel Missionary Archives of Ghana," EC 1/33.

"Enquiry into Disputed Land Questions Between Jakites and Begoro 4 July 1876," ADM 11/1440.

"Mate Kole Family Papers" (SC-8).

"T. B. Freeman Family Papers" (SC-4)

Balme Library, University of Ghana, Legon. The Furley Collection of translations, transcriptions and abstracts from Dutch and Danish archival sources.

Institute of African Studies (IAS), Legon.

Gold Coast and Ghana Gazette (An Official Document).

United Kingdom

British Parliamentary Papers

1842: *C. 551-II Report from the Select Committee on the West Coast of Africa*, Part II, Appendix and Index (Accounts and Papers, XII).

1864: *C. 385 Despatches from the Governor of the Gold Coast, explaining the cause of war with the King of Ashanti* (Accounts and Papers, XLI).

1865: *C. 170 Report of Colonel Ord, appointed to enquire into the condition of the British Settlements on the Western Coast of Africa* (Accounts and Papers, XXXVII).

1873: *C. 819 Further Correspondence respecting the Ashanti Invasion* (Accounts and Papers, XLIX).

1874: *C. 890 Part I: Further Papers Relating to the Ashantee Invasion.*

1874: *C. 891 Part II: Further Correspondence Respecting the Ashantee Invasion.*

1874: *C. 892 Part III: Further Correspondence Respecting The Ashantee Invasion.*

1874: *C. 893 Part IV; Further Correspondence Respecting the Ashantee Invasion* (Accounts and Papers XLVI).

1874: *C. 962 Asante Invasion: Report by Captain Glover, R.N., on the Conduct of the Deputy Commissioners, Officers, and Men, April 1874.*

1875: *C. 1139 Correspondence relating to the Queen's Jurisdiction on the Gold Coast and the Abolition of Slavery within the Protectorate* (Accounts and Papers, LII).

1875: *C. 1140 Correspondence relating to the Affairs of the Gold Coast* (Accounts and Papers, LII).

1876: *C. 1343 Papers relating to Her Majesty's Possessions in West Africa* (Accounts and Papers, LII).

1876: *C. 1402 Papers relating to Her Majesty's Possessions in West Africa* (Accounts and Papers, LII).

1881: *C. 3064 Affairs of the Gold Coast and threatened Ashanti Invasion* (Accounts and Papers, LXV).

1882: *C. 3386 Further Correspondence regarding Affairs of the Gold Coast* (Accounts and Papers, XLVI).

1883: *C. 3386 Further Correspondence regarding Affairs of the Gold Coast* (Accounts and Papers, XLVIII).
1884: *C. 4052 Further Correspondence regarding the Affairs of the Gold Coast* (Accounts and Papers, LVI).
1885: *C. 4477 Further Correspondence respecting the Affairs of the Gold Coast* (Accounts and Papers, LV).
1886: *C. 4906 Further Correspondence respecting the Affairs of the Gold Coast* (Accounts and Papers, XLVII).
1887: *C. 5357 Further Correspondence respecting the Affairs of the Gold Coast* (Accounts and Papers, LXXV).
1888: *C. 5615 Further Correspondence respecting the Affairs of the Gold Coast* (Accounts and Papers, LXXV).

Public Record Office, (PRO)

Treasury Papers, T-70
Colonial Office Papers, (CO)

All references are given in full in the notes

Denmark

National Archives, Copenhagen

All References are cited in full in the notes

Switzerland

Basel Mission Archives:

Der Evangelisches Heidenboten der Basler Mission
Evangelische Missionsgesellschaft der Basel
Jahresberichete der Basler Mission
Jahresbericht - Evangelische Missionsegesllschaft
Jahresbericht der evangelischen Missions-Gesellschaft zu Basel
Evangelisches Missions-Magazine, Basel

All references are cited in full in the notes.

Field Materials

The field notes collected by the author (1973-74, 1983-84) are on deposit at the University of California, Los Angeles, African Studies Library.

Unpublished Materials

Field, Margaret, J. "The Krobo Constitution in Relation to the Nyewe-Ogome Dispute and the Significance of Priestly Stools." May 1942. (Copy provided by Hugo Huber.)

Sutherland, Donald A. "A History of the Manya Krobo State." 1934. (Copy provided by Konor Azzu Mate Kole.)

Newspapers

The Gold Coast Chronicle (Accra)
The Gold Coast Times (Cape Coast)
The Royal Gold Coast Gazette (Cape Coast)

MONOGRAPHS IN INTERNATIONAL STUDIES

ISBN Prefix 0-89680-

Africa Series

36. Fadiman, Jeffrey A. THE MOMENT OF CONQUEST: Meru, Kenya, 1907. 1979. 70pp.
    081-4 $ 5.50*

37. Wright, Donald R. ORAL TRADITIONS FROM THE GAMBIA: Volume I, Mandinka Griots. 1979. 176pp.
    083-0 $15.00*

38. Wright, Donald R. ORAL TRADITIONS FROM THE GAMBIA: Volume II, Family Elders. 1980. 200pp.
    084-9 $15.00*

41. Lindfors, Bernth. MAZUNGUMZO: Interviews with East African Writers, Publishers, Editors, and Scholars. 1981. 179pp.
    108-X $13.00*

43. Harik, Elsa M. and Donald G. Schilling. THE POLITICS OF EDUCATION IN COLONIAL ALGERIA AND KENYA. 1984. 102pp.
    117-9 $12.50*

44. Smith, Daniel R. THE INFLUENCE OF THE FABIAN COLONIAL BUREAU ON THE INDEPENDENCE MOVEMENT IN TANGANYIKA. 1985. x, 98pp.
    125-X $11.00*

45. Keto, C. Tsehloane. AMERICAN-SOUTH AFRICAN RELATIONS 1784-1980: Review and Select Bibliography. 1985. 159pp.
    128-4 $11.00*

46. Burness, Don, and Mary-Lou Burness, ed. WANASEMA: Conversations with African Writers. 1985. 95pp.
129-2 $11.00*

47. Switzer, Les. MEDIA AND DEPENDENCY IN SOUTH AFRICA: A Case Study of the Press and the Ciskei "Homeland". 1985. 80pp.
130-6 $10.00*

48. Heggoy, Alf Andrew. THE FRENCH CONQUEST OF ALGIERS, 1830: An Algerian Oral Tradition. 1986. 101pp.
131-4 $11.00*

49. Hart, Ursula Kingsmill. TWO LADIES OF COLONIAL ALGERIA: The Lives and Times of Aurelie Picard and Isabelle Eberhardt. 1987. 156pp.
143-8 $11.00*

50. Voeltz, Richard A. GERMAN COLONIALISM AND THE SOUTH WEST AFRICA COMPANY, 1894-1914. 1988. 143pp.
146-2 $12.00*

51. Clayton, Anthony, and David Killingray. KHAKI AND BLUE: Military and Police in British Colonial Africa. 1989. 235pp.
147-0 $18.00*

52. Northrup, David. BEYOND THE BEND IN THE RIVER: African Labor in Eastern Zaire, 1865-1940. 1988. 195pp.
151-9 $15.00*

53. Makinde, M. Akin. AFRICAN PHILOSOPHY, CULTURE, AND TRADITIONAL MEDICINE. 1988. 175pp.
152-7 $13.00*

54. Parson, Jack, ed. SUCCESSION TO HIGH OFFICE IN BOTSWANA. Three Case Studies. 1990. 443pp.
157-8 $20.00*

55. Burness, Don. A HORSE OF WHITE CLOUDS. 1989. 193pp.
158-6 $12.00*

56. Staudinger, Paul. IN THE HEART OF THE HAUSA STATES. Tr. by Johanna Moody. 1990. 2 vols. 653pp.
160-8 $35.00*

57. Sikainga, Ahmad Alawad. THE WESTERN BAHR AL-GHAZAL UNDER BRITISH RULE: 1898-1956. 1991. 183pp.
161-6 $15.00*

58. Wilson, Louis E. THE KROBO PEOPLE OF GHANA TO 1892: A Political and Social History. 1991. 254pp.
164-0 $20.00*

Latin America Series

8. Clayton, Lawrence A. CAULKERS AND CARPENTERS IN A NEW WORLD: The Shipyards of Colonial Guayaquil. 1980. 189pp., illus.
103-9 $15.00*

9. Tata, Robert J. STRUCTURAL CHANGES IN PUERTO RICO'S ECONOMY: 1947-1976. 1981. xiv, 104pp.
107-1 $12.00*

11. O'Shaughnessy, Laura N., and Louis H. Serra. CHURCH AND REVOLUTION IN NICARAGUA. 1986. 118pp.
126-8 $12.00*

12. Wallace, Brian. OWNERSHIP AND DEVELOPMENT: A Comparison of Domestic and Foreign Investment in Columbian Manufacturing. 1987. 186pp.
145-4 $10.00*

13. Henderson, James D. CONSERVATIVE THOUGHT IN LATIN AMERICA: The Ideas of Laureano Gomez. 1988. 150pp.
148-9 $13.00*

14. Summ, G. Harvey, and Tom Kelly. THE GOOD NEIGHBORS: America, Panama, and the 1977 Canal Treaties. 1988. 135pp.
149-7 $13.00*

15. Peritore, Patrick. SOCIALISM, COMMUNISM, AND LIBERATION THEOLOGY IN BRAZIL: An Opinion Survey Using Q-Methodology. 1990. 245pp.
156-X $15.00*

17. Mijeski, Kenneth J., ed. THE NICARAGUAN CONSTITUTION OF 1987: English Translation and Commentary. 1990. 355 pp.
165-9 $25.00*

Southeast Asia Series

31. Nash, Manning. PEASANT CITIZENS: Politics, Religion, and Modernization in Kelantan, Malaysia. 1974. 181pp.
018-0 $12.00*

38. Bailey, Conner. BROKER, MEDIATOR, PATRON, AND KINSMAN: An Historical Analysis of Key Leadership Roles in a Rural Malaysian District. 1976. 79pp.
024-5 $ 8.00*

44. Collier, William L., et al. INCOME, EMPLOYMENT AND FOOD SYSTEMS IN JAVANESE COASTAL VILLAGES. 1977. 160pp.
031-8 $10.00*

45. Chew, Sock Foon and MacDougall, John A. FOREVER PLURAL: The Perception and Practice of Inter-Communal Marriage in Singapore. 1977. 61pp.
030-X $ 8.00*

47. Wessing, Robert. COSMOLOGY AND SOCIAL BEHAVIOR IN A WEST JAVANESE SETTLEMENT. 1978. 200pp.
072-5 $12.00*

48. Willer, Thomas F., ed. SOUTHEAST ASIAN REFERENCES IN THE BRITISH PARLIAMENTARY PAPERS, 1801-1972/73: An Index. 1978. 110pp.
033-4 $ 8.50*

49. Durrenberger, E. Paul. AGRICULTURAL PRODUCTION AND HOUSEHOLD BUDGETS IN A SHAN PEASANT VILLAGE IN NORTHWESTERN THAILAND: A Quantitative Description. 1978. 142pp.
071-7 $10.00*

50. Echauz, Robustiano. SKETCHES OF THE ISLAND OF NEGROS. 1978. 174pp.
070-9 $12.00*

51. Krannich, Ronald L. MAYORS AND MANAGERS IN THAILAND: The Struggle for Political Life in Administrative Settings. 1978. 139pp.
073-3 $11.00*

56A. Duiker, William J. VIETNAM SINCE THE FALL OF SAIGON. Updated edition. 1989. 383pp.
162-4 $17.00*

59. Foster, Brian L. COMMERCE AND ETHNIC DIFFERENCES: The Case of the Mons in Thailand. 1982. x, 93pp.
112-8 $10.00*

60. Frederick, William H., and John H. McGlynn. REFLECTIONS ON REBELLION: Stories from the Indonesian Upheavals of 1948 and 1965. 1983. vi, 168pp.
111-X $ 9.00*

61. Cady, John F. CONTACTS WITH BURMA, 1935-1949: A Personal Account. 1983. x, 117pp.
114-4 $ 9.00*

63. Carstens, Sharon, ed. CULTURAL IDENTITY IN NORTHERN PENINSULAR MALAYSIA. 1986. 91pp.
116-0 $ 9.00*

64. Dardjowidjojo, Soenjono. VOCABULARY BUILDING IN INDONESIAN: An Advanced Reader. 1984. xviii, 256pp.
118-7 $26.00*

65. Errington, J. Joseph. LANGUAGE AND SOCIAL CHANGE IN JAVA: Linguistic Reflexes of Modernization in a Traditional Royal Polity. 1985. xiv, 198pp.
120-9 $20.00*

66. Binh, Tran Tu. THE RED EARTH: A Vietnamese Memoir of Life on a Colonial Rubber Plantation. Tr. by John Spragens. Ed. by David Marr. 1985. xii, 98pp.
119-5 $11.00*

68. Syukri, Ibrahim. HISTORY OF THE MALAY KINGDOM OF PATANI. Tr. by Conner Bailey and John N. Miksic. 1985. xix, 113pp.
123-3 $12.00*

69. Keeler, Ward. JAVANESE: A Cultural Approach. 1984. xxxvi, 523pp.
121-7 $18.00*

70. Wilson, Constance M., and Lucien M. Hanks. BURMA-THAILAND FRONTIER OVER SIXTEEN DECADES: Three Descriptive Documents. 1985. x, 128pp.
124-1 $11.00*

71. Thomas, Lynn L., and Franz von Benda-Beckmann, eds. CHANGE AND CONTINUITY IN MINANGKABAU: Local, Regional, and Historical Perspectives on West Sumatra. 1986. 363pp.
127-6 $16.00*

72. Reid, Anthony, and Oki Akira, eds. THE JAPANESE EXPERIENCE IN INDONESIA: Selected Memoirs of 1942-1945. 1986. 411pp., 20 illus.
132-2 $20.00*

73. Smirenskaia, Zhanna D. PEASANTS IN ASIA: Social Consciousness and Social Struggle. Tr. by Michael J. Buckley. 1987. 248pp.
134-9 $14.00

74. McArthur, M.S.H. REPORT ON BRUNEI IN 1904. Ed. by A.V.M. Horton. 1987. 304pp.
135-7 $15.00

75. Lockard, Craig Alan. FROM KAMPUNG TO CITY. A Social History of Kuching Malaysia 1820-1970. 1987. 311pp.
136-5 $16.00*

76. McGinn, Richard. STUDIES IN AUSTRONESIAN LINGUISTICS. 1988. 492pp.
137-3 $20.00*

77. Muego, Benjamin N. SPECTATOR SOCIETY: The Philippines Under Martial Rule. 1988. 232pp.
138-1 $15.00*

78. Chew, Sock Foon. ETHNICITY AND NATIONALITY IN SINGAPORE. 1987. 229pp.
139-X $12.50*

79. Walton, Susan Pratt. MODE IN JAVANESE MUSIC. 1987. 279pp.
144-6 $15.00*

80. Nguyen Anh Tuan. SOUTH VIETNAM TRIAL AND EXPERIENCE: A Challenge for Development. 1987. 482pp.
141-1 $18.00*

81. Van der Veur, Paul W., ed. TOWARD A GLORIOUS INDONESIA: Reminiscences and Observations of Dr. Soetomo. 1987. 367pp.
142-X $16.00*

82. Spores, John C. RUNNING AMOK: An Historical Inquiry. 1988. 190pp.
140-3 $14.00*

83. Tan Malaka. FROM JAIL TO JAIL. Tr. and ed. by Helen Jarvis. 1990. 3 vols. 1,226pp.
150-0 $55.00*

84. Devas, Nick. FINANCING LOCAL GOVERNMENT IN INDONESIA. 1989. 344pp.
153-5 $16.00*

85. Suryadinata, Leo. MILITARY ASCENDANCY AND POLITICAL CULTURE: A Study of Indonesia's Golkar. 1989. 222pp.
179-9 $15.00*

86. Williams, Michael. COMMUNISM, RELIGION, AND REVOLT IN BANTEN. 1990. 356pp.
155-1 $16.00*

87. Hudak, Thomas John. THE INDIGENIZATION OF PALI METERS IN THAI POETRY. 1990. 237pp.
159-4 $15.00*

88. Lay, Ma Ma. NOT OUT OF HATE: A Novel of Burma. Tr. by Margaret Aung-Thwin. Ed. by William Frederick. 1991. 222pp.
167-5 $20.00*

ORDERING INFORMATION

Orders for titles in the Monographs in International Studies series may be placed through the Ohio University Press, Scott Quadrangle, Athens, Ohio 45701-2979 or through any local bookstore. Individuals should remit payment by check, VISA, MasterCard, or American Express. People ordering from the United Kingdom, Continental Europe, the Middle East, and Africa should order through Academic and University Publishers Group, 1 Gower Street, London WC1E, England. Orders from the Pacific Region, Asia, Australia, and New Zealand should be sent to East-West Export Books, c/o the University of Hawaii Press, 2840 Kolowalu Street, Honolulu, Hawaii 96822, USA.

Other individuals ordering from outside of the U.S. should remit in U.S. funds to the Ohio University Press either by International Money Order or by a check drawn on a U.S. bank. Most out-of-print titles may be ordered from University Microfilms, Inc., 300 North Zeeb Road, Ann Arbor, Michigan 48106, USA.

Prices do not include shipping charges and are subject to change without notice.

Milton Keynes UK
Ingram Content Group UK Ltd.
UKHW011819280923
429583UK00001B/90